International Library of Anthropology

Editor: Adam Kuper, University College, London

ArborScieniae
Arbor Vitae

A catalogue of other Social Science books published by Routledge & Kegan Paul will be found at the end of this volume.

Robber noblemen

Robber noblemen

A study of the political system of the Sikh Jats

Joyce Pettigrew
Department of Social Anthropology,
Queen's University of Belfast

Routledge & Kegan Paul
London and Boston

First published in 1975
by Routledge & Kegan Paul Ltd
Broadway House, 68–74 Carter Lane,
London EC4V 5EL and
9 Park Street,
Boston, Mass. 02108, USA
Set in Monotype Times
and printed in Great Britain by
Western Printing Services Ltd, Bristol
© Joyce Pettigrew 1975

ISBN 0 7100 7999 0
Library of Congress Catalog Card No. 74–84172

Here is my gift, not roses on your grave,
Not sticks burning incense.
(Anna Akhmatova)

To my beloved aunt, Isabelle Pettigrew,
in special memory.

Contents

Maps

Foreword

At the time when Dr Pettigrew went to study social life among the Sikhs in the Punjab, social anthropologists had for a few years become interested in the politics of factionalism. The alignment of persons in factions had not figured extensively in reports on African and Oceanian societies: factions became a focus of interest to anthropologists working in Asia, and in Central America and the Caribbean. To some extent, I believe that this new focus came out of the field material; partly, too, it came from the use of the term, rather than from a new kind of interest in a new form of politicking. As far back as the 1930s, those of us working in South Africa had found a general cleavage within tribes in terms of those sections of the population whom we call Christian or 'schooled' people, and the 'pagans', in their reaction, in some situations, to White authority and culture. So we had the making of a factional division—but on the whole, the alignments of people in a series of situations seemed to be so shifting that it was inappropriate to speak of 'factions', in the sense that this term was applied to the Blues and the Greens in Byzantium, or the Guelphs and Ghibellines in medieval Italy. Within indigenous politicking, the competition between parties seemed to produce alignments, in all studies of sub-Saharan societies, in terms of institutionalized groupings, such as lineages, associations of various kinds, sectors linked to princes, and the like. Political divisions in Asian and Central American villages did not seem to have this institutionalized framework: they were more *ad hoc*, and all the studies of that period, as cited by Dr Pettigrew in her text, emphasized both changing membership of rather ephemeral factions and the fact that they were defined by their allegiance to particular leaders—and that a faction disintegrated with the departure, overthrow, or death of a leader. In the experience of Africanists, the leader was representative of an already established group, competing with like groups, and the position of the leader depended on his position within each group. Hence the term 'faction' was not used of these major units engaged in political competition; and even what might be called 'factions' within each major group, emerged out of the institutionalized cleavages within each group.

I consider that another factor influenced the analyses of these societies. Western anthropologists, and their colleagues from Africa itself, were still engaged in working out the major institutionalized structures of the societies under study; and these varied structures had to be analysed before studies could be pushed into factional alignments within them. It was after this that the study of factions became important. The first studies of this kind concentrated, as Dr Pettigrew cites, on factions within villages in Indian and in other regions; and this concentration influenced the general propositions which were formulated, and which are discussed by Dr Pettigrew in her chapter 6 on the structure of factions. She emphasizes there that the factions she observed in struggle among the Sikhs of the Punjab were less ephemeral in themselves, lasting for a long period, more stable in their membership, larger in scale, and less dependent on particular local leaders for their continuance, than those studied by her predecessors working in this field, some of whose studies were reported in a symposium introduced by Professor (later Sir) Raymond Firth (*British Journal of Sociology*, 1957). She argues that these differences arise from the fact that the Sikhs' local factions were linked into political organization at the level of the State, within the Union of India. Major politicians and parties had to seek to get the support, in terms of votes, of factions which had developed in local areas out of competition for land, and later licences, quotas and permits for industrial commodities, as well as honour and prestige. In turn, these local factions felt they needed to secure the support of those powerful in the State for protection from the administration, and the police and even the judiciary, both to gain advantages and to secure themselves from prosecution. Hence the book develops its analysis of factionalism in terms both of local political competition and of major political struggle at the level of the State, and between Sikhs and Hindus as 'communities'. The bases of alignment are different, at these various levels; and they, and the extent to which links between State leaders and local leaders develop, are beautifully analysed.

This book therefore brings together two developments in Indian studies: first, the study of local factionalism; and second, the development of what have been called 'brokers' delivering votes, the 'political bosses' of other contexts. Dr Pettigrew indeed suggests that earlier studies (save for a couple) of village factionalism, by isolating the village, overlooked the link of local factions into wider political competition, even though these old links were not only there, but also were relevant to an understanding of village politics. I myself am not sure that this is a correct assessment. I am inclined to feel that no intelligent anthropologist, settled in a village, would miss such important connections, and I consider that it is more likely that one of two things differentiated the Punjab from other regions of India. First, Dr Pettigrew herself argues that the Punjab has always, because it lay on a main invasion route into India from the north, been marked by uncertainty of life and by arbitrary and changing rulers. Hence early on Sikhs developed private armies, themselves congeries of private armed bands, for protection. Second, in all newly independent countries political developments have been very rapid. I would expect that over the period of almost twenty years between Indian independence and Dr Pettigrew's own study, there would have been major developments in the linking of village politics into state politics. The accelerating effort to speed technical and economic development must have offered more goods to compete for, in addition to the fact, documented by Dr Pettigrew, that the Punjab had all the problems of re-settling expelled Sikhs and Hindus on land in its turn vacated by fleeing Moslems, creating special problems. This she has described effectively. Thus I feel that earlier studies may have dealt with an earlier phase of factionalism in villages in India.

The Punjab was always a turbulent area, under its Rajas and under the British, and something of this situation continued into the period considered here. Dr Pettigrew was a member of a Sikh family and thus, maybe, had an inside view of the politics of a local area and the connections, or attempts at building connections, with leading men in State politics. This inside knowledge, illuminated by anthropological training, has produced a very vivid account of factional strife at all levels, and of the methods, and alleged methods, of inimical factional leaders and members to do one another down. It is a graphic and a sad story, particularly that of Kairon, a State leader who was in the end assassinated: he strove to support Nehru's attempts to keep India united despite its multiple cleavages and to develop the Punjab economically. Working with what was at hand, he felt he had to work with those who were locally powerful. Dr Pettigrew's analysis of his dilemmas and difficulties, as well as his achievements, adds a new dimension to our understanding of India and its politics. I commend it warmly to anyone interested in politics anywhere, and especially in the political problems of the countries recently made independent, within boundaries drawn by colonial conquests.

On behalf of the Department of Social Anthropology, University of Manchester, I thank most sincerely the Department of Sociology in the University of Delhi for the help they so generously gave Dr Pettigrew in her studies.

MAX GLUCKMAN

Department of Anthropology,
Victoria University of Manchester

Preface

Anthropologists have observed the characteristics of factions in a succession of village studies and on the basis of these have derived certain conclusions regarding the concept of faction as such. This book, however, is intended to be a contribution to our understanding of factions in the setting of local area and state, rather than of village, politics. Following on my observations in units beyond the village, certain modifications to the concept of 'faction' have necessarily emerged. These I discuss in chapter 6. It is hoped, therefore, that the book will make a contribution to the developing literature on factionalism in social anthropology, and perhaps also in political science.

The focus of the analysis centres on the manner in which factions among the Sikh Jats in a particular local area of the Central Punjab are manipulated by a political leader at state level to eliminate political rivals and competitors in an attempt to centralize power. In this context I examine the relationship of the faction as a traditional form of political organization to the social structure of the Sikh rural areas. Divisions within the family and rivalries and alignments between families are seen as forming a basis for factional alliances and enmities. Concepts central to the Jat value system such as honour, prestige, respect and reputation, sustain this mode of organization. Moreover, it is factions rather than castes or classes that compete for available political and economic resources. Historically, too, the faction has been the typical form of political coalition which has supported leaders at different periods. Nowadays it significantly hinders the establishment of unitary rule. One purpose of the book is therefore to attempt to analyse why the faction, as a typical form of coalition supporting the political leadership, prevents the effective centralization of power.

The faction operates at three levels—village, local area and state—and my main interest is in the vertical linkages within the faction and the points at which, and occasions on which, the vertical links operate. I am concerned to try to analyse how the levels of the political system become integrated through the medium of the faction. The book is thus oriented towards understanding a particular political system and uses the faction as a tool in this respect. The 'faction', stretching across the levels of the state political system, is not merely a formal construct, but has to be examined in its several operational aspects. I believe this mode of approach gives a representative picture of the political system, since the type of contacts seen to exist between the Chief Minister of the state and the leaders in the specific local area where I did my fieldwork existed also between the Chief Minister and leaders in many other areas of the province.

An oral history of factional alignments and oppositions in the fieldwork are as given in chapters 11 to 15. Certain statements made by participants in the factionalism express beliefs and rationalizations about, rather than actual knowledge of, the motivations and activities of their opponents. These have been incorporated as 'facts' in so far as they provide part of the context in which enmities and alliances occur and on the basis of which action was taken. They also can be considered as 'facts' in that the kinds of alignments and kinds of situation to which they refer are typical of systems functioning on a patronage basis. The implication of opponents in court cases, allegations of financial corruption and of the co-operation of the administration with political leaders and their supporters are the accepted means by which the factional competition that characterizes the struggle for power in the Punjab is carried out. The information contained in statements describing this situation was of relatively easy access. Jats, who dominated the political scene of the Punjab, were connected to each other by a complicated web of ties based on family, affinity, friendship and faction membership. This, combined with the smallness of the state, in fact meant that inter-personal relations existed on the level of the society itself. The associations, reactions, attitudes to certain occurrences on the part of anyone participating in the factionalism, whether in the village, or local area, or within the state as such, were difficult to conceal on account of the network of links that seemed to connect all Jats if not on one basis, then on another, and if not at one time, then at another.

At certain points in the analysis it may appear as if the book concerns the period of rule of a certain Chief Minister of the Punjab.

If indeed this were so, the chapters commenting on political inter-actions at state level could certainly be criticized as being unduly short and of decidedly insufficient depth. My main purpose is, how-ever, to portray the nature of the political system in its relationship to the social organization of the Jats. Because I am an anthropologist, the bulk of the data has been gathered in villages and the political system has been viewed from the standpoint of local leaders and village participants in the political process. The book in fact rep-resents the second attempt by a social anthropologist to understand the workings of a state political system in India using the techniques of his own discipline.

Acknowledgments

My book is based on twenty-two months of fieldwork in the Punjab, India, from August 1965 until June 1967. The fieldwork was made possible by a Commonwealth Scholarship given by the Association of Commonwealth Universities to whom I am grateful for financing my research.

I wish to thank those in the Department of Sociology, Delhi School of Economics, from whom I received help; particularly Dr André Beteille. For initial guidance in writing up my data I also thank the following: Dr Paul Baxter; Professor Adrian Mayer, for reading through the first draft of my thesis; and two of my friends— Kathleen Johnston and Fernando Fuenzalida. I am indebted, too, to Professor W. H. McLeod of the Department of History, University of Otago, for reading the manuscript and offering his advice on chapter 3. It has been a long, difficult process publishing this book and many individuals over the years have given me their help. In this respect I would like to thank Alastair Maclean of Shaw Maclean and Company and Mr Peter Hopkins of Routledge & Kegan Paul and to particularly mention Professor T. D. Weinshall of the Graduate School of Business Studies at Tel Aviv University, Professor John Blacking and Dr Adam Kuper. I especially thank Dr Kuper for being enthusiastic enough about the Sikh Jats to promote the publication of the book.

It is, however, to Professor Max Gluckman that I am particularly obligated, not only for his many detailed comments and criticisms and his continuous encouragement while writing, but also for being a very friendly godfather through three very hard years.

In all humility I not only acknowledge, but will never forget, the many Punjabis (especially the Sikh Jats) who, by their interest, by their active co-operation, or by their hospitality, aided me in collecting my data. Co-operation was so extensive that I cannot list all names here. But I would like to mention especially the following:

Giani Ajmer S., Secretary of the Shiromani Akali Dal; S. Harbans S., Head of the Department of Religious Studies, Punjabi University, Patiala; S. Amar S. Ambalvi, Advocate, High Court, Chandigarh; S. Harbans S., Gujral Advocate, High Court, Chandigarh; S. Ajaib S. Sandhu, M.L.A.; S. Ujaggar S., Advocate Ludhiana; S. Birinder S., Advocate, Delhi; S. Joginder S. Cheema, Advocate, Karnal; the late S. Anup S., member of the Upper House of Parliament; S. Jai Inder S., formerly President of the Urban District Congress Committee, Amritsar; S. Bhan S. of the Sikh Museum; S. Raghbir S. of the Public Relations Department, Government of Punjab; D. S. Garewal, formerly Deputy Inspector General, Punjab Armed Police; Mrs Sarbrinder Garewal, Ludhiana; and Sirdar Harchand S. of Gobindpura, Payal, landlord. I remember too the friendliness shown to me by the late Master Tara S. because of my interest in his community. Lastly, I may say two 'pukka Sikhs' were always in the background to give a helping hand and some hilarity when necessary, namely S. Khushwant S., writer and journalist; and S. Satindra S., journalist, New Delhi.

I would also like to mention Surendra Sehgal and Mr and Mrs Narinder Mehra.

Although many Jats would have been proud to see their names in print, most names have in fact been changed. This was, however, merely to comply with standard anthropological practice.

Glossary of Punjabi terms

Block	A development area usually covering a hundred villages
Block samiti	An elected group of members representing the block
Goonda	Colloquial term for lawless person
Goondaism	Lawlessness
Got	Clan
Granth	The Sikh scriptures
Granthi	Reader of the scriptures
Gurudwara	Sikh temple
Ilaaqa	District
Izzat	Honour; ideas and values concerning what is honourable
Lakh	A hundred thousand
Lok Sabha	Lower House of Parliament in Delhi
Morcha	Mass demonstration
Paarti	The Punjabi word denoting the unit which I call a faction
Pancayat	Village council
Sarpanc	Head of the village council
Sirdar	Chief, lord: used by Hindus to connote a Sikh
Vidhan Sabha	The State Legislative Assembly
Zilla parishad	District council

Abbreviations

BDO	Block Development Officer
CM	Chief Minister
DC	Deputy Commissioner
IAS	Indian Administrative Service
INA	Indian National Army
MLA	Member of Legislative Assembly or State Parliament
MP	Member of National Parliament
PCS	Punjab Civil Service
PEPSU	Patiala and East Punjab States Union
'S.' before a proper name	Sirdar
'S.' after a proper name	Singh
SGPC	Shiromani Gurudwara Parbhandhak Committee
SHO	Station House Officer—the police officer in charge of a subdivision of a district
SP	Superintendent of Police
UP	Uttar Pradesh—the state to the east of Delhi

Part one
The environment

IN THE LAND OF THE FIVE RIVERS

If you want real freedom for the Punjab, i.e., a Punjab in
which every community will have its due share in the economic
and administrative fields as partners in a common concern,
then that Punjab will not be Pakistan, but just Punjab, land
of the five rivers; Punjab is Punjab and will always remain
Punjab whatever anybody may say.

Speech in the Punjab Legislative Assembly, 11 March 1941, by Sir
Sikander Hayat Khan, Unionist Party Leader and Chief Minister of
United Undivided Punjab.

1 Introduction

The physical setting

(i) *The people and their pattern of life*

Punjab, as the land of the five rivers, is one region. Geographically, it is the western extension of the Ganges plain through which flow the five tributaries of the River Indus, the Jhelum, Chenab, Ravi, Beas and Sutlej; a natural area stretching from the Khyber Pass to Delhi and from the Himalayan ranges to the deserts of Sind and Rajasthan. It is a land almost uniformly level, watered by a network of canals; a land of flat green fields producing crops of wheat, cotton, sugar cane and maize. Its wide, extensive and open plains, ringed by the Himalayas, are criss-crossed by a dense pattern of metalled roads[1] lined by tall trees. From mid-April until mid-September, plains and people are burnt up by a revengeful heat, the temperatures reaching 115°F. during June and July, accompanied by dust storms. All heavy work is completed before noon and at night it is common practice to sleep on the topmost courtyard of the house to catch a breeze. The heat of the area in summer is one reason why the houses are built of mud (which is cooling) in the southern districts of the Punjab rather than of brick and cement as in the Central Punjab. As the end of September approaches the season changes abruptly, with cold dry winds blowing down from the mountains. From November until mid-February temperatures rise to 60°F. in the late morning and early afternoon but men and women alike wrap themselves up in shawls to protect themselves from the wind, and at night, when temperatures fall below freezing-point, sleep indoors beneath a heavy quilt or *razaiyee*. It is not a temperate climate.

The flat expanses of plain have always facilitated easy movement of armies and of fleeing populations. Their very exposed nature, while making the entire province vulnerable to invasion, has also

3

increased communication among its people. As the plains are open
and stretch on and on into the far distance, so the networks of most
Punjabis (though Jat Sikhs in particular) are un-delimited by any
ideological principle and open out in every direction to include all
persons who can be of use. Historically its people share one past:
the experience of continual invasion. Across the province have
streamed the armies of Greeks, Turks, Persians, Mongols and
Afghans. Being thus the main gateway into India for over three
thousand years it has been a land of strife. The themes invariably
mentioned in all historical accounts of the province are its violence
and disorder. Historically, too, its contacts and ties have been with
peoples on its western border.[2]

Although it is one region, the Punjab is at present divided into
three, each area being the home of a religious community. In 1947,
the province was partitioned into two. The larger part, the West
Punjab, then richer in terms of existing agricultural assets, agricultural potential[3] and mineral wealth, became Pakistan with a
Muslim majority. Subsequently, in November 1966, the Indian
Punjab was divided to secure a Sikh majority area within the Central
Punjab. These divisions take little account of the similar culture in
which all three communities—Muslim, Sikh and Hindu—share, nor
of the uniqueness of the area as such from the rest of the sub-
continent.[4] The social organization and value system, especially of
the rural Punjab, differ from that of Hindu India. The prevailing
form of social co-operation and the type of political solidarity bear
no reference to 'caste' and to rules of purity and pollution,[5] but
rather to the family unit and to the values pertaining to that unit,
namely, honour, pride and equality, reputation, shame and insult.

In the sphere of occupational preference, similarities are again
obvious. There is high status attached to army and administrative
service throughout the region. A man's preferred occupations are
those which will involve him in constant physical activity whether
as an administrator touring a district, as a policeman dashing after
border smugglers or as an army officer on active service. This
activism has innumerable other empirical manifestations. It can be
seen, for example, in the way people walk—with a confident and
determined sway. The clothes that are worn are designed for an
active life. A woman's traditional dress in the rural areas is not a
saree but a *salwar kameez*; a wide skirt which is worn over the top
of loose-fitting trousers which fall in folds gathered at the ankles.

Housing accommodation is more or less the same throughout the rural areas. A large square building houses an extended family and is divided into sections, each section being the private premises of a nuclear family unit. All rooms open out onto a wide open courtyard surrounded by a high wall. Each nuclear family section usually also has its own private courtyard. The windows, invariably, have iron grilles over them. The objects one sees around the house are the same: the *charpoy* (string bed), kitchen utensils of brass and copper, steel trunks in which valuable objects are stored, and different kinds of earthen pots for cooking. These are the basic items of every Punjab household. They are all transportable. As will be stressed later, particularly with reference to the Sikh Jats, though it applies to all Punjabis living in the rural areas, there has been much insecurity with respect of property. Very few Punjabis would have an experience to parallel that of the Madrasi civil servant I knew who told me that his own children had been rocked in the same cradle as had at least five generations of his family before them.

Moreover, among all Punjabis certain behavioural characteristics and habits are very common. Extremity is not a feature pertaining to the climate alone.[6] It operates with reference to people and their loyalties. One must be faithful to a friend no matter what this involves one in: reward him extravagantly when one has the place and position to do so. One must treat one's enemies unmercifully, and flagrantly demonstrate that one is doing so. People are either enemies whom one hates or friends whom one loves. Feelings are direct and uncomplicated, a decisiveness which in many respects is reflected in the political formation of the 'paarti' or faction, i.e., there are always only two 'paartis'—that to which one's friends belong and that of one's enemies. Extremism as a principle extends into colours traditionally accepted for clothes. These were bright orange and yellow, purple and dark vivid greens, all of which are now branded by westernized urbanites as *fazuul* (garish). However, colours customarily chosen were not mellow and shading into one another, but definite and clashing. With food, the emphasis has been on having rich strong flavours rather than on achieving a subtle blend of flavours. In relationships, in clothes and in food, the concept is present that whatever one does, one must do thoroughly, otherwise it is better not to do it at all. If one wants to get from one place to another one goes as fast as one can, and if one wants to entertain someone, entertain them lavishly—don't place one glass of whisky in front of them but the whole bottle. These are basic behavioural characteristics visible in most Punjabis.

Throughout the entire Punjab, each family's defence is still its own responsibility. Making private agreements for its own defence may be dangerous and certainly requires bravery but it implies no sacrifice of independence. The system of power distribution through-out the Punjab still takes into account the unwillingness of farmers and landlords to be ruled and of their desire for private power over an area. Only on one occasion in the past (aside from the period under British rule) has a large part of the territory of the undivided Punjab been under the control of one man—namely Maharajah Ranjit Singh. He then apportioned it out among loyal followers who distributed it to those who had served them. They were thereby converted from being equals who helped to conquer the territory into dependants who, overnight, could be dispossessed of everything, if the Maharajah willed. This was one reason why the Sikh chiefs south of the Sutlej river co-operated with the British against Ranjit Singh. The British were prepared to guarantee their right to remain masters in their own territory. Punjab today, either East or West, cannot be ruled without those who are in power in the state govern-ment co-operating with those who are in power in various local areas. It is this political system which is discussed in the remainder of the book specifically with reference to East Punjab and the Jat Sikh community.

(ii) The land

The Punjab, as it is at present constituted, is divided into three areas—Majha, Doaba and Malwa—which are the names for the three areas between the rivers Ravi and Beas, Beas and Sutlej, and Sutlej and Jumna. These rivers, especially the Beas and the Sutlej, are the main sources of water for irrigating the farms and of hydro-electric power in the state. Soils are a mixture of sand and clay. The climate is semi-arid. Rain falls principally in the months of July and August, decreasing from thirty-five inches near the hills until it is only eighteen inches near the borders with Rajasthan. Low rainfall is gradually ceasing to be an important factor for agricultural production, as almost 55 per cent of the net area sown is irrigated either by canal or tube well. Tube wells may be private property or government owned. There is indeed no shortage of water, but rather the main problem is that of intensive irrigation from canal water causing soil salinity and water-logging in certain areas.

The harvest is thus sufficiently protected from drought and fluctuates little from year to year. The whole of Punjab is a food surplus area and it exports grain, particularly wheat, to other parts of India, being at present the second largest wheat-producing area in the Union. In 1959–60, India was receiving on average only seven maunds of wheat per acre (i.e., 580 lbs). In the same year, the highest yield per acre for wheat in the Punjab was just over eighty-three maunds. These wheat yields were the highest in the country. Since then wheat yields have risen steadily with the intensive use of purchased inputs, fertilizers, insecticides, seed drills, air-tight metal storage bins, and, above all, use of the new high-yielding varieties of wheat such as PV-18 and Kalyan.

Each year there are two main harvests: the *rabi*, or spring harvest, in which wheat and grams sown in November are reaped in the months of April and May; and the *kharif*, or autumn harvest, in which cotton, millet and maize are sown in the period June to August and reaped from October until mid-December. Sugar cane is being increasingly grown. It is sown in March and cut and harvested at the end of November.

An upper limit of thirty standard acres, not exceeding eighty ordinary acres, has been set by statute on the ownership of land.[7] The productivity of the land, as affected by the texture of the soil and irrigation facilities, was the major criterion in determining what was a standard acre. An acre of land which could yield ten to eleven maunds of wheat (828 lbs)[8] was given the value of 1 rupee and was termed a standard acre. The physical area of a standard acre thus varied. In rain-fed areas (*barani*) the valuation of one acre was 4 annas, and four ordinary acres went to one standard acre. In tracts irrigated by canal or by well, where the value of one acre was 1 rupee, an ordinary acre was the equivalent of one standard acre. The ceiling therefore differed according to the quality of the land. It applied to individuals and not to the aggregate area held by a family. Hence ownership of land, especially in the case of those with large landholdings, was distributed among family members. This, however, is no longer allowed under the new law (1971) which allows only 17½ acres for a family of five. There was exemption from the ceiling for specialized farms, e.g., seed farms, dairy farms, orchards.

Categories of population and the institutional framework

The population of Punjab, which was just over eleven million, almost one-fifth of whom were urban,[9] was divided on the basis of community, of language, and of urban or rural residence. The Sikhs approached 60 per cent of the total population, and approximately five-sixths of the Sikh community were concentrated in the rural areas. They spoke Punjabi, and the language was written in the Gurumukhi script. According to their religious tradition the script had been invented by their second religious prophet in the sixteenth century. Hindus formed approximately 40 per cent of the population, and at least one-third of their total numbers[10] were found in the four major cities of Patiala, Ludhiana, Jullundur and Amritsar and in the innumerable market towns. The Hindu percentage of the total urban population in the three major districts of the Central Punjab was 67·7. Many Hindus spoke Punjabi at home and at work but for census purposes always declared Hindi in Devanagari script to be their mother tongue. Languages were thus associated with specific religious communities, while the urban-rural cleavage also tended to be a cleavage on the basis of community, Sikh interests being dominantly rural interests.

The state had very little mineral wealth but it had considerable industry. Ludhiana, for example, with a population of 244,032, was the biggest centre in India for hosiery goods, hosiery machines and textiles. It was also prominent in the production of woollens and sewing-machines. Amritsar, fifteen miles from the border with Pakistan, had a population of 376,295 and was important in manufacturing carpets for export, and in cotton dyeing and printing. Much of this industry was controlled by Hindus, and this was one reason why Sikhs were to be found mainly in transport, in the motor spare parts industry and in the manufacture of machine tools. Industrial development was chiefly in the small-scale sector and it has been commented that a notable feature of the Punjab industrial pattern is the predominance of small units.

In 1969 the average *per capita* income was 575 rupees, as compared with the average for India of 422 rupees.[11]

I now set out briefly the institutional framework of the province, since much of the data which I shall later present on factionalism are embedded in a number of institutional contexts, viz. those of the judiciary, the civil administration, the police administration, and the State Assembly.

(i) *The judiciary*

The high courts stand at the head of the judicial administration in the states of the Union. Every high court consists of a Chief Justice and a number of judges determined by the President of India according to the needs of the state concerned. The President appoints judges in the high court in consultation with the Chief Justice of India and the Governor of the State concerned, though the latter relies greatly on the advice of the Chief Minister (CM). The high court has both original and appellate jurisdiction in civil and criminal matters and superintends the work of all courts within the state. The most important of these are the district courts, whose personnel are appointed by the state Governor with the advice of members of the high court and whose postings and promotions are now under the control of the latter. Beneath the district courts are a number of courts of subordinate judges, who deal with cases relating to civil matters having a value, for purposes of jurisdiction, of up to 10,000 rupees. Also beneath the district courts are the magistrates' courts, dealing with specifically criminal matters. Over the magistrates there is a chief judicial magistrate at district headquarters, who has power of withdrawing cases from the magistrates' courts and transferring them to the district court. Cases of a serious nature, e.g., murder, rape, armed robbery and forgery, are tried by a sessions judge at district headquarters. Apart from trying such cases, the sessions judge hears appeals from the orders of magistrates.

(ii) *The administration*

Administratively, Punjab is divided into eleven districts[12] and at the head of each there is a Deputy Commissioner (DC) and a Superintendent of Police (SP). Each district is further subdivided into units known as 'tehsils', there being usually three to six tehsils to a district. Attached to each tehsil is an official whose duties are the collection of land revenue, the checking of revenue records to recover loans and the superintending of transfers of land. Beneath him are a number of clerks, each of whom is in charge of the land records of a number of villages. Both the official in charge of the tehsil and his subordinates were key persons in the rural areas, since they determined how official documents would record ownership of land. It is the DC and the official in charge of a tehsil who, in their respective units, empower the police to take action in case of failure to comply with their orders, and, who, in times of a state of emergency, rule respectively the district and the tehsil.

The DC and the SP are ultimately recruited by what is known as the Union Public Services Commission. This is a statutory body which conducts examinations and interviews for recruitment to the administrative services of the Union, of which the most important are the Indian Administrative Service (IAS), the Indian Foreign Services and the Indian Police Service. The equivalent body for the state of Punjab was the Punjab Public Services Commission. Parliament in the Union, or the Assembly in the state, can regulate the recruitment and conditions of service of the persons appointed by the Union Public Services Commission or the public services commission of any one of the states; appointments can be taken out of the purview of the latter by Parliament and the legislature in their respective areas of control. A member of the civil service of the state can be dismissed, however, only by the Governor, though this rule does not apply if the person is dismissed or reduced in rank on grounds of conduct which has led to his conviction on a criminal charge. The CM of a state also, although he cannot technically dismiss an IAS officer, can get a charge made against an officer or enter a bad report on his file. The chairman of any public services commission in a state is appointed by the Governor, and half of the members of the Commission itself are supposed to have served for ten years in the government of the state in another capacity prior to their appointment. In Punjab the CM had a large say in the appointments of such persons and in the appointments made by them.

At the head of the CID, the Punjab Armed Police and the district police is the Inspector General of Police, Punjab. Beneath him are two deputy inspector generals in charge of the Punjab Armed Police: one dealing with the border districts of Amritsar, Ferozepur and Gurdaspur, the other at police headquarters at Jullundur. Another deputy inspector general heads the CID, whose function when Congress was the ruling party was to watch over political parties other than the Congress, private associations and those Congress MLAs who did not belong to the CM's group. The heads of the CID in each district are not under the SP or the DC but are responsible directly to the deputy inspector general of the CID. A Vigilance Department is attached to the CID. This department has nothing to do with direct law enforcement but is purely concerned with making investigations and enquiries into the conduct of administrative officers. Officers of the Vigilance Department are stationed at the state capital of Chandigarh, though some are deputed by the deputy inspector general of the CID to go out into the districts and enquire into individual cases. After the CID has investigated a case, it is checked by the Director of Vigilance and, thirdly, it is reviewed by the departmental secretary. Subsequently the CM decides if a case is to be instituted. Such a case is then customarily heard and judged in the presence of two enquiry officers of the civil service. Those technical experts of all administrative departments who have a reputation for reliability and honesty are taken onto the vigilance staff to make enquiries regarding complaints against officers of their own department. In the period of tenure in office of one CM— Partap S. Kairon—they were also used to collect private and confidential information for the CM on the personal weaknesses of IAS officers, which would facilitate their removal should they be obstructive to him.

(iii) Elective institutions

During the period of my fieldwork, Punjab was territorially divided into 104 Assembly constituencies with representatives known as MLAs sitting in the Vidhan Sabha, or State Assembly, in Chandigarh and thirteen parliamentary constituencies, with representatives known as MPs sitting in the Lok Sabha, or Lower House of Parliament, in Delhi. There were eight assembly constituencies to each parliamentary one. All bills passed in the State Assembly were deemed to be law. The powers of the state government, however, regarding law and order, education beyond the primary stage, health and economic development overlap with those of the Union and in effect only land reform and agricultural taxation are the sole prerogatives of the state government.

In agriculture, minor irrigation works, primary education and local communication, the state government had devolved all its functions on a three-tier structure of elected bodies. These were respectively the pancayats (village councils), the block samiti and the zilla parishad (district council). The block samiti consisted of certain heads of village pancayats and certain co-opted members representing women and scheduled castes. The system of blocks aimed at raising standards of agricultural production, improving sanitation, paving village streets and providing connecting roads between villages. One block covered one hundred villages, and in Ludhiana district, where I did my fieldwork, there were ten blocks. A block development officer (BDO) was appointed to each block, and attached to him there were certain experts in agriculture, health and engineering. Before the block samitis came into force in 1962 the BDO would formulate, organize and execute schemes for rural areas. Since then, however, a BDO has only advised the technical standing committees attached to the block samiti (one in finance, one in health, two in education, three in agricultural production). The presidents of all block samitis of a district formed, together with members of the state legislature for a district and various technical personnel, the zilla parishad.

Part two
Sikh Jats

2 Perspective on community studies

The fieldwork area

The bulk of the participants in the factions I later discuss were Sikh, and they came from that section of the community known as the Jats, the majority of whom lived in villages in the rural areas where they were landowners. During my fieldwork I did not reside permanently in one particular village. My purpose being to study factions on a state-wide basis, the fieldwork area was not only that of a village or a group of villages located in a particular area. Facts pertaining to leaders of factions at state level had also to be gathered, principally from interviews, historical records, documents, reports and letters. Thus a considerable part of my time was spent in the state capital of Chandigarh.

That part of my fieldwork, however, which was conducted using the traditional anthropological methods of observation, participation and casual interview, was carried out in what was known as the Doraha–Payal–Sirhind area. This area was part of the Central Punjab and had originally been included in PEPSU, an area comprising the territories formerly ruled over by the Sikh princes and which had its own legislature and high court until 1956. It was fifteen to forty miles distant from one of Punjab's major cities—Ludhiana— and coincided approximately with the four assembly constituencies of Payal, Khanna, Sirhind and Amloh (see Map 3). It contained approximately 250 villages. Much of my information was collected in a small market town (*mandi*), Doraha, which was one of the principal centres of factional activity, and in two small villages near Payal. Doraha itself was situated where the famous Sirhind canal met and cut across the main road leading from Amritsar via Ambala to Delhi. Sirhind (approximately twenty-two miles away) and Gobindgarh (seventeen miles away), two other major centres of factional activity, were situated along the same road. Payal, a fourth centre of factionalism, was approximately twelve miles from Doraha.

15

The area had been repeatedly sacked and plundered during the Moghul period. Ludhiana tehsil, an area approximately coinciding with the Doraha–Payal–Khanna area, had also a tradition of high recruitment to the army. Thirty per cent of male Jat Sikhs of Ludhiana district had enlisted in the First World War, and Ludhiana tehsil had been the principal recruiting ground for these. This tradition of high enlistment into the army continues.[1]

(i) *Punjabi villages and southern European communities*

There are several reasons why, in the Punjab, an anthropological study cannot be confined to a single village or to villages as such. Only in a certain empirical situation can villages be seen to be units, the relevant variables in this connexion being: the existence of strong ties to a particular locality; the endogamy of local communities; the physical separation of these communities from one another by the area's natural topography; the concentration of power, both political and economic, and of education in the towns and its association with a particular class, who also place a premium on urban residence. One reason for the now sufficiently numerous community studies done in southern Europe (as well as in Turkey and other parts of the Middle East) is that in varying degrees all these characteristics were present and thus, as well as it being methodologically easier to concentrate on small units, it could not be proved theoretically invalid. Southern European communities are socially (by the stratification pattern)[2] and geographically (by physical topography)[3] isolated and the evidence that they are so is that they structure their relationships with those in towns via mediators. This, however, is a complete contrast to the situation in Punjab where there is no concept of the superiority of urban residence, where exogamy prevails rather than endogamy and where there is no rigid stratification. Principles of kinship and affinity are important rather than ties of locality and class, and different social formations are the result. The social networks of Punjabi society, together with those aspects of its history and value system as have affected their maintenance, determine what are the relevant units on which to focus in the Punjabi milieu. Specifically, certain structural features (to be developed in subsequent chapters) explain why the units of the family and the faction rather than the village are of significance.

(ii) *The unimportance attached to ties of locality and of class among the Jats*

For purposes of elucidation only, this situation may be contrasted with Andalucia where, as Pitt Rivers describes, bonds of locality[4] are so strong that the people of the pueblo have no links beyond it. Their interactional system is thus within a defined spatial area. Endogamy results in any additional ties and links being made within the village and the concept of neighbourhood therefore develops only with reference to a small area. Such ties link by kinship, affinity and friendship, people of approximately equivalent status who have little access to relationships beyond the village. These features of the rural social system in southern Spain clearly contribute to lack of contact and connexion between villages and between village and town, and hence favour their analytical treatment as units. The inegalitarian nature of the societies of which they are a part especially renders them readily isolable. For a village represents a distinct type of social world and whoever lives in a village portrays socially identifiable characteristics—poverty, illiteracy—while usually also they are either tenants or labourers. In the rural Punjab, however, the two features which would isolate a village as a unit, namely, the existence of strong ties on a territorial basis and upper-class solidarity in the towns, are not present. Neither are there, for example, the wide cultural differences between rural settlements and the towns described by Stirling throughout his book *A Turkish Village*, which will facilitate the isolation of the villages as a unit.

(iii) *Exogamy*

Jats usually marry out of their own village and frequently out of the village of their mother; also out of their father and mother's clan. Normally a man not only uses his wife's immediate relatives, but also her family's entire set of connexions, in addition to the set of connexions of the extended family to which he belongs and all the connexions of the extended families into which his daughters and sisters are married. Distant affinal relatives help their kin on request and indeed, since they may be in the army or police administrative officers, expect to be asked for favours.[5] Because of the nature of exogamy in the Punjab, 'family' consists of a state-wide network of relatives.[6] Without such a family a Jat is considered to have no protection and, in effect, to be homeless. Within the text, many examples are noted of how affinal kin are used, and how persons profit and suffer at various times as a result of their political associations. One consequence of exogamy therefore and the nature of the family unit that it establishes is that the Jat community is closely knit. The Jat villages are not.

(iv) Friendship and enmity

Those ties that do exist within a village are based not on common residence there nor on sharing any like position, but on friendship, the social evidence of which is being a member of the same faction and being loyal to all those within the faction. Everyone is a neighbour who is a friend. It is not only therefore on an affinal and kin basis that there is a constant interaction beyond the village. These interconnexions also occur due to friendship and, by implication, due to enmity since one's friends' enemies become one's own as well. As will be seen in later chapters, there is no inhibition about involving state leaders in local disputes and these leaders do not offer any resistance to being so involved. Their supporters come from a variety of villages and mix in that capacity. Usually half of the members of any village are tied laterally to members of other villages throughout their own local area (and maybe further afield as well —see chapter 11) and linked vertically to one or more state-level political leaders (see chapter 12). The lateral ties and vertical links established by this structure create a unit which cuts across villages. Empirically one is therefore dealing in the Punjab with a state-wide, rather than a village, reality. Any Jat knows, feels himself to be and is, as much part of the state as of his own village.

(v) The value system sustaining the social networks of family and faction

The value system: the requirements of honour and prestige and the meaning attributed to independence and equality encourage widespread linkages in the community.

Equality does not mean, as it has so often meant in western Europe, the extension of privilege. It has no such connotations of 'sameness'. To be equal means to be independent and independence means having one's freedom within one's own area. If one does not have such independence one is less than an equal and does not share in the equality which other men possess. One has therefore been insulted— hence lowered. A man's equality thus depends on his reputation not to be 'subject to insult'. Such independence/equality can only be safeguarded by interdependence. Families trade what they have to offer each other in terms of material wealth and political protection. Other kinds of exchange are also incorporated under the same value. For example, a certain very high police official used to confide in an old friend, who was in politics, at moments of extreme pressure from his political boss. In return for this favour of trust on one occasion he had passed on his intelligence record to him. Friendship crosses many lines. This bargaining and exchange is not against a man's independence because it preserves his freedom. Reciprocation is part of the concept of honour and this is also one reason why leaders involve themselves in local quarrels.

The refusal to submit to threats is a sign of independence, and also an indication that ties of interdependence in the form of the faction exist. Factions, so far as the Jats are concerned, exist to provide a collective protection to each individual family in its friendships and enmities, and thereby to protect their honour and their reputation and hence their parity of standing with all other families. Factions, which are, in one guise, state-wide family alliances with a political object, then also exist to protect the values to which Jats are faithful. These values require the existence of a wide variety of allegiances for the protection of what Jats regard to be the repository of honour, that is, the family. The existence of these allegiances makes it impossible to concentrate on a village as a unit since doing so would give no picture of the ties and connexions which extend far beyond its boundaries.

(vi) The nature of the patronage tie

Punjab's patrons do not have their position ascribed; their position is achieved. The patronage tie presumes an equality by virtue of the fact that what it involves between two persons is reciprocal protection of the other's sphere of influence. 'Clients' in the Punjab are not those to whom favours are done, the victims of a system of charity that makes piecemeal adjustments to the inequalities of life. They have the capability to reciprocate for what they receive from a

patron who is different from them only in that he has more power
at that one moment in time when they ask for a favour. Leaders
are always approachable and there is no structural distance between
them and their supporters. It is indeed a basic feature of Jat society,
if not its most important feature, that everyone is contactable to
everyone else, for all purposes. Patronage dispensed by a political
patron within the faction therefore creates rural solidarity rather
than village solidarity since his followers are not only from his own
local area but from all local areas. Political patrons never lose
contact with the areas in which they were born and reared, rarely
lose contact with their old schoolfriends and their parents, their
relatives wherever they might be (unless, of course, they are in the
opposing faction). Even though he may be an MLA, resident in the
state capital of Chandigarh and his supporters and any who want to
see him are in their villages, he can never be separated off in any way.
One MLA I knew found his garden crowded each day with persons
demanding that he accompany them to the various administrative
offices. His wife had to provide beds and food for them all. The
common values which all Jats share sustain this lack of social
distance. All Jats alike are brought up to be proud irrespective of
what they possess in terms of education, wealth or power. No Jat
defines himself as subservient and none can actually be trampled
upon. All alike are bound by these norms, a feature which does not
characterize most of the southern European villages studied and
which as noted many times hence marks them out as units which are
distinguishable and separate.

To sum up. Actual political power and the contenders for it were
dispersed throughout a number of units, each headed by a political
leader with supporters and followers in a specific local area. No
corporate village intervened. A man conceived himself as belonging
first to a family and then to a 'paarti'. Jats were linked by ties of
blood, or affinity, and in the reciprocity relationships binding friends
and leaders and their supporters. A village was important to a man
only in so far as his land happened to be there and therefore he
resided there. Villages, as such, only came into the political picture
at all because the political interests and activities of their leading
members invariably linked them into the larger territorial political
unit of the state. In this context the village is important as one of
many 'gathering grounds' of recruitment for political support. With
the prime importance of the kinship, affinity and friendship principles,

neighbourhood ties become unimportant and the scene is set, potentially, for far and wider-reaching allegiances. Families ally on the basis of these principles to operate in a faction. If, then, a study is limited to a village, it will provide neither an accurate picture of Jat family units and their widely ramifying ties and networks, nor of the factions through which they function politically in the structure of state politics. In southern Europe the isolation and incommunicability of communities were the two main reasons why they were traditionally suitable for study as wholes. In the Punjab, where the city can be distinguished neither as the home of a cultural tradition nor as the home of an *élite* nor as the locus of political and administrative power, it is, beyond doubt, impossible to define villages as units or parts of the political system.

Village studies in theoretical perspective

Whether villages can be considered units is also, however, a theoretical problem or, at least, must be treated as such, in view of the number of monographs that have appeared stating, for various reasons, the relevance of small community studies. Pitt Rivers, in *People of the Sierra*, implies that anthropological techniques are not suitable for the analysis of wider units and this being so 'one delimits the area of one's data according to the techniques one wants to use', (p. 208). Similarly, Stirling, at the beginning of his book, claims that his training suits him only for the study of small communities. Both statements focus attention on the fact that the kind of unit it is convenient for a fieldworker to observe, and what it is realistic and appropriate to observe simply because it exists, do not necessarily coincide. One should not disregard actually important social and political processes simply in order to do the kind of analysis for which one has received professional training. Frequently, however, this has occurred.

Lopreato (in *Peasants No More*) and Banfield (in *The Moral Basis of a Backward Society*), for example, although working in areas of southern Italy where the Mafia is known to operate, that is respectively Calabria and Lucania, manage to restrict the scope of their work to local communities. Key characteristics of the social and political systems are thereby excluded from mention. A study of the linkages of that system would have been theoretically relevant. As it is, one is left with the problem as to how the various coalitions which the Mafia is composed and which are referred to by Blok in his article 'The Mafia and peasant rebellion as contrasting factors in Sicilian Latifundism', fit in with the pattern of community studies done by most anthropologists. Can the Mafia only be studied by novelists (Puzo, *The Godfather*; Maxwell, *God Protect Me from my Friends*; Lewis, *The Honoured Society*) and social reformers (Dolci, *To Feed the Hungry, The Outlaws of Partinico*, and *Waste*)?

With respect to studies which have been done in the Indian sub-continent, Bailey (in *Politics and Social Change*),[7] to take one example, does not look at the political activity of a single small unit but attempts to understand the political processes at work in the state. I try to do similarly. The differences in our respective approaches only stem from the different content of our data. For Bailey (in 'Two villages in Orissa', pp. 78–9) explicitly states that

> If the explanatory value of analysing the social structure of the village becomes very low, and a relatively large number of factors have to be taken as 'given', then the social anthropologist must be prepared to select ... those 'given' elements which seem susceptible to social analysis by his own techniques ... otherwise he runs the risk of losing touch with contemporary reality.

He has also noted earlier that the boundaries he seeks to draw with reference to the two villages he studied and their relationships to outsiders apply only to his own research. Bailey (*Politics and Social Change*) sees the two villages in which he did intensive research, and the constituency of which these villages are a part, as units. Concerning Bailey's data at what he calls 'the constituency level', one problem seems to be that the constituency is a level at election times only. The nature of my own data prevented me from classifying the constituency as 'a level'. The corresponding term I used, if it can be called that, is 'the local area', which consisted of four constituencies. It may, in fact, have contained fewer constituencies than this or, alternatively, more, but as it happened these four constituencies were the active sphere of influence of a particular state political leader and an area of combat between him and the CM of the state. I demarcated it for study on this basis and used the two opposed chains of links into which political leaders, their supporters in the local area, and their followings, aligned themselves, on a semi-permanent basis, to understand the political system. Since it was such units that I isolated out as being crucial parts of the political system, I did not have the problem, as Bailey[8] did, of whether the villages I chose were typical or not as I had not specified them to be parts of that system which I have indicated earlier—families and factions—extended across the state. The same type of semi-permanent linkages existed in all localities of the province.

Families and factions were both non-local units and the arena for their political activity was the state itself. The supporting evidence for these statements from chapter 11 onwards can be contrasted with the views of Morrison who, on the evidence obtained from a single village in the northern part of the Karnal district, believes villages to be 'isolable political wholes'.[9] He states that 'the political system described here is a closed one. Its territorial base is the village itself.'[10] It is difficult to judge whether or not this set of facts has emerged and is a consequence of a certain prior methodological approach and set of assumptions. Anthropologists going out to do fieldwork in India have received prior theoretical and conceptual conditioning that the village is the context of relevance and they have regarded its boundaries as establishing a unit within which to observe political activity. The problem that ethnographers who worked in the Punjab therefore gave themselves was that of relating villages to the political life of the state. Izmirlian, for example, describes his work as 'a detailed examination of the political relations between a Punjab village and the larger society of its region'.[11] Similarly, Morrison, because he conceived of villages as encapsulated entities and the wider society and its political system as external, immediately defined his problem as being their relation to the state political system. With respect to the Punjab, as has been seen, this would appear to be a problem that bears no relation to socio-political reality; an invented problem in that the unit in which political activity actually takes place is a state-wide unit—the faction. The problem also owes its existence to the structuralist school in social anthropology which selected small communities for study and sought to discover and relate every aspect of their life. In many respects, as Steward remarks, it treated the wider society as if it did not exist.[12] Even when structuralists did not treat small communities as self-contained wholes, their manner of connecting them to the wider society was to focus on the formal political framework, for example, in this case, the pancayat, the block, the district council, and totally to neglect the units functioning within and across this total structure. In Punjab these were factions. Thus the criticisms made by Dumont and Pocock ('Village Studies', pp. 23–41) of Marriott ('Village India') that by posing the problem of the representativeness and relevance of village studies he has given the village a 'sociological reality' (p. 25), would apply to those who have worked in the Punjab. To some extent any work in the Punjab should have bypassed this problem of 'the relevance of the village' by virtue of the existence of certain structures already described of very wide span. The real problem is—how can one person cope with an ethnographic unit of such expansion?

One describes a factional network 'because it is there'. But, if one has the presuppositions these works evidence, one clearly will not see it to be there. In this respect the rules which have guided some anthropological research in India (for example, to regard the village as 'an invaluable observation centre')[13] have resulted in observations that are, at the most, factually wrong, and, at least, harmless and irrelevant. On a philosophical level they are the very crude evidence of 'the primacy of the abstract' to quote the title of an article by Friedrick Hayek. For riveted, as they are from the very beginning, to certain themes they thereby impose a set of meanings which are not necessarily relevant to a situation. Indeed, when one encounters these village studies one is almost prepared to welcome the empiricism so much criticized in the same book in a joint article by Piaget and Inhelder ('The gaps in empiricism', pp. 118–60).[14] When cognitive mechanisms become so divorced from reality one is clearly on a treasure hunt for what one cannot find.

Wider issues are thus raised in that it would appear that observations cannot necessarily be accepted as ethnographic facts and that 'writings do not necessarily represent ethnographic realities'.[15]

3 Significant events in Jat history

In this chapter I endeavour to show the historical continuity between the organization of factions in the past and in the present. I relate a relevant section of the history of the Jats in order to illustrate the historical persistence of the faction as a traditional mode of political organization in the rural areas.

Sikhs numbered ten million in all, most of whom were settled in the Punjab. The word Sikh, etymologically meaning 'learner' or 'disciple', was a term signifying both the follower of a religion and membership of a community. Anyone who believed in the ten gurus, the religious prophets of the Sikhs, and in their writings as contained in the Granth Sahib, or holy book, was designated a Sikh. Sociologically and culturally a Sikh was a member of a community who wore the five symbols which were the visible identification marks of belonging to the community. These were a *kirpan* (steel dagger), a *kara* (steel bangle), *kachchh* (short breeches), a *kanghha* (comb) and *kes* (uncut hair). Why these particular symbols should have been chosen to show distinctiveness is not completely clear. According to religious tradition they were given in 1699 when the tenth and last of the Sikh gurus—Govind S.—had established what was known as the Khalsa, a collective term for all those who, on baptism, had taken the common surname of Singh[1] in the case of men and Kaur[2] in the case of women, who wore the five aforementioned symbols, and who renounced their previous occupation for military pursuits. The pursuit of arms was rendered the religious duty of the Sikhs. However, it would be historically more accurate to say that these symbols, which in the course of time came to be regarded as distinctively Sikh symbols, were evolved during the events of the eighteenth century and were associated with the influx of Jats into the community. Uncut hair was a Jat custom,[3] while a thick kara and the turban were worn for protection in warfare.

The Jats were mainly small proprietors and tenants, a few were

25

landowners. When the sixth guru had succeeded in building up an army the recruits had been drawn from the Jats. Similarly, Govind's attempt to turn a small band of religious believers into a political community similarly coincided with a large influx of the Jats of Majha into the Khalsa. The essentially mystic and non-sectarian philosophy of Nanak, acknowledged by Sikhs to be the founder of their faith, was appropriated by a defined social category with a distinct historical identity and became an effective medium through which their opposition to Rajput landowners and Muslim rulers alike was expressed and unified.[4] The rise of militant Sikhism in the Punjab was, in effect, the rise of the Jats.[5] The ranks and leadership of the Khalsa, from this period onwards until the nineteenth century, were predominantly Jat.[6] The history that follows, therefore, is primarily the history of the Jat section of the Sikh community.

The history of the Jats during the eighteenth century appears to have been characterized by uniformity in the pattern of political allegiance and in the type of political situation generally current at any given time. 'Factionalism' in the form in which I am to describe it in part three has been an historically important phenomenon and has represented for the Jats a relatively persistent and typical mode of organization. The prevalent situation has been that no effective operative unit—either of village or caste—has intervened between the extended families and such governmental rule as existed. In the absence of such units the significant linkages of men have been into factional coalitions which were more frequently engaged in conflict with each other,[7] and which were only sporadically united against the Muslims. A faction was seen by its members as offering them protection, and once in power over a given area it would challenge the ability of other units constituted on the same structural principle to protect within that area. Historically this has been the only permanent form of organization that has persisted in rural areas through the frequent collapses of central rule. Historically the type of situation that has been continuous, and to this extent characteristic, has been that of emergency—emergency in the form of repeated invasions and in the form of predatory acts of one or more families in alliance with particular officials in government and administration against other families aligned with an opposing coalition. The section of historical data that follows presents the essence of the Punjab environment, to which the factional mode of organization seems to correspond. I am, of course, here conceptually postulating

an objectively historical link of present forms of political organization with past forms of organization, a link of which Jats show no
awareness. I first give a general account of the history subsequent
to the death of Govind S. and before the ascent of Maharajah
Ranjit S.; and then I cite a small number of examples from this
history to illustrate the general points I have made.[8]

After the death of Govind S. there were innumerable further
conflicts with the Moghul empire. Sikhs incited peasant uprisings
against local officials and Muslim landlords, and held Punjab
intermittently from 1710 to 1715. In that year they were defeated by
the then Moghul emperor, Jahandar Shah, the grandson of Aurungzeb, and an edict was issued that wherever found they were to be
apprehended and killed. Many fled to inaccessible areas of the hills,
leaving their land and womenfolk in the care of relatives. In the hills
they lived the life of outlaws, existing by plunder, but—in combination with one another when it was profitable—they took villages
under their protection. A central fighting force—the Dal Khalsa—
was established in 1735. It reflected a pattern of organization in
which various plundering bands, each headed by a chief or sirdar,
had complete freedom of action and were expected to combine in
the event of danger to the community as a whole. In 1738 the province
was invaded by the Persian, General Nadir Shah; but the Sikh
sirdars did not combine their followings to face him in open combat,
and in the absence of such unity the capacity of each small band was
sufficient only to raid for plunder. While Moghuls and Persians
fought each other the Sikhs plundered units of the Persian army and
wealthy people, who, in terror of the war, fled from the towns.

There followed nine Afghan invasions in the period 1745–67,
under Nadir Shah's most trusted general, Ahmed Shah Abdali.
These were plundering expeditions and were in no way successful in
establishing a settled government. It was during this period that the
Sikhs grouped themselves into misls.[9]

In 1748 the army or Dal Khalsa was divided into eleven misls,[10]
which were mainly found to the north of the Sutlej, that is, in the
Majha area. The twelfth misl (that of Phulkia) was not part of the
Dal Khalsa and was the only misl in the Malwa area. Each misl was
associated with a specific territorial area which was the sphere of
influence of a particular chief (sirdar). Each sirdar put into the field
a certain number of fighting men, mainly cavalry, with himself as
leader, to form one of the army's regiments. Each misl was

considered the equal of the others, though the fighting strength of each was not equal. Within the sphere of its control every misl was free to act in the way it chose, and they were bound to combine in alliance and take united action only when they faced a common danger. Not only was every misl free to choose its alliances but each fighting man was free to join any misl he chose, i.e., to choose his leader. He received no regular pay from the sirdar and in fact was not under any obligation to obey beyond what was required in his own interests. During the period of the invasions, Moghuls and Afghans fought for control of the province, which remained without a government. In this situation some misls routed Abdali every time he crossed the Punjab, others collaborated with the Moghuls, while yet others offered to undertake to protect the peasantry of certain areas against plunder, in return for payment of one-fifth of their takings, twice yearly, at the end of each harvest. The relationships of co-operation of the Sikh chiefs were with whoever would repay them with land and territory.

The economic backing to the system was not solely plunder and the levying of tribute. The Sikhs were themselves landowners, though during this period irrigation by canals remained in a very rudimentary stage: the interfluves between the rivers were semi-desert, and when rain did not fall in adequate quantities, famines occurred. No fighting was done in the rainy season (July to September) but for the rest of the year there appears to have been a division of labour. At harvest time, for example, some members of the family would be harvesting the produce of their own land while others would be roaming elsewhere to collect tribute. Many Hindu zamindars (landlords) co-operated with and joined the Sikh bands in their neighbourhood at this period. They suffered excessive taxation as well as maltreatment from marauding army units and were tempted by expectations of plunder and hopes of seizing land. The Jats of Majha had embraced Sikhism earlier, but it was during this period that many Malwa Jats from the Sirhind area—an area bordering on and including part of the fieldwork area—became Sikhs. The Moghul empire was crumbling, and joining the Khalsa was one means of obtaining independence and power. When Abdali left, Sikhs remained in undisputed possession of the province. Each separate band under a chief expanded as far as it could until it met the areas under the control of other chiefs.

As soon as the province was free of Afghans and there was no danger from invasion, the misl organization began to fall apart. The only reason why the followers of a sirdar continued to owe allegiance to a misl was to safeguard and add to their possessions. When Abdali vacated the Punjab, there was a situation when temporarily there was much territory to seize. The sirdars began quarrelling among themselves and aggrandizing themselves at one another's expense.[11] Not until the last years of the eighteenth century were the sirdars eventually reduced from equality and rivalry; then they were subjected by Ranjit S., who was formally invested with the title of Maharajah of the Punjab in 1801. Between the death of Ranjit S. in 1839 and the annexation of the province ten years later, anarchy similar to that I have just described again returned, and the civil administration disappeared amidst internecine struggles.

It is in the function of the misl that parallels can be seen with factional coalitions in the present—at least as I saw them operating in my fieldwork area. When a misl sirdar acquired territories, he first reserved a sufficient portion of these for himself, and then subordinate sirdars who had fought with him were given their share. These held the land on condition of continued military service. In turn they partitioned the land among their dependants. Otherwise, payment took the form of a share of the plunder after an expedition of conquest, and a follower would desert if he considered he had not received enough of the booty. This tiered structure of the misl was very similar to that of the faction at present. Joining a misl chief and rendering him services in war in return for protection, was one method of gaining an ally in periods of political upheaval. Only the content of the loyalty given to a leader in the present situation has changed, since it is now political loyalty and support that is offered, and not military support. Another method mentioned[12] of securing alliances was to marry one's daughters and sons into nearby villages so that one's affines were not too far distant and could readily give help. These two modes of forming an alliance continue to be, in the present, the most significant politically, for reasons discussed.

In one respect the wider situation in which the misl operated, however, was totally different from that in which the factional coalition has to operate at present: there was no stable central political authority to which it had permanently to refer its activities and within whose framework it had to carry out its plans, outside the local area in which it operated. At times the complete absence of such an authority made of the misl no more than a confederacy of chiefs who agreed to follow the general orders of the most powerful among them only in the event of a common threat and who otherwise were constantly quarrelling. Because, also, of the plurality of possible masters, it was easy for a follower of one of these chiefs to desert. The greater degree of impermanence in the structure of the misl at this time was thus related to the availability in number of those who had it in their power to dominate, and this in turn was related to the lack of a strongly centralized rule. It was in the context of an absence of an identifiably strong and permanent ruling power that the various chiefs in different parts of the province constantly changed their allegiances and alliances. I illustrate this with respect to the alliance formed by one Ala S., whose territory encroached on and in some places covered part of my fieldwork area. Ala S. headed the Phulkian misl, a misl composed of a group of chiefs descended from a common ancestor and represented now by the Maharajah of Patiala and the Rajas of Jind and Nabha.

In 1714 Ala S. had succeeded to thirty villages in the neighbourhood of Patiala. In his first military campaign he had combined with the misl leaders to seize the nearby town of Barnala (1727–8). The Rajput chiefs of the neighbourhood had allied themselves to the military commander (*faujdar*) of the Jullundur Doab, feeling threatened by Ala S.'s growing power as represented in his seizure of the territory of others, but they had been defeated. In 1745 Ala S. allied himself with the Moghul governor of Sirhind to expropriate the lands of a powerful Rajput chief whose influence was growing and whom both therefore wanted to check. Ala S. continued for a time to take help from the Moghuls and fought under the emperor against Abdali in 1747. In the next ten years, however, he extended his possessions, principally with the help of the other misls, in 1757 allying himself with twelve thousand of the Dal Khalsa, this time against the Moghul governor of Sirhind. Subsequently he relinquished his alliance with the emperor to avoid any agreement that would prevent him from sharing in the acquisition of territory along with the Majha Sikhs. In 1761 he got himself confirmed in these possessions as a result of paying submission to Abdali, and his misl was the only misl that did not fight against the Afghan invader in the famous battle of the Ghallughara in February 1762. Once Abdali had left the Punjab, however, he renewed his alliance with the misl chiefs of Majha to seize the territory of Sirhind.[13]

The motive that lay behind all Ala S.'s changes of allegiance was to place himself always under the protection of the powerful, whoever that might be at any given moment, so that he was able to retain the ascendancy in a particular area himself. There was no ideology behind his alliances, no rationale other than the seeking of protection so that he would be secure in his aggrandizements. From his base of power, locally very strong, he extorted titles from the emperor at Delhi, and finally from Abdali to put a seal on that power. This ensured that his existing followers would be less likely to desert, while smaller chiefs then attached themselves to him to escape forcible absorption. He, in turn, offered protection to them in return for military service. Now, the motive behind alliances with political leaders is the same, namely a search for protection from the influence that a leader has built up through exercise of his coercive power. The difference is that although in the present a leader at state level has certainly to come to terms with those who have control in rural areas, the latter cannot coerce him to the same extent as Ala S. coerced Abdali and the emperor, simply because the degree of dependence of the state political leader on any one of these local leaders in a centralized system is not so great. However, just as Ala S. attracted more followers once his power was confirmed, so also it will be seen that those controlling rural areas at present have retained much of their support only when their political patronage has been continuous.

In the province's recent past, when power was concentrated in one person for eight years, the power of the faction existed and persisted only by grace of his patronage. In this period of unitary rule, ties within the faction were stronger and the faction itself was more cohesive. It began to crumble and to lose some of its key participants only when its political patron at state level had also lost his power. When the latter event took place, a similar situation to that in which the misl operated arose, with the leaders of the faction concerned seeking for political patronage wherever they could.

The pattern of a misl's external relationships with units of like nature in the same locality was also comparable to those maintained by factional coalitions in the present. Thus in 1776 a quarrel arose between the chiefs of two misls—the sirdar of the Kanheyas and the sirdar of the Ramgarhias[14]—both of whose lands lay interspersed in the upper portions of the Bari and Jullundur Doabs. The quarrel was over the division of the revenues of certain territories. To help him in this quarrel, the sirdar of the Kanheyas sought outside help and made common cause with another misl leader (Jassa S. Ahluwalia,[15] the supreme commander of the Dal Khalsa) who was already inimical to the Ramgarhia sirdar because he feared the Ramgarhia was becoming so powerful that he was about to seize his (Jassa's) lands. This pattern, of a local leader and his followers from a particular area allying themselves with those opposed to their enemy, was one whose repetition can be noted later with respect to events in the fieldwork area. In this particular battle the Kanheya sirdar won and the Ramgarhia sirdar was forced to flee from his lands in the Jullundur Doab and to relinquish his control over the hill state of Kangra, which he had made tributary in 1770. The Kanheya victory was, however, due to treachery among the followers of the Ramgarhia sirdar at Batala (then only a large village). The Ramgarhia rule was unpopular, and in the siege of Batala some of them had supplied the Kanheyas with provisions and horses and finally had opened the gates of the fort to let them in. There was, likewise, a continuation of this pattern in the present, with followers of one faction inside a village conspiring with those favourable to it from outside.

It is specifically this historical period between the death of Govind and the rise of Ranjit S., i.e., the period 1708–99, that may be isolated as being representative of a quality of life which appears to have been the historic mean for the province and which certainly characterizes conditions in certain rural areas of the province nowadays, for example the border areas. Of this period one reads: 'The cultivator followed the plough with a sword in his hand.' In the rural areas of the districts of Ferozepur, Amritsar, Bhatinda and Sangrur any difference in the situation now is one of content only, i.e., a farmer drives his tractor with a rifle slung across his shoulder or a revolver beside him, and rarely leaves home without a weapon of defence in his possession. Moreover in the rural areas a consciousness of the instability and insecurity of life and property persist; the feeling of a lack of rootedness of home and its possible loss. There has never been in Punjab a period of peace long enough to allow a forgetfulness of the contingent. One link with the past, therefore, is the actual and felt continuation of the same conditions in the rural areas as seen in a lack of public order and a lack of acceptance of central rule and authority.

It has been seen that the individual Sikh chieftains followed their own interests and made offers of submission to, conspired with, or opposed those in power according to their own interests and ambitions. These arose from their competition with other Sikh chiefs and the necessity to gain support and favour in case of defeat. The consequence was that internecine strife within the community persisted despite the ideal of a united Khalsa. Throughout history the community has been broken into various political coalitions and never represented by any single political allegiance or alliance. Unwittingly, the effect of this pattern has always been that it has been pregnant with the possibilities of guarding the community on all fronts or of betraying it on all fronts.

In the misl, men sought the protection of the strong, and the leader of a misl would attempt to contain the growing power or undermine the established power of another misl leader despite the need for unity against Afghans and Moghuls. Similarly, in the recent past and present, despite movements to unite the Sikhs in the defence and protection of their cultural heritage, power continues to be dispersed among coalitions of men, consisting of a political patron, his lieutenants and their followers, which are opposed to each other and whose role and effect is the same to that of the misl. Now, as in the past, the withdrawal or the commitment of support by a central or state authority to those controlling rural areas disturbs relationships of power in those areas, and, according to this factor, one factional coalition manages to take advantage of the situation to obtain more resources at the expense of the other. Gains made through various forms of illegality can be more lasting so long as political protection is secured. In a situation thus characterized by an absence of any acceptance of the legitimate rights of others, usurpation continues to have its customary historical lack of meaning. Perhaps it is because conditions in the rural areas of the province have not radically changed that the modes of organization, which were important historically, in gathering and mobilizing support for leaders, persist.

4 Patterns of allegiance I

Chapters 4 and 5 depict the social structure of the Sikh rural areas to which the factionalism among the Jats relates. I consider the ties which bind the Jats together and enumerate three kinds of tie as being important: kinship, affinity and the patron-client tie. I note that there is no set hierarchy among the Jat clans and that clan is not a basis for any kind of political alliance. I also report that there is no status differentiation between rich and poor among the Jats and that combinations on a class basis are almost non-existent. Nor have Jats any political solidarity on a caste basis. The family is a fundamental institution and affinal ties are used to link these families in advantageous combinations, both outside and inside the coalitions which I call factions.

Village links

The pattern of settlement in the Punjab had traditionally testified to the lawlessness of the province. The population was clustered in large nucleated villages and there were few isolated houses. Defence against invading armies had historically been the principal reason for concentration. In the fieldwork area the villages were generally one or two miles distant from one another. Many of them had been founded by a number of Jat clan heads, who originally came from different areas and who had united for convenience against outsiders in order to defend the land they had seized. Village solidarity had traditionally depended on co-operation between these groups on the basis of mutual interest; it was not a matter of kinship. Referring to the manner of dividing each village, Gupta remarks that 'the Sikh conquests were made by confederated bands. Every village was proportionately shared according to the number of horsemen present. . . . The single free Sikh horseman fighting on his

34

own account was entitled to his horse share.'[1] This practice and the invasions had a very disruptive effect on village solidarity. It has been noted that after the fourth invasion of Ahmed Shah 'from Lahore to Sirhind not a village was left tenanted'[2] and that 'deserted sites . . . still tell how even the strongest villagers had to abandon the spot where their fathers had lived'.[3] It is against this background of the uprooting of villages that one has to understand the lack of any conception of strong ties in villages as such. Solidarity on a village basis was not an adequate defence and seems to have been short-lived. The villages of the fieldwork area had been repeatedly sacked and plundered.

Now, factions divide villages and cut across village boundaries. This is a continuance of the historical pattern of a lack of political cohesion in each village unit. Villages are thus not to be considered as segments of the political system that are connected to the political and administrative structures at state level by their representatives. They have no such representatives who perform this function. Rather, certain prominent persons belonging to a faction in a particular local area and, having links in the administration and with political leaders at state level, attract followers from the various villages of that area. The significant political unit is therefore one which includes villagers, local area leaders and state political leaders.

Clan affiliation among the Jats

The factionalism I shall speak of occurred within that section of the Sikh community which owned land and which was economically and politically dominant in the rural areas, namely the Jats. According to the 1931 census, Jats formed just over 50 per cent of the total Sikh population.[4] They were the hereditary landowning section of the Sikh community, who traditionally had known no occupation but war and agriculture. In Maharajah Ranjit S.'s time they had constituted the ruling aristocracy and had continued to prosper under British rule. Canal colonies were developed at Lyallpur (1892), Sargodha (1897) and Montgomery (1912) and the colonists for those lands were Jat; it was they who were responsible for clearing the land, digging the canals and making some of the investment. The land of Sargodha canal colony was given in grants to Jat military officers, and as a response to their willingness to serve as soldiers the

British Raj passed the Land Alienation Act, whereby the transfer of landed property henceforth became limited to the agricultural classes.

The Jats, whether Hindu, Sikh or Muslim, have formed the back-bone of the agricultural community in Punjab, in the neighbouring provinces of Rajasthan and Sind, and in the western portion of the Gangetic Doab. They divide themselves into a number of clans known as 'gots', each of which has the tradition of descent from a Rajput ancestor[5] and of having come to the Punjab in the sixteenth century. The Jat section of the Sikh community is customarily endogamous[6] but their clans are exogamous.[7] There is no established hierarchy among the clans: they are unequal in size[8] but not ranked, and which Jat clan is regarded as being superior has seemed to vary according to the criteria selected for differentiation by the Jats as such. For example, at present, Garewals are admitted by other clans to be superior because a large number of them are in military service and administration. Traditionally their women have not worked in the fields, which is unique among the Sikh clans. Originally Garewals also considered themselves superior because of their tradition of descent from a Rajput prince. The oldest clan in the Punjab south and east of the Sutlej is that of the Sidhus. The premier Sikh prince —the Maharajah of Patiala—is a Sidhu, and his family traced its descent from 1526, while another Sidhu house in Majha—the Attari —traced its descent to the fourteenth century. Sidhus had played a prominent role in Sikh history, and the exploits of some Sidhu families were said to have raised the clan to a position of prominence in Sikh eyes. There was, however, a proverb which denied them their supremacy: 'Sandhu, Sidhu, ik baraabar, Gills tore uchera (Sandhus and Sidhus are equal but Gills are a bit superior to both).' There was also a tradition that the clans of Maan, Chahal, Bhullar were '*asal Jats*', that is, genuine Jats, and that all others were degraded from Rajputs.

Thus among the Jats there is no universally accepted hierarchy of clans. The clans are also not arranged spatially. Not only are adjacent villages of different clan, but also in some areas, such as the fieldwork area, different sections within the same village are also of different clan. Jat clans are therefore, in many instances, not localized kinship groupings.[9] There is now no further division into smaller units within the clan, nor is there any conception of clan solidarity as such. Clans among the Jats are merely divisions which are recognized by the Jats themselves for marriage purposes. Some families concerned with the 'lineage' (a term synonymous simply with background) of another family might be interested in the 'blue blood' of the Sidhus. Simply being a Sidhu, however, counts for nothing. Likewise, the Garewals have become associated with high administrative and political position, but a man cannot 'get' anything out of merely being a Garewal.

Class

The Jats live in rural areas, in large compact villages.[10] Almost a third of their villages were provided with an electricity supply at the time of my visit in 1965-7. Most of the villages in Central Punjab— i.e., in the districts of Amritsar, Ludhiana and Jullundur—are connected to one another by some form of road. This area is the province's most intensively irrigated belt and hence its most prosperous part.

As seen in the fieldwork area, there was no difference in way of life between the categories usually called landlord, middle-class farmer and small proprietor. They ate the same food—a basic diet of wheat, raw sugar (*gur*), milk, butter (*ghee*), fresh vegetables, lentils (*daal*) and occasionally meat and rice, and oranges in season. In the villages, food was usually cooked in the open and eaten in the open. Frequently there was an equal lack of toilet facilities in their houses. The conception of a house was that it was a shelter. The house of a landlord Jat, i.e., a Jat owning upwards of 200 acres of land, was certainly larger than its neighbours, all its portions, including those where cattle were kept, being made of stone or brick. But even this was rapidly ceasing to be a differentiating factor, especially between the landlord and the middle-class farmer. In addition, many small proprietors had that part of the house in which they lived built of brick and cement. Also, in the houses of small proprietors and landlords alike there was a lack of decoration, and ornaments were not displayed but locked up in steel trunks. These three categories of landlord, middle-class farmer and small proprietors could not be clearly distinguished by their outside connexions: it was not a pattern, for example, that small proprietors had some family members *only* employed in such jobs as bus conductor, lorry driver, in the ranks of the army, or as teachers, while those with large landholdings would have those of their family members working off the

land in high administrative and political positions. Many of those
in the latter positions had, indeed, small landholdings.

The main means of differentiating the middle-class farmer, i.e., a
farmer owning between fifty and a hundred acres of land, from the
small proprietor was in the former's possession of a car and certain
agricultural implements. Jats in the landlord category could be
distinguished from middle-class farmers by the number of household servants they employed, as also by the finer clothes, design
and quantity of jewellery, and finer looks of their womenfolk. Not
infrequently, too, their sons and daughters were educated at board-
ing school. By virtue of his connexions and his money, a larger
landowner was also more likely to be able to remove himself from
the monotony of village life whenever he wished, but again this was
becoming a less exclusive privilege. Moreover, during the harvesting
periods he participated in the same gruelling labour as did smaller
landholders. The way of life of the Jats was essentially the same
whether they were rich or poor.

Membership of these categories was, in any case, fluid, as the
amount of land in a family's possession was not constant. It was
specifically the system of land division on the death of the head of
the family and the customary inheritance of equal shares by his sons
that led to difficulty in conserving wealth. If, for example, the four
sons of a middle-class farmer who had eighty acres of land decided
on inheriting their father's property to divide it, each would then
have only twenty acres, i.e., they would have sunk to the category of
small proprietors. The categories of landlord, middle-class farmer
and small proprietor did not have anything like stable membership,
and families were not securely in any one category. Ranking on the
basis of the amount of land owned was also continually being disturbed by land disputes and land seizures, which were initiated by
persons as soon as they had an affinal linkage or political connexion
to give them protection. One cannot, therefore, postulate three
strata, each with definite characteristics, for the whole of the province.[11] Moreover, each family had at least two or three important
relatives whom they frequently used, and these relationships, often
distant, may be said to have formed a link between the highest and
lowest among the Jats. The links provided by affinal relationships
stretched across the system and affinal links were especially nurtured
when they offered possibility of a connexion upwards in the political
system. Active use of these ties may be associated with the lack of

a firmly established class system. It was also believed by the Jats that they could all ultimately trace links with one another, an idea expressed in the proverb, '*Jat jatan dee salee wichhe ghale male.*' ('Jats are all connected with one another through their wives' brothers.')

In the villages the significant economic division among the Jats was the division between those who were in a position to lend money and those who were dependent on these loans. To this I now turn.

Dependency ties

Small landowning proprietors[12] were often bound in so much debt to the landlord that they could not repay in their lifetime. Debt mainly affected small proprietors wanting to improve their general living conditions. They were often unable to seek supplementary sources of income because that would mean neglecting the land, causing yields to fall. Money was lent for such purposes as building brick houses or obtaining pumping sets and seed, and for expenditure on marriages. Litigation was also a major source of debt in Central Punjab.

Technically, money could be borrowed from two sources. The first of these was the rural co-operative bank. All rural co-operative banks of the area were under the Central Co-operative Bank in Ludhiana, and in villages were generally under the control of the sarpanc (head of the village pancayat). A man became a member of a bank by a deposit of 100 rupees. A loan in excess of 100 rupees or in excess of what a man's deposit eventually became was given at the rate of 7 per cent. A member could only borrow up to 2,000 rupees. For any amount in excess he therefore had to run to the landlord, who was the second source of money in the village. It was particularly to his friends that a landlord would lend from the co-operative bank; to those opposed to him or whom he disliked for some reason, he himself would give the loan. The landlord lent at the rate of 30 per cent and generally he lent up to the value of the borrower's land, the latter pledging his land as security. If small proprietors could not pay back the loan quickly enough, existing land assets were mortgaged. Most of the indebtedness of small proprietors in villages I was acquainted with had been running for over fifteen years. In many cases a landlord would not take over a small proprietor's land even when he was justified in doing so according to the terms of their agreement: he did not want to antagonize potential or actual

supporters. Moreover, landlords often could not take over their
clients' land formally because they already held land in excess of the
prescribed thirty standard acres; thus if they did take the land, they
shortly afterwards sold it and invested the money in some form of
property elsewhere. In some cases, also, the landlord did not always
have his eyes on the land. In one instance I know of, the landlord
concerned, instead of taking to court the small proprietor who had
defaulted on his interest payments—in which instance, while fighting
the case he would have lost the interest payments anyway, and
maybe eventually also the case—struck a bargain with his client that
he should vacate his house. From time to time he would allow
default in interest payments as a favour. In one village in which I
stayed for four months, a large landlord, who was also a sarpanc,
had, in the 1962 election, negotiated further loans for small proprietors at cheaper rates of interest from the Central Co-operative
Bank, which could lend up to 8,000 rupees. The local MLA, campaigning for re-election at the time, had been a director of the
Central Co-operative Bank and agreed that loans be temporarily
given at cheaper rates, since he knew that certain small proprietors,
being indebted to the sarpanc, would vote the way the latter directed,
i.e., for himself. There was no need to antagonize a set of small
proprietors who could be used as a more or less permanent nucleus
of support, and the landlord, one may say, obtained their gratitude
for nothing.

The tie between a landlord and a small proprietor was a vertical
tie. The horizontal ties of class and clan were noticeable by their
absence, as also were strong horizontal relationships on the basis of
caste.

The Jats and their relationships to non-Jats

In Punjab each major caste is broadly associated with an economic
category. Broadly, the landowners are Jats; the middlemen, shopkeepers and businessmen are Aroras and Khatris; a high percentage
of labourers in industry and on the land are Mazhbis (scheduled
castes). Jats are, however, prominent in the transport industry and
in the manufacture of machine tools, while Mazhbis, traditionally
landless, *were* becoming tenants on government land and would
eventually acquire this land. Caste did not necessarily determine
occupation. But land tended to circulate among the Jats,[13] and

very little has in fact passed into non-Jat hands. Aroras and Khatris, for example, are legally excluded from the purchase of land by the Land Alienation Act, while the distribution of power in villages has effectively meant that Mazhbis have never had the resources to purchase land. No members of a caste in Punjab have aspired to 'jump into' the status of another, with the exception of certain members of the Mazhbi caste.[14] They, in fact, aspired to become Jat, as was indicated by their adoption of Jat clan names.

(i) Jats and city dwellers

The Jats considered themselves to be 'born Sikhs' and did not think other Sikhs deserved the title of sirdar. Each Jat felt tremendous pride that it was *his* section of the community that had built up the military organization which led to the establishment of Sikh rule in the Punjab. He felt that prestige lay with the Jats because of this. The Aroras, who formed 9 per cent of the Sikh population and who generally supplied most of Punjab's petty traders and small shop-keepers, were spoken of as *kiraar* (coward) by the Jats. Originally the Arora section of the Sikh community had been principally found in West Punjab, in the districts to the west of Lahore. Jats from my fieldwork area, which was part of Malwa, often commented to me that, until 1947, they had never seen a Sikh who was a shop-keeper by profession. This, they said, was the trade of Hindus, whom they despised, and generally they undoubtedly associated Sikh Aroras with their Hindu counterparts. They had traditionally, however, given respect to the Khatris, and particularly to those Khatri families to which the Sikh gurus belonged: the Bedis, Trehans, Sodhis and Bhallas. The Khatris until recently had exclusively provided the intelligentsia in the professions and education, and they were also prominent in business. An idea of essential nobility under-lay the Jat ethos. Jat families had the longest tradition of adherence to Sikhism. In 1699, when Govind S. had established the Khalsa, many non-Jat believers in the religion of Sikhism living in urban areas had not joined its ranks. They did not adopt the Sikh symbols until the period of Maharajah Ranjit S.'s rule, when they felt it prudent to identify themselves with the ruling class, which was Jat. Griffin (in *The Law of Inheritance to Chiefships* . . .) noted that the supply of candidates to become Sikh fluctuated with estimates of the advantage or disadvantage of joining the community. In the Punjab census report of 1881, another observer—a British commissioner of Amritsar district—reported that 'Sikhs decline in number in years of peace'. The 1931 census also mentioned that Hindu Jats become Sikhs to get their sons into the army, which during British rule showed a preference for Sikhs.

Jats pictured the townsman as lacking in physical bravery. They also had an image of him as grasping, greedy and lacking in dignity. Their outlook was epitomized in the proverb characterizing the city businessman as praying to God and saying, '*Jhooth vi bolney aan, ghut vi tolney aan, par tera naan vi taan laney aan* (We tell lies, we cheat, but we pray to you too)'. In the Arora-Khatri Sikh community of the towns, the ideal was that of the educated merchant and director of a large business firm who had travelled abroad and who bestowed money on gurudwaras; the aspirations of the Jats were towards military service, large landholding and high administrative position. They were people with a passion for dominance. More than three-quarters of the members of the Legislative Assembly are now Jats, and of the nine Sikhs representing Punjab in Delhi, eight are Jat. Of the nine Sikhs who were ministers before the general elections of 1967, seven were Jats. Similarly, of the six Sikhs who were secretaries to the government of Punjab at the same time, five were Jats. Jats also dominated in the Sikh percentage of the officer class of the Indian army.

Jat stereotypes regarding the Aroras and Khatris were a reflection of their economic antagonism to the urban section of the population, whether Sikh or Hindu. The clash of economic interest between the two had been brought into relief as far back as 1901, at the time of the Land Alienation Act, when large amounts of land were passing into the hands of money lenders, who were principally Aroras and Khatris. Formerly, also, the army had recruited only Jats and had been closed as an occupation to Aroras and Khatris. More recently the opposed interests of the urban and rural sections of the population became evident when a predominantly Jat government came to power in February 1967 and fixed a stable price for wheat. This was in accordance with rural demands that middlemen in the food grains market, who were predominantly Khatris or Aroras, should not be allowed to take undue profit out of the small farmer's hard labour and that there should not be a wide yearly fluctuation in food grain prices, as small proprietors themselves had to buy from the market in the lean months from December to March.

It is clear that the Jats did not function on a caste basis with respect to the Aroras and Khatris of the towns and that their caste was not a basis of solidarity among them. Their interests, however, as the rural landowning section of the community were opposed to the interests of certain sections of the business community (who happened to be of Arora–Khatri caste) in the cities.

(ii) *Jats and labourers*

Labourers on the land of others were mainly members of scheduled castes, known as Mazhbis, who owned no land. Jats traditionally laboured only on their own land, and laboured for payment on the land of other Jats only in circumstances of extreme social and economic crisis. It is impossible to estimate the numbers of Jats that were 'servants' at any one moment in time. In the area where I worked, farms exceeding thirty acres in size were always worked with the help of a tractor. But irrespective of the size of landholding most Jats recruited landless labourers to work with them either on a daily basis (*dihari*) or on a yearly basis (*biit*). The relationship was purely contractual, and hereditary relationships between landlord and labourer or small proprietor and labourer were not customary. Daily labourers were hired on a sunrise-to-sunset basis and were given a fixed money payment at the end of each day. Labourers on a yearly basis were paid either in money or were given a certain percentage of the crop twice yearly at Lohri (13 January) and Nawani (13–14 June). The wives of these labourers were expected to give free service in the houses for which their husbands were working and they used to sweep out the courtyard, make dung cakes and collect vegetables for cooking. On a farm between sixty and a hundred acres in size, which had high yields and a dependent family of nine, generally 15 per cent of the wheat crop and the same percentage of the maize crop would be given in payment to the labourers, with 5 per cent being kept for home consumption and 80 per cent of the farm's entire produce being sold for cash. Such a farm would be buying in from the outside only such food as a few vegetables, bananas and tea to supplement the basic diet built up on wheat, milk, sugar and home-grown vegetables such as spinach, potatoes and carrots.

The busy season was that between the beginning of October and the end of December, when wheat was being sown, cotton and maize were being harvested, and sugar cane was cut. Labour needs were never met at this time, and three to four hours' sleep at night was normal. There was a proverb that during this season it was permissible for a Jat even to refuse to attend his mother's funeral rites. January and February were free months with relatively little work to do. The Mazhbi population of any village, which apportioned itself out among the various Jat owners of land, could often only get work at harvest time. They sometimes tided over economic hardship by making shoes, which was their traditional occupation,[15] and by selling them in towns, while a small percentage of them also had sons working in factories in the cities or, occasionally, in the ranks of the army.

Jats dominated relationships between themselves and the Mazhbis through control of the economic resources of the village and the pancayat system. Jats misused Mazhbi women when they got the opportunity, and they had been known to beat their Mazhbi labourers, though this was not a common occurrence. They could and did cause hardship to the Mazhbis if it was in their interest; for instance, they used to threaten Mazhbis that they would deprive them of the right to take sugar cane and spinach (an important item of diet during the winter) from Jat fields, and fodder for Mazhbi cattle, if the Mazhbis did not vote in a particular way at elections. The general prevailing pattern in the villages of the fieldwork area was that the Mazhbi labourers had to co-operate with the Jats to get themselves employed as permanent labourers and to gain access to the land for vegetables and fodder for their cattle. A labourer was automatically associated with the Jat proprietor who had his services; the interest of both was to get produce out of the land. Mazhbis were not organized on a caste basis but were divided, as were the Jats, according to the pattern of their ties of political and economic dependence.

Caste solidarity in Punjab rarely operated in practice. None of the castes discussed were politically organized on a state-wide basis. The only customs in which any solidarity was expressed among the Jats on a caste basis was that in the village they did not visit the houses of Mazhbis, take food from them, eat with them[16] or intermarry with them. Jats, Khatris, Aroras, all ate with one another and there was also an increasing number of cases of intermarriage between them. In villages, neither Jats nor Mazhbis had any solidarity on a caste basis. Jat landlords, on antagonistic terms with one another, forced those Mazhbis whom they had recruited to work for them to support them politically. Allegiances were thus cross-caste allegiances, and it is more helpful to look at them in terms of a patron attaching himself to certain clients who, relative to him, are in an economically depressed situation. For the same relationships that a powerful Jat had with his Mazhbi labourers, he also had with small proprietors who were in some way indebted to him, or with tenants. Moreover, labourers, whether Jat or Mazhbi, were treated exactly alike by their Jat employers. The core of the relationship was the same in all these instances and unaffected by caste.

The absence of a caste system among the Sikhs

A caste system is one which gives sanction to, and justifies on a religious basis, the principles of inequality and hierarchy and which is accepted as a model by the entire society.[17] Mandelbaum notes that 'villagers of all levels hold to the belief in a social hierarchy based on ritual standards'.[18] In Punjab, however, the Sikh community officially and in its system of religious belief repudiates the concept of caste. It also shows no recognition of the concept of hierarchy as such.

The non-acceptance of hierarchy[19] is expressed in the value system by the principle of equality, a principle which is supported and sustained by other traditional, customary values such as reputation, respect and prestige. Exclusion, implying as it does an evaluation on a hierarchical basis, is not characteristic of social relationships. The social expression of the egalitarian principle is indeed that the very varied and totally different sets of relationships that a man has are not seen as excluding or contradicting one another. Social networks include multiple ties with men of different types. In the political system this is exhibited in the formation of factions—collaborative relationships between families for the purpose of sharing power and influence. These relationships are established and maintained as a recognition of mutual interdependence and interest. The stability of these political combinations is very much affected by the non-acceptance of hierarchy, and the actual working of the political system in turn reinforces such non-acceptance. For a leader's power depends on those who have given it to him. His power has legitimacy so long as he receives their continued support. This he does receive so long as he uses his own resources and those of the political system to bestow benefits. The leader thus has no legitimacy unless he is constantly dispensing power and protecting in power his followers within a faction. The prevailing belief in equality, the fact that it is not basically accepted that leaders have the power they do, thus has some correspondence to an actual situation where leaders are constantly losing that power and where a man can, by a manipulation of ties and relationships, put himself into an equivalent position. Political leaders are not given the distinct type of deference that acknowledges superiority. They are given a strategic regard that arises out of an assessment of the situation that they have more power and can accordingly be useful or dangerous. The political reality that it is difficult to maintain positions of power, though not difficult to achieve them, corresponds to the pattern of values held by the society. Leadership and political position, implying as they do more power for a man, also imply that the abilities and achievements of other families have been excelled, and thereby that these families have been insulted and dishonoured. If they allow this situation to continue and do not attempt to regain their honour by opposition, they lose reputation and prestige.[20] The opposition and competition between families that ensues thus brings about in reality the equality that people subscribe to. In and by such competition the non-acceptance and the non-legitimacy of the leader's ascendancy is also revealed. Socio-political reality, especially the difficulty of maintaining political position, is reflected in a pattern of values where political and economic accumulation is held to be unjustifiable both on grounds of the premium set on equality and in terms of the value of honour. It is in this context that the stress placed on achieved position and the emphasis on work and independent effort has significance.

It will be apparent from the above how the values, concepts and social reality of the Sikh rural areas of the Punjab differ from those of Hindu India, at least as these have been depicted in ethnographic writing. There nevertheless has been a bland assumption on the part of certain writers that castes, as political segments, exist within the Punjab as they do in other parts of India. Although, for example, Izmirlian notes that castes are not cohesive units, it is evident he ascribes importance to caste units for he states that he chose his village for study because 'it contained a representative number of castes'.[21] The assumption that castes are significant politically has no doubt arisen because Punjab, existing as it does within the formal political framework of the Indian Union is thought of as having a similar socio-cultural and political system. This is, however, to deny the very varied cultural influences coming from countries on the province's western border and to which it has been continually exposed for centuries. On the basis of his fieldwork in the Malwa area of Madhya Pradesh, Mayer states 'Caste membership is pivotal to the actions of Indian villagers'.[22] The very reference to '*Indian villagers*' implicitly assumes that because India is one politically it is also one culturally.

5   Patterns of allegiance II
—Sikh Jat families

One of the most immediately noticeable features of rural Jat Sikh society is the separation of the sexes. This separation reflects the strength of consanguinal bonds, and of the companionship of men and the weakness of conjugal ties. The empirical evidences of this separation are evident in the different activities men and women perform, separate sitting places and separate eating places.

Women rise before men, do the milking, churn the milk to obtain butter and *lussee* (buttermilk), then prepare food. They pump water into buckets so that the men can wash (though some families have showers installed). After the men have washed they take their food, usually around the *chula* or hearth. Throughout the day the women remain in the house doing embroidery and weaving blankets or rugs. A young wife is usually given the hardest chores to perform, for example, cleaning the dishes with ashes. Women go out of the house only for some specific purpose: to take food to the labourers in the fields, to go to the gurudwara, or to pick cotton when it is in season. If a woman is married to a landlord and not an ordinary farmer there is nothing for her to do during the day as her children are often at schools in the hills while servants do the cooking in the house. Her only relief from boredom is to talk to relatives who come to visit her or to whose houses her husband may take her in his car.

After breakfast a landlord may see people who have come to enquire about the personnel in the district offices and courts, to whom they are related and to whose 'paarti' they belong, etc. When he leaves the house at eight he may do so on foot to catch a bus, by car or by tractor. These visits may be: to the courts, for his own purposes or to express solidarity with a friend; to the local police chief and to the tehsildar; or to attend the meeting of an elective body. He may go to the market to sell his sugar cane or, if it is harvest time, he will be on his land. After the wheat harvest when the hot weather settles in, he will return to the house in the late morning having done any small errands, and lie on his bed under the fan.

In the evenings a landlord may or may not bring back guests to the house. If he does not, the family is usually in bed by eight, but if he does, the men usually sit drinking until twelve in a long hall which may be said to be the men's room. The women wait around the *chula* with food. Rarely do the men come out in advance to give any sort of prior notice as to when they want food to be served, but when they shout for it, it is an order to bring it at once. Either one of the younger men will come out and take the food in, a male child will carry it in, or one of the women will go to the door, knock, and a relative will come out and take the food from her.

Those inside may be political supporters, friends, affines. The basis of inviting a man to one's house is not 'he's like us', 'he'll fit in'. Differences are not seen as contradictions in Jat society, but as complementing each other in some way. And usually the persons who meet for long drinking bouts and to enjoy each other's hospitality are linked only by the fact that they can help one another in some way. It is accepted that maintaining such contacts is not always agreeable and can be taxing. A function of the high alcohol consumption seems to be, as one Jat put it, that 'drink makes you like the person sitting beside you much more than you otherwise would'. It is expected a landlord will have varied contacts since a man sees himself and is viewed by others primarily as a head of a family. It is in this capacity that he has the right and the duty to look after that family, especially its women, and through those women, of its connexions and prestige. The talk at such evening 'get togethers' is about politics: new political intrigues and the ousting of opponents through defamation, slander, court action or in elections. Accordingly, any evidences of recent acts of unfaithfulness on the part of the wives of opponents are discussed and the affairs of one man, the drunkenness of another or his financial dishonesty noted. Strategic alliances for a man's daughters are planned; a man sometimes arranges to marry one of his daughters or sisters to his friend if he finds out through conversation and in the course of the acquaintanceship that he and his family are reliable. An implication of this type of social gathering is that a man's slightest mishap is known over a wide area and to a wide variety of people. They know that if they are true friends they have got to give him their support. Men become extensively involved with one another through these meetings.

Just as men sit indoors in a very diverse gathering, so also, outside at the *chula*, among the women, there is this same juxtaposition of people of different types and of the educated and uneducated. For example, a young wife may have a BA degree, but she still has to respect her husband's sisters, irrespective of their qualifications, and revere her probably illiterate mother-in-law.

The complete separation from men thus portrayed: not sitting with men, not talking to men, not eating with men, not publicly recognizing male members of one's own family when one meets them on the road, rarely indeed going out with them at all and when one does, walking behind or walking in front with one's children or with another woman, are the empirical evidences of the concept of purdah. Purdah enjoins a woman to conduct her life separately from men. However, as the Pathans say, 'purdah is in the heart'[1] and it therefore does not solely mean separating oneself from men by veiling oneself and by avoidance. These are only two realizations of a concept which requires a situation of distance and separation between men and women (except mother and son) in all spheres of life. According to local circumstances this may be more or less evident. Among the Sikh Jats, the most that is now covered is the head, upper part of the body, and the top parts of the arms, by a *dupatta* or long scarf, usually of chiffon. Sometimes the face is veiled publicly and before an elder brother-in-law or father-in-law. These rules are rarely adhered to when shopping in towns. Jats are practical people and they laugh at the consequences of purdah rules. One man's mother was taking food out to the labourers. When she was walking down the *gali* (village lane), seeing a man approach, she abruptly pulled down her veil to conceal her face. In the process she walked into a pool of mud. Her son who had come out of the house at that moment found it extremely amusing and passed some derogatory comment about her intelligence.

The gradual disappearance of veiling is, however, not an indication that purdah has vanished from the mind and feeling. The expressions of it are now more subtle and discreet. For example, when a woman is talking to a man she is very careful not to be too polite, not to joke and laugh unless there is a considerable age gap. She generally averts her gaze from the face of the man, or lowers her eyes. These are the modern indications of purdah. They are so uncomfortable to observe and create such a situation of unease that many women deliberately restrict their movements. None of the unmarried women in the families I knew would go into a café in Ludhiana to refresh themselves with iced coffee on a burning hot day even when there were a few of them together. They were afraid that they would be seen by someone who would gossip about their presence there in an insinuating manner. It was an insult to a family if the name of one of its women came onto a stranger's lips. Women could be talked about when they went out with their brothers or cousins. These rumours were started by a family's opponents. Their effect was to reduce the number of times male and female relatives went out together.

Rules of separation between men and women are, therefore, also related to the honour of the family of which a woman becomes a part. Links with other families are established through women and if the honour of a family's women is lost so also is the family's entire public position. Her children are also affected because no one would want to marry the children of a woman who was dishonourable because they would 'come from bad blood'. Men thus spend most of their time with men, and women most of their time in the company of other women. In the process they develop varying degrees of trust for each other. When a feeling of fondness develops between two women they will call each other sister, whether they are sisters or not. Within the family strong bonds will develop between a woman and her sister-in-law. Women will arrange affairs for a beloved *bhabi* (brother's wife) when she is lonely and if she is in their own house on a visit may lend her their own husband if they are not too possessive. Whereas a man offering his wife to a friend can often imply indebtedness, a woman who offers her husband to another woman does so as an expression of silent solidarity. Sisterhood is the complement to brotherhood. It is almost a natural instinct for young women to protect each other. For example, if an unmarried brother-in-law asks one to go and visit the family of a girl he would like to marry with a view to finding out her suitability and one finds out that she is too good for him, one protects 'one's sister' by stressing her inadequacies.

A second consequence of the long hours spent without male company is that women become very emotionally dependent on their sons who, in turn, reciprocate this feeling and throughout most of their lives are loyal to it. The intensity of feeling in the mother–son relationship is indeed why a woman hates her daughter-in-law if she does not look after her son. In any dispute the son is always right. If the son is not behaving properly *vis-à-vis*, his mother—'giving proper respect'—it will be blamed on the wife. If a son and his wife are becoming too close, a man's mother will attempt to put the wife in a position of disgrace.

The alliance between a man and his mother on the one hand, and that of his wife and their children on the other, is the major line of structural division in the Sikh Jat family. A man's duties and responsibilities and sometimes also his affective ties, are primarily to his brothers and sisters and to his mother. A woman's bonds are with her own children, especially her male children, rather than with her husband. Her sons are the source of any influence and power she has in the household, and in time they become her supporters in the struggle for power within the family against her husband and his mother. Sleeping patterns within the household reflect these patterns of opposition. A woman sleeps with her children and not with her husband. Often sons do sleep with their mothers until they are twelve and a woman in fact encourages the development of strong emotional bonds between herself and her children because her position of future dominance in the household depends on the control she has over her sons.

Thus, although men dominate, they are not free, because women mould them as children and control them thereafter, thereby perpetuating the traditional structures (but only because they have no other psychological outlet). They are greatly aided in this by the fact that the menfolk of the house are rarely at home, and when at home associate little with them.

The Jats perceive three types of relationship as important: kinship ties, affinal ties and ties of reciprocity, between friends and between a leader and his supporters. All are evidence of the companionship of men. Whether kin, affines or those come to ask a favour, everything is given to him who is a friend. Once a friendship tie operates between two men, other aspects of their character are forgotten and their other activities discounted.

The Jat family usually consists of a number of brothers, their wives and children. The relationship between real brothers was ideally the closest of all relationships. It was brothers who worked the land together and lived together in the one house or in close local proximity; it was brothers who were supposed to look after and defend sisters; it was brothers who sometimes shared a wife. When a man died, it was frequently his brother's responsibility to look after the widow and her children.

In the area where I worked I came across numerous instances of a woman being married to one brother, usually the eldest, but being shared by those brothers younger than him, in some cases maybe four or five. Sexual access to the wife of the eldest brother reduced, in some cases, the likelihood of other brothers marrying. In many instances I know of, it was a permanent arrangement and none of the other brothers would marry. In the fieldwork area, it seemed to be a practice associated with less well-to-do families owning under ten acres of land. It was said that it was associated with the need to keep small landholdings undivided, as, if there was only one woman, and there was an arrangement among the brothers themselves to hold her in common, it was unlikely that during their lifetime the land would be divided. Also, there was a shortage of women.[2]

Women then were regarded as the possession of the family, and in rural areas where the family lived jointly, the wife of a man was known as *adi-karwali* (half-wife) for all his younger unmarried brothers. Hence the saying that 'if one Jat boy in a family is married, all are'. Sometimes a man would hand over his wife to a younger (though married) brother while he was on active service with the army. A woman was especially accessible to her younger brother-in-law. Customarily, if a woman's husband died she was passed to her husband's younger brother and the word *deevar*, meaning husband's younger brother, comes from the Sanskrit *duivar* meaning 'second husband'. If a man's brother died it was his family duty to take over his brother's widow although he might have a wife himself, this practice being known as *karewa*. With respect to the inheritance of land, the majority of cases in which brothers had obtained preference to widows were those in which the widow had been remarried to one of them.[3] *Karewa* marriage was therefore a custom entitling brothers to succeed and achieved the purpose of keeping land within the family and prevented women from causing succession disputes between brothers. When widows tried to hold on to property rights as individuals, frequently they were murdered.

Both *karewa* and *adi-karwali* customs are prevalent among the Jats in all rural areas of the Punjab though they are dying out quickly. Both practices were associated with the strength of consanguinal ties and, in more recent times, were an indication of closeness between brothers. These practices, initially associated with the undivided joint family and communal living premises where there was no legality on individual possession until the father died or the brothers agreed to divide the property, are often adhered to now for affective reasons, i.e., married or unmarried, a man sleeps with his brother's wife if she is beautiful. Traditionally women do belong to the family as such, while the principle of '*ghar di izzat ghar wichh ha*' ('the honour of the family remains within the family') is so firmly felt and well established in Jat Sikh society that, for reasons other than family honour, there is still considerable sanction behind the continuance of these customs.

There is enormous respect for the kinship tie and closeness between brothers in such an ideal that those of a man's companions of whom he is extremely fond become his *sakhi bra* (true brother; or brother in faith and trust), and are expected to help each other as if they were real brothers. In so far as such practices extend the family even further than it is already extended by affinal ties, the family as a unit has a very vague outline and this is yet another factor which widens the arena in which all Jats can make connexions and cooperate.

Despite the solidarity which brothers sometimes have and which it is their society's ideal for them to have, it would be erroneous to picture internal family life as being idyllic. It has been earlier mentioned that women sleep with their sons. If, however, a woman has several male children, her mother-in-law will generally sleep with one of them or maybe even two and it is not unknown for her to incite the children against their mother. One then has a situation where there are two sets of brothers, one set under the influence of their mother and another under the influence of their paternal grandmother. The influence male children come under while young is one of the facts responsible for divisions that take place within the family between brothers, which may emerge at the time of property division.[4] These family enmities and antagonisms may be expressed in opposing factional alignments.

In the area where I worked, Jats, during the 1960s, had developed a practical and active interest in agriculture. Farmers had begun to be very concerned about land improvement and conservation. Fertilizers were widely used, and many farmers visited the Agricultural University in Ludhiana to take courses on how to improve their farming technique.

Attachment to the land was glorified. It was a Jat's dearest possession, which he was committed to secure and enlarge. This was his main preoccupation, but connected with it were two other dominating concerns: the marriage of his sisters and daughters and the development of influential contacts. All three were interrelated; all contributed to achieving family power, family honour.

Among the Jats the question was not that of survival to the next harvest but of the threat felt from others to the security of life and possession, whether these others be invaders from Pakistan or, more commonly, the opposite faction in a village or particular rural area. It is in this context that the concern of the Jats for family power has to be set. Family was to be perpetuated, defended, made powerful and enriched by all the means available. To this end, given the historic and still continuing conditions of instability, power had to be achieved. Behind the emphasis placed on achievement of some kind, whether in the form of material acquisition, high rank in the army or high administrative position, was the concern to improve family position by making it powerful. Power was the means by which a man guaranteed not only the security of his family in certain situational contingencies but also, when he was economically beyond the stage of scarcity, by being a rich landlord or middle-class farmer, it was the means by which he considered he honoured that family and made it impregnable.

Family power was dependent on and achieved through the local concentration of the family in one place, in combination with the possession of a large landholding and a wide network of linkages outside the village built up through affinal connexions and through factional contacts. In the first place, family power was related to keeping the men of the family physically concentrated in the one place. Some of the power of the head of one of the factions in the fieldwork area was attributed to the fact that he had five brothers behind him, as the two following comments show:

Generally, if in one family in a village all are big, strong, healthy and living together, they manage to dominate that village.
(Pancayat officer, Doraha, March 1966)

When six tall, well-built brothers are living together and not

mutually quarrelling they are a very powerful force. They can
fight about a hundred men who are not brothers.

(General Mohan S., April 1967)

In the second place, a family's prestige was measured by the size of
its landholding. Family was the unit which defended and extended
rights in land. Strong families arose and were needed for this purpose.
The amount of land in a family's possession, however, was never
constant, because of the inheritance rules and because of disputes
over and seizures of land. To protect landholding, therefore,
alliances were formed through marriage with other families and by
joining factions. Political links were sought primarily to give security
in the possession of economic resources in the form of land, and
possession of such resources enabled a man to disperse his daughters
through a number of connexions useful to him. Development of such
connexions was, indeed, not only a material necessity but also a
duty. Marriage was an arrangement providing for the mitigation of
the family's risks and the enhancement of its opportunities. A large
progeny was therefore damaging to a family only if that family had
little land. A large family on a large landholding allowed a wider
network of useful ties through marriage to be built up. The political
system operated on a patronage basis, and frequently much wealth
flowed along affinal channels. Affinal relationships for the Jats
were both a mode of securing influential contacts and a mode of
dispensing the benefits of power.[5]

Jat families were not in functional dependence on one another in
any way; with the exception of debt relationships, very few forms of
dependency outside the family existed. Affinity connected families
otherwise isolated and placed a whole network of links at the disposal
of each of their members. Factions, as I will introduce them in the
next chapter, also established a form of co-operation between
different families.

Among the Jats factions were the least situational and least
impermanent of allegiances. They were a means whereby certain
powerful families attempted to consolidate their power and whereby
certain weaker families were provided with links necessary for the
preservation of their property and other interests. Ideally, the
faction was seen as providing a shelter, a collective defence for its
members in their private enmities. Together with affinal ties these
relationships were less ephemeral than most, and they were the only

relationships, aside from blood ties, that Jats could rely on—if only for a period of some years—as a form of support. A man viewed it as dangerous to put himself in the position of being a follower to a leader. He felt that he would thereby antagonize the leader's opponent and his supporters. Equally, however, a man felt that if to give support was a danger, not to place himself under the protection of a leader was dangerous.

Followers of a leader invariably believed that they did him a service and favour by helping him to rise to power, and they expected some sort of repayment. In fact they usually did get some. But it seemed that they did not feel themselves to be followers. Traditionally every man saw himself as a leader. Whenever a man had enough economic resources, and the political conditions were suitable, he could aspire to collect a following around himself. It was this sort of actual development that in the past provoked comments from observers such as, 'There are more leaders than followers', and, 'The Jats bow the knee only to themselves and God.' The Jats showed a marked lack of respect for those in positions of power—an irreverence aptly illustrated by the classic reply of the rebelling army to the wife of Maharajah Ranjit S.—acting as regent after the Maharajah's death—when she asked for their support: 'Give us gifts, your rule depends on us.' Political circumstances—the frequent changes of political rule in which an individual could create his power, make the utmost use of, or augment the power he had, fostered a particular cultural tradition among the Jats: they did not regard themselves as subordinate to any other person. The cultural tradition was expressed in and reinforced by religious conceptions that each was an equal member of the Khalsa and was responsible to no one but God; God alone was his master.

Using affinal and factional relationships, each Jat tried to strengthen his family. A Jat already in a prominent position in his own home area, the area in which he held land, believed that he alone should dominate. If he saw another from that area succeeding in establishing wealth or position, he considered it prudent and necessary, and also honourable, to plot with that man's enemies to achieve his downfall. Resistance was offered not only to those who seized a tiny part of one's property and undermined one's influence but also to those who potentially might do so. This was done not only for self-protection but also out of jealousy and to spoil the triumph of another family.

The capacity of a family to dominate depended on control of men, economic resources and political institutions. In this struggle, violence was taken for granted and Jats often commented that it had a positive influence in that it kept up the martial spirit. It was accepted that, depending on a man's successful or unsuccessful use of his coercive power and on his manipulation of outside ties, he might find himself with more possessions and influence tomorrow than he had today or, alternatively, with none at all. A proverb coined in the time of the invasions of Ahmed Shah Abdali has certainly lost none of its relevance since: '*Khadda pitha lahada, Rehnda Ahmed Shahida.*' It means that only that which is eaten and drunk in one day is a man's own and can be said to belong to him, for the rest will be stolen by Ahmed Shah. It neatly epitomized the often variable fortunes of one man in his lifetime.[6] Power was transient, possessions were transient, and the basis of both power and wealth was force. The ideology of the proverb remained to mirror the experiences of existent life, reflecting its quality of perpetual uncertainty.

Relationships of extreme friendship and hostility between families were actively involved with the philosophy of life embodied in the conception of *izzat*[7]—the complex of values regarding what was honourable. If a Jat achieved power for his family he automatically enhanced family honour. Power was honour and honour was power. In a situation where a family had no power it was inconceivable that it could have 'honour', as it would not be able to defend the content of that honour from another family. The rise to power of a family into an 'honourable' position was inevitably accompanied by threats and litigation, and sometimes also by violence and murder.

That aspect of izzat according to which the relationships between families were supposed to be ordered emphasized the principle of equivalence in all things, i.e., not only equality in giving but also equality in vengeance. Izzat was in fact the principle of reciprocity of gifts, plus the rule of an eye for an eye and a tooth for a tooth. Giving was an attempt to bring a man of another family into one's debt, and acceptance of the gift involved the recipient in making a return, not necessarily in kind or immediately, but at the moment appropriate to the donor. Not making the return could break relationships and develop future hostility. Izzat enjoined aid to those who had helped one. It also enjoined that revenge be exacted for personal insults and damage to person or property. If a man was threatened he must at least threaten back, for not to do so would be weakness. The appropriate revenge for murder was likewise murder. Izzat was also associated with sanctioned resistance to another who trespassed into what was regarded as the sphere of influence of one's family. This 'other' might be other Jats belonging to the opposing faction; in the past it also applied to the state and foreign powers. The honour and pride of the Jats was expressed in opposition to their rivals within their own family and in other families, and in hospitality and co-operation to their friends. In non-submission to threats they expressed their own dignity and their respect. Thus the concepts central to the Jat system of values, notably honour, respect, reputation, shame, prestige, which pertain to relationships between families and the status of these families *vis-à-vis* one another, can be seen as sustaining factional divisions.

It is important to note the feeling of the imminence and closeness of death, figuratively, often actually, and certainly potentially, to those families living in areas where there has been both a tradition of feuding and a high percentage of men enlisting in the army—namely the former PEPSU state, of which my fieldwork area had been a part, and the districts of Ferozepur and Amritsar. 'Death' for families living in these areas was within the range of the immediately possible. It was a tragedy only for sisters and for mothers. But for men, young and old, death was excitement, drama, a proof of their daring, their bravery, as true sons of the Khalsa. The legitimation of killing and violence was historical and cultural. Courage, the willingness to take risks, the absence in the ideology of any concept of defeat and submission and the capacity to impose oneself on others, were major values of the culture. The archetypes for such conduct were the two historical figures of Guru Govind S. and Maharajah Ranjit S.: on both personalities Jats had a fixation. Legitimation of killing and violence, was, however, fundamentally based on power. Violence had always been the traditional accompaniment of dominance in a village or small local area and in the state. Moreover, the security achieved by dominance was conceived to be, and in fact often was, only temporary, and therefore required permanent guarding. This led to further violence. In my fieldwork area killing and violence were facts of existence that had to be lived with.[8] They were not sensational news and were thought about unemotionally. For this reason I have treated the murders and violence that occur in subsequent chapters almost incidentally. Also, too, the violence that accompanied factional disputes in the Doraha–Payal–Sirhind area was not typical of all areas and districts of the Punjab though factions as a mode of political organization were widespread.

Part three
Factionalism

6 The structure of coalitions —factions at all levels

In this chapter I discuss the structure and internal dynamics of Punjabi coalitions. I call these coalitions 'factions' and believe I am justified in so doing in view of how the term 'faction' has been used in previous studies by social anthropologists and political scientists.

Previous studies of factions by anthropologists have been done in villages. My own study, however, was not conducted exclusively in a village and I was looking at factions in the context of state politics. I also viewed the two specific factions with which I deal in this book, over a span of ten years, while the background information to their present activities extends to up to seventeen years. I believe that any modifications I make to the concept of 'faction' are, therefore, in part a product of the unit in which I made observations and the period over which I considered the factionalism. Seen over this longer period of time, and in this larger unit, the allegiances of individuals to factions seemed less ephemeral and the alignments more predictable, while the factions themselves took on a more stable appearance. I do not think it is a coincidence that I find applicable also to the Punjab two of the features which Brass attributes to factions in Uttar Pradesh, namely:[1]

Factions are vertical structures of power oriented towards influence, that is, towards the establishment of links which will provide for the transmission of favours and services.

Personal enmity is the primary organizing principle of factional conflict in the Uttar Pradesh Congress.[2]

I consider that we found the same situation because we were both observing the political process from a level in society other than the village.[3]

Anthropologists have distinguished 'factions' from other forms of association by some six characteristics, which I here set out, with brief comments which I shall develop in the second part of this chapter and validate in later chapters.

Nicholas, Benedict and Pocock describe factions as 'conflicting' units, operating in the political field, which are part of a larger whole. For example, Benedict[4] takes over Lasswell's view of a faction as 'any constituent group of a larger unit which works for the advancement of particular persons or policies'. Pocock specifically states that[5]

> The behaviour of a faction is such that it attempts to bend the power and potentiality of the whole of which it is a part to its own particular interests and to dominate the other faction or factions which are similarly motivated.

Clearly, this is true of any 'company of persons' we may call 'a faction', and I shall subsequently discuss how the Punjabi faction, at different levels and in different contexts, is part of quite different 'wholes'.

Factions operate in the framework of the rules, values and ideals of the larger whole. This point has been little emphasized in previous anthropological studies of factions made particularly in villages. Members of one faction criticize and condemn others for breaches of the wider code. In the Punjab, at state level, members of a faction attempt to justify their actions and policies by reference to the 'public good', while members of the faction in the villages and local areas relate their actions to the performance of izzat.

Factions, like all political units, are seen to be in competition for control over the resources, in material goods, offices and personnel, of the whole within which they operate. These form the property of the 'corporate whole' within which the factions compete, and the faction that is in power has control over the distribution of these resources.

In a social system characterized by class divisions and in which, for certain cultural and historical reasons, a one-party system prevails, the factions that exist inside that party take on an ideological complexion and are committed to and pursue different political policies.[6] In such a situation, since each faction recruits different 'types' of person as supporters, the resources which the winning faction secures after an electoral victory are used to benefit the specific class in the population that it represents. Punjabi factions drew their support from socially similar units and hence the successful Punjabi faction merely benefited a different set of persons as distinct from a different category of persons.

Pocock states it as a general proposition that factions are 'relative to particular circumstances' and their membership is determined 'by the precise circumstances of their occurrence'.[7] In his 'Introduction' to the symposium in which Pocock wrote the above, Firth (at p. 292) endorses this view: factions 'tend to be activated on specific occasions'. If this were so, observers would be right in concluding that factions are ephemeral. Benedict also frequently notes that the composition of factions, and the factions themselves, are 'ephemeral', changing according to the issues involved and over time, though he points out that this pattern was observable in some, but not all, village units.[8]

Because of this general agreement on ephemerality, Morris decided not to apply the term 'faction' to the 'communal' groups he studied among Indians in Uganda:[9]

... for if a faction is considered to be a group organised to deal with a specific but temporary situation, then the term is not always appropriate to the circumstances I am about to describe.

It may well be that 'faction' is correctly applied to ephemeral combinations to deal with a specific but temporary situation. This may well further our understanding of political strife. However, such historical cases as the struggle between the houses of Lancaster and York, or between the Guelphs and the Ghibellines in twelfth-century Florence, accord far more with Nicholas's statement that there is 'continuity of conflict, which keeps factions alive and maintains the personnel in surprisingly unchanging alignments over long periods of time'.[10] Some factions, and the strife between them, endure for many decades and we are faced with problems in defining the situations in which ephemeral and enduring factions occur, and in examining the varying dynamics of their internal structure. It is probable that the factions are the more enduring the larger the unit in which they operate.

The two specific factions which I consider in the present study have existed over a number of years and have mobilized on numerous occasions. Each of these occasions may be seen as one in a whole series; and the series gives significance to each particular mobilization, in the same way that each killing between two feuding groups is one in the whole record of their historical relationships. Given this record, factional strife itself moves persons to action: scoring off members of the other faction becomes an end in itself, for it aims to reduce their strength. I shall view the relationships of these Punjabi factions over a span of ten years, on which I have considerable data, while I use information relevant to their present activities drawn from a further seven years. I have suggested in chapter 3 that the factionalism has still deeper roots in the history of the Punjab.

Most observers of the faction consider that the leader is the central organizing focus of the faction: 'factions are clusters of men around a leader'; and 'factions are largely held together by leaders'; 'factions are leader-based', to quote Mayer on factions in Fiji.[11] In the 'Introduction' to the special issue of the *British Journal of Sociology* in which this and other articles on 'factions' appeared, Firth also concludes that factions are mobilized by a leader. Similarly, in his general article 'Factions: a comparative analysis', Nicholas remarks that 'there is neither a structural principle nor common interest to hold together faction members in the absence of a leader'.[12] Bailey also notes that 'the point of unity . . . is the leader . . . without him there can be no group'.[13] It is probable that most factions do have a leader, or clique of leaders, among whom there is a first. But theoretically it is possible to have a faction within which there is no clear leader. We shall see that the assassination of the Chief Minister of the Punjab did not destroy his faction: this persisted in being.

The purposes and reasons why any person associates himself with a particular faction are diverse: 'Their [factions'] bases of recruitment are usually structurally diverse—they may rest upon kin ties, patron–client relations, religious or politico-economic ties or any combination of these'. This is Firth's statement.[14] But even if the reasons for persons becoming members of a particular faction vary, I do not feel that it is correct to speak of factions as 'unstable', as Firth does.[15] Other anthropological observers of factions in villages have reached the same conclusion as Firth. They have stressed the qualities of relativity and impermanence as features denoting the faction.

The problem has been raised as to the relation of 'faction' to the concepts of 'group', 'quasi-group' and 'action-set' as used in anthropological analysis. Mayer,[16] for example, suggests that the quasi-group can be called a faction. Whether or not this is so with respect to Punjabi factions, I believe, will depend on the structure of the coalition and the situation in which it mobilizes. Rivalry in a village over a given period of time may persistently mobilize the same set of people around a leader: the resulting formation may be called a quasi-group. Or persons may be mobilized thus to meet a specific contingency and constitute an action-set. But the enduring coalitions of Kairon and Rarewala in Punjabi politics which are organized to pursue political power within larger wholes are, though they are named after their leaders, more than ego-centred, as I will show.

With these theoretical points in mind, I proceed to present an outline of the coalitions which have dominated Punjabi politics: later chapters will fill in this outline.

For the Punjab, therefore, I use the term 'faction' to denote a coalition that is in opposition to a unit of like nature within a larger whole. Over the Punjab as a whole, a faction is composed of combinations of persons at different levels of the political system, who are vertically linked and who together form the core of the state-wide faction. The term 'faction' as I use it throughout the book will refer to the chain of links that vertically connects certain individuals of this coalition at the levels of state, local area and village. These individuals are usually a political leader (or leaders) at state level, functioning more or less actively as a patron, and connected through a chain of links to a number of brokers[17] in a specific local area of the province who are able to commit a following in the villages of that area. The structure of each faction extends across the state political system. Factions in villages and local areas become attached to leaders in wider units. Beyond state level, in the framework of national politics, factions converge on the Prime Minister and other central leaders. The colloquial Punjabi word to denote the faction in the sense I have outlined above is 'paarti'. The indigenous term 'paarti' and the analytic term 'faction', cover units that are exactly similar in span and refer to the same type of unit, i.e., to a semi-permanent chain of links connecting certain persons on a vertical basis. I use the word 'paarti' when viewing these relationships as relationships formed on the basis of sharing enmity in common, since it is in such terms that Jats explain their alignment to a 'paarti'. I used the word 'faction' when seeing these relationships as having their basis in certain types of exchanges which operate along them. For example, the objectives and goals of the political patron of a faction differ from those of his lieutenants and their following in a specific local area. Their interests are interdependent by virtue of the fact that each has control over resources that the other needs, or lacks resources which the other possesses. I illustrate this point on pages 74–6, when, with respect to the Chief Minister's faction, I summarize the nature and content of the link between the Prime Minister of India, the Chief Minister of the Punjab, his lieutenants in a specific local area and their followings in villages.

Faction, as a coalition, is a state-wide unit, and I will now detail in what respects Punjabi factions operating in a state-wide arena resemble or differ in their characteristics from the characteristics of factions that have been depicted by observers as operating only in villages. I will do so with respect to the six major features that have emerged from studies of village factionalism as being important attributes of the faction and which I have outlined earlier.

The first three of these attributes, namely that factions are units competing in the political sphere, that they are part of a larger unit and operate in terms of the accepted values of this larger unit, un-equivocally apply to the state-wide factions I analysed in the Punjab. The factions which I will describe were part of, and competed within, larger units, such as the Punjab state, the Sikh community, the Congress party and the state administration. The importance of these wider units as settings for the factions was indicated by the way in which faction leaders slandered one another for alleged failure to fulfil the ideals of larger units, such as the unity of the Punjab, or the unity of the Khalsa, or personal honesty and im-partiality in the making of governmental decisions. The presence of such a wider unit was also indicated by the struggle of factions for control over the disposal of the various forms of patronage which belonged to the group or organization concerned. The faction, as a faction, no matter within what unit it exists, has relatively little property, meagre funds and no offices. In the Punjab, at state level, certain departments in the government and/or certain positions in the ruling party at any one moment may be in the control of persons belonging to a particular faction. Similarly, in the areas and villages of the province, families belonging to the dominant faction may, for a period, be able to accumulate land, retain their monopoly in trucking, control the block samitis, and become sarpancs in the villages. The faction, however, cannot permanently retain control of these institutions, offices and resources. There are no permanent positions in the faction. There are, however, permanent positions in the group which contains factions, and it is over these that the factions are in competition and struggle. Factions, in the Punjab state, exist to gain access to, to make use of and to maintain relationships with the persons who are in the offices that allow them to control and organize the distribution of property through the disposal of offices, permits, loans, quotas and licences.

As the fourth attribute of faction will evidence, an intrinsic part of the concept of faction as elaborated in village studies is that it is activated on specific occasions. Factions are seen to operate on occasions—particularly elections of one sort or another—simply because these elections are public contests for the control of resources. A faction has no permanent hold over these resources, which belong to the wider unit of which the faction is a part. Hence I consider it is more useful to see the factions as enduring beyond such occasions. The unit of which the faction is a part is a permanent one, and therefore competition between the factions for its resources also persists, as Lasswell and others cited emphasize. The occasions when factions mobilize in the Punjab are so frequent and so interrelated that they cannot be considered as isolated situations; they form a continuous series and at times almost create a continuous situation. In the Doraha–Payal–Sirhind area between the years 1956 and 1965 there was a perpetual struggle, clearly observable in slander, court litigation, intervention in village disputes, intimidation, assaults, conspiracies to murder and actual murder. It was particularly court litigation and intervention in village disputes that kept local factional struggles alive. Preparations for lawsuits ran into months and they would be followed by counter-lawsuits. This involved not only members of a faction but also those of their relatives, affines and friends who acted as prosecution or defence witnesses; court cases would, in turn, be instituted against them. On a continuous basis, the leaders of the faction in the local area were also trying, or pretending to try, to do villagers small favours; and over each favour, rumoured or actual, however small, that was done for a man there would be a contest. The publicizing of abuse and slander against key members of the opposing faction, and the frequent meetings of elective institutions on which prominent faction members were represented, kept the factionalism alive. Therefore to conceive of factions as operating on several 'neat' occasions is to cut the factionalism off from the life of the area and to over-simplify greatly.

Thus it is not particularly helpful to the understanding of Punjabi factions to view most allegiances as changing over a period of years and with respect to such variables as the nature of the dispute. Most participants in the factionalism did not regard their links to a paarti as being temporary. Local area leaders and villagers saw their links, and those of others, as persisting because those linked together were members of *saadi paarti* (our party); they did not see their links with a paarti as existing solely on each occasion when they were mobilized together. In some instances the concept of *saadi paarti* would break down when the exchange relationship which was, analytically, at the basis of a man's linkage to a local area leader also broke down. However, the fact that local area leaders and village participants alike thought of the paarti as a whole unit had an effect on the way in which they operated their links; thus vertical links continued to persist even when they were apparently not being used, since the linked persons acted as though they were in a continuing relationship with one another because they were members of the same paarti.

In most instances vertical links had been of long standing, dating back and operating over a period of at least ten to twelve years. On most of the occasions when factions operated, the members of the core of the state-wide faction were always involved. Any variation in the personnel actively participating in the factionalism covered those outside the core. The absence of active participation in the faction on any one occasion on the part of a man who had previously been actively involved did not necessarily imply that a man's allegiance had been temporary; factionalism entered into a variety of contexts. The members mobilized actively on any one occasion varied, save for the core who had developed a key interest in the factional struggle itself. When looking at the structure of the faction I think it is more appropriate, with respect to particular cases, to look at the conditions favouring the maintenance and the use of links, and the circumstances in which they cease to be used. That the Chief Minister of the Punjab, for example, allowed his relationship to one of his lieutenants in a certain local area to lie inactive on specific occasions was a consequence of his structural position as CM of the state, and of the demands and requirements that his upward link imposed on him: it was part of his technique of leadership. But such lieutenants in the local area were always 'his men': they were so regarded by themselves, by others, and by the CM himself. Because he was so powerful, it was the CM's privilege to stress or play down his involvement with a faction as it suited him. If not always its active leader, he was certainly its potential leader in so far as at any one moment he might see his own goals and interests as interdependent with those whom he called his men and who thought of themselves as his men. When the CM did not use his link down to one of his lieutenants in a specific local area, it did not imply that such a link would not, in the future, still be there to be used. It is inadequate, therefore, to point solely to the fact that the composition of the faction changes from occasion to occasion without further examining the allegiances concerned in terms of the contexts that led to people not using, or to breaking, particular links.

The fifth and sixth characteristics attributed to the faction are that it is leader-centred and that the purposes and reasons for any individual's linkage to a faction are diverse. I will now discuss these two points concurrently in the course of considering whether the Punjabi faction is a group or a quasi-group.

State-wide factions of the Punjab are similar to the village factions discussed by other anthropologists in that the motives behind each linkage in a faction are various. This, indeed, is one reason why a faction cannot be called a corporate group. Factions in the Punjab certainly have group-like characteristics: faction members interact with one another; they define themselves as being members of a paarti; they are defined by others as belonging to that paarti. In a group, however, the links joining persons have multiple exchanges running along them, while each person is also not necessarily linked to any one particular person in the structure but can be linked to all. The faction differs from the group of which it is a part also in so far as its members are not related to one another mainly through sharing a common purpose; each member has his own private interest to serve. The faction is a unit whose members have varied aims, and the links connecting its members are not alike in type because they are links characterized by different exchange interests. In a group the links connecting individuals are characterized by manifold, if specialized as well as general, exchanges; in a faction each connecting link in itself is different in nature from the other because each is characterized by a possibly unique transaction and exchange.

The specificity of each linkage which is alike a characteristic of all factions, no matter the type of unit in which they operate, is also a reason why factions can be looked upon as quasi-groups. A quasi-group, according to Mayer,[18] has the following characteristics: it consists of a number of linkages connecting people either directly or indirectly to an ego; the links are created by ego; the bases for them are very diverse and specific to each and hence those involved cannot be bound by any common rights or obligations; the linkages exist and operate only on specific occasions. These are also the features of the action-set. Mayer distinguishes the quasi-group from the action-set only on the basis that it does not exist solely on particular occasions but persists through a series of occasions and often has a repetitive membership over a period of time. A quasi-group is in fact formed when the same series of linkages of an action-set are used successively.

Factions in the Punjab consist of persons tied horizontally and linked vertically to one another on a variety of bases. The chains of links that connect the various combinations of persons at different levels of the political system are of a semi-permanent nature, and in this respect the faction can also be seen as a quasi-group as defined by Mayer. The most important attribute of the quasi-group is that it is ego-centred. With reference to one of the two factions I studied, I specify below in exactly what sense it can be characterized as such.

The link connecting a CM of a state to the Prime Minister of India was a link focusing exclusively on the person of the Prime Minister, and a link operating between a leader in a local area of the state and the CM ultimately tended to be of a similar character. Members of the core surrounding the CM were sometimes the focus of links from below, but not in any independent sense, as they could act only with the CM's knowledge. The type of vertical link between persons in villages and a political leader's lieutenants in the local area focused, in both factions, on a core of persons. Each member of the core did not have his own personal following but shared in a general following coming from the villages; the support accrued belonged to the core as a whole. Analytically, there was thus a variation in the pattern of the linkages within the faction.

The CM's faction would apparently seem to be ego-centred in that it exhibited tendencies to disintegrate on the death of its political patron: on that occasion it lost two of its local area leaders and a third was subsequently assassinated. That the faction portrayed a tendency to break up at this particular juncture was primarily because of the power vacuum existing in the state after a period of strongly centralized rule; its political patron had been the incumbent of a powerful position, a position that gave the occupant an opportunity to control and manipulate several kinds of links as well as other resources. In the situation created by the death of the CM, the remaining members of his faction in the local area attached themselves to the new incumbent of the chief ministership and to at least one other subsidiary person. The structure of the faction thus did not remain constant over a period of time; after the death of the CM it had three political patrons. But most of the CM's adherents continued to be associated in political struggles after his death.

I think it is at this point helpful to clarify how a member of a faction looked at his allegiance. There was a continuous consciousness of being a member of either *Kairon di paarti* or *Rarewala di paarti*. 'We are not for Rarewala or Kairon,' the dominating local leader of the Kairon faction once told me, rather earnestly, 'we are for *saadi paarti* [our party].' When faction participants talked in this vein it was not simply a way of categorizing themselves *vis-à-vis* others, so to speak, a way of defining their position. A man explained his allegiance with reference to this enmity to particular persons and used this allegiance to further his interests against those of his actual opponents, who were also opponents of his paarti. When asked why he was a member of a particular paarti a man said that he shared with certain others the same enmities. A man saw paarti as being the unit that would be behind him in his own specific contingencies. Actually, the links of villagers, local area leaders and the CM, or whoever was the senior political leader, were based on certain types of exchange. These exchanges obviously continued only so long as they were beneficial to all involved; but in addition they could continue only so long as the unit of which all three were a part retained the image and the reality of power, and appeared to be strong. It was in this sense that the faction centred on its leader: a faction had as much power as its political patron. The leaders of the faction could not retain effective control of their own downward links were they without political patronage. In this sense the CM was a determining factor in the degree of cohesion that his faction possessed. After the CM's assassination, for a period of almost two years those that remained of the local area core had no clear and unequivocal political backing. The faction did not, however, collapse on the death of the CM, but it ceased to be the faction in power. The fact that it did persist after its important upward link had been finally severed reveals that it is not completely an ego-centred unit.[19]

One reason for the continuance of the faction after the death of its
leader is that a man believes he can obtain resources only by being a
member of a paarti. He has in fact often had many favours done to
him through links with people whom he associates with his paarti.
Fearing the loss of these resources, many of which have been,
technically, illegally obtained, he considers that he can retain them
only through continuing to be a member of a paarti. In the circumstances of a leader's death it is the existence of an effective
nucleus that 'saves' the faction; if such a nucleus then 'hitches on' to
and makes itself useful to another state-level leader, the mutually
beneficial system of exchange can continue.

'Faction', therefore, cannot be completely fitted into the category
of quasi-group as Mayer defines it. Though factional allegiances
lead to a political patron at state level, certain of the constituent
elements at local area level persist beyond his death. 'Faction' can
be seen as persisting at local level in the form of a coalition, by
virtue of the fact that its members are bound to one another by
different kinds of interdependent ties. Hence it is best spoken of as
a coalition of families linked together both by differing exchange
interests and by the ideology of paarti.

The Punjabi faction, as a coalition, operated through both vertical
links and horizontal ties. The horizontal ties of leaders of the faction
in the local area developed and became interdependent with respect
to the enlistment of support from below (downward links) and of
support from above (upward links). The key to the structure of the
faction lay in the fact that the local leaders had to maintain their
upward links in order to retain their downward links, and vice versa.
I consider this structure from the national level downwards and not
from the village level upwards, because the relative strength of the
two factions in the Doraha–Payal–Sirhind area depended on two
factors in the external situation. The first was who exercised central
control and direction over how the state should be governed. The
second was the degree of effective control possessed by a CM over
the state administration, judiciary and legislature, and his relationships with other leaders at state level at any one moment in time. It
was in terms of the rivalry at state level that struggles in each small
unit or village of the Doraha–Payal–Sirhind area were given a
common political value within wider factional competition and
allegiances.

The links connecting political patrons, local area lieutenants and villagers differed in their nature and content. The link between the Prime Minister of India and the Chief Minister of Punjab was characterized by mutual reliance, faith and trust. In crisis situations this link became stronger, the Prime Minister loyally sustaining the Chief Minister's power even when the latter lost control over the political resources in the state. The strength of the link was largely explicable in terms of its content. Nehru had an ideological, strategic and policy interest in the perpetuation of his link with the CM: first, the latter was an avowed believer in the philosophy of secularism; second, he was committed to the same social and economic policies; third, his base of support was unequivocally strong. The two men were also personal friends. The Prime Minister never sacrificed the CM, and the link was broken only by the former's death. The links of the opposing faction leader in the Doraha–Payal–Sirhind area—Rarewala—with certain central leaders were different in their character, in that they were one-purpose links: they aimed solely at preventing the power of the Chief Minister of Punjab from becoming more effective at national level. They also aimed at ousting him from the position of CM of the state. These other central leaders were jealous of the CM's special relation with the Prime Minister,[20] and this was one among several reasons why they supported the opposition to the CM in the state.

The link between the CM and local area leaders was important for the CM's policy of eliminating political competitors with bases of power in specific areas by building up the support of their local rivals. These local leaders were thereby confirmed in their rise to positions of prominence in these areas and used their connexion to gain new assets. In the CM's faction, however, the link between the CM and local area leaders was a very variable one which operated only under certain conditions. The CM was not so dependent on this link as on his upward link, and hence he treated the local area leaders instrumentally. It was a feature common to both factions, however, that upward links were necessary for the retention by local area leaders of support in the villages. Leaders in the local area were valued in terms of their links with their respective political patrons: without these they were valueless to the villagers. They could not therefore be in complete control of their links downwards into the villages, since villagers found it useful to approach and contact them only while they remained under the patronage of a powerful politician.

The CM could not sever his links with the local leaders completely
and permanently because these were his principal means of con-
tacting political support and rooting out opposition among voters.
But he did stop openly supporting his lieutenants in the local area on
certain definite occasions, namely when they threatened his upward
link and when he conceived a local area lieutenant to be powerful
enough to rise upwards, and no longer be a dependent, so that he
could no longer control him. In the CM's faction links were periodi-
cally ineffective in that area which concerned the relationship of the
CM with his local lieutenants because the local leader, in fulfilling the
demands of his patron, inevitably also acted against the CM's interests,
in so far as the CM had to appear to abide by rules. This situation
arose out of the nature of the requirement of the local leaders' upward link which demanded that an effective opposition to the head
of the opposing faction in the local area be built up. The demonstration of effective opposition in the Jat rural areas was the use of
violence, and this conflicted with the conditions favourable to the
retention of the patronage of the upward link. The CM's power was
itself sustained by an upward link, and acts of violence committed
by his supporters were used by opposing faction leaders in the state
to build up a reputation for the CM as a patron of 'badmashes' (bad
characters) in an attempt to discredit him in the eyes of the national
leadership. It was precisely because the CM had to fulfil the demands
of his own upward link regarding the crushing of a political party
(the Akali Dal) opposed to the Congress that he had to court high-
ranking police officers and dissociate himself from the actions of his
lieutenants when they clashed with the subordinates of these officers.
The actions of local area leaders, therefore, threatened the CM's
upward link when they compromised him by clashing with those
responsible for sustaining any one of his means of maintaining power
in the state.

I observed a number of differences in structure between the two
factions operating over the Doraha–Payal–Sirhind area. First, the
structure of the faction that was in power in the state, namely the
CM's faction, was larger. As I point out in chapter 8, the CM's faction
consisted of all those in the various local areas of the province, in
the administration, judiciary and legislature who saw themselves
as being aligned to him. The CM's link with his lieutenants in the
Doraha–Payal–Sirhind area was one of many such links which he
maintained with local leaders in other areas of the province.[21] The

different local leaders belonging to the Kairon faction also knew one another.

The Rarewala faction was much smaller and consisted of Rarewala's followers from his own local area, together with such supporters in the administration who had formerly served in PEPSU, where Rarewala had once been CM.

Rarewala had fewer links converging on him than had the CM of the Punjab. When, however, the opposition to the faction in power in the state gathered momentum the Rarewala faction joined in and became part of the wider opposition to secure the downfall of the faction in power.

A second feature distinguishing the structure of the two factions was that the upward links of the CM, Kairon, were more enduring than were those of Rarewala, in his capacity as a state minister, and this made their respective factions less than equivalent in terms of the resources at their disposal.

Third, it was because the CM's upward link to Nehru was so crucial that his links to his supporters in the local areas were on occasions expendable. The state to local area link was a weak one in the CM's faction, whereas this was not the case in the Rarewala faction. It was mainly Rarewala's upward link that was weak. This link was, indeed, only temporarily activated on those occasions when it would embarrass the CM, since Rarewala tended to be distrusted by some of the top leaders of Congress. It was because Rarewala's upward link was not stable that he had in fact little more power than his lieutenants in the local area.

7 Vertical links of a state leader with a national leader

In the period 1957–64 the Chief Minister of the Punjab, Partap S. Kairon, had a very close relationship with the Prime Minister of India, Pandit Nehru. Kairon attempted to concentrate state political power in his own hands in order to fulfil Nehru's requirements that fissiparous communal forces be crushed, that the Congress party in the state be strengthened, and that the Punjab, as a border state, be made stable and economically progressive.

For the central government, a communal group was an interest group formed on a religious basis and oriented towards securing preferential treatment for its members simply because they were its members. The two communities of this type in Punjab were Sikhs and Hindus. Sikhs formed just over one third of Punjab's total population after partition of the province in 1947 and before the second division of the province in November 1966. A certain section of them wanted an area to be carved out of the then constituted Punjab on the basis that it was predominantly Punjabi-speaking; this in fact coincided with an area where they were in a numerical majority. Hindus were opposed to their demand. What Nehru meant by the stability he expected Kairon to ensure was, therefore, that the province remain undisturbed by Sikh demands for changes in the Punjab's boundaries, and that any bitterness and tension between the two communities arising from the Sikhs' pursuit of their demand be prevented from causing open strife. Nehru selected Kairon, supported and patronized him, in a situation where the historical and cultural trend towards separatism in the Sikh community was being exploited by a political party known as the Akali Dal. It strove to reconstitute the Punjab so as to include only Punjabi-speaking areas because it would then be able to unseat the Congress and gain political power.

Therefore I will describe first such evidences of communal strife as there were between Sikhs and Hindus and its association with the

Sikh conception of their identity, the Hindu fear of the Sikhs, and the exploitation of both by the Akali Dal. Kairon was made CM to crush communalism and to control his own community. Nehru liked him personally, but Kairon's retention of the chief ministership specifically depended upon his effectiveness in containing communal strife; and it was his success here that led Nehru to sustain his power. In what follows I am not cataloguing events from a particular section of history but I am providing the context for the formation of the vertical link between the CM at state level and the Prime Minister of India. I am seeking to explain the conditions in which Kairon, the leader of a factional coalition at state level, established an all-important vertical link and maintained it. Three months after Nehru's death, Kairon was compelled to resign, and six months later he was assassinated. I examine how the repercussions affected the position of his faction in the Doraha–Payal–Sirhind area and in the villages of that area in chapters 12, 14 and 15. Ten months after the CM's death, in the power vacuum that resulted, the leader of his faction in the Doraha–Payal–Sirhind area was also assassinated.

The meaning of 'community'

As has been explained, the term 'Sikh' denotes a follower of a particular religion and a member of a specific community. This community is visibly identified by the wearing of five symbols. All those who wear the symbols form the Khalsa—a fusion of individuals into a community on the basis of these symbols, a common religious belief, a common language and a common history.[1] More particularly, it was the tradition of sharing for close on three centuries a common way of life, religiously enjoined and centring on military pursuits,[2] which formed the historical and cultural foundation for many Sikh attitudes and values and led to the development of their feeling that they had a distinct and unique identity. The exclusiveness of the community was also evident in distinct forms of address. When Sikhs meet they address each other with the words '*Sat Sri Akal*', or 'God is truth'; and the form of Sikh address to people congregated for social purposes is '*Khalsaji*' ('the chosen'). Such social occasions were always opened and closed with '*Waheguru ji ka Khalsa*; *Waheguru ji ki Fateh*', meaning 'We are the chosen of God, victory be to our God'.

A Sikh's conception of his community was one which had evolved historically. Common historical experience was the major factor cementing community relationships *vis-à-vis* Hindus and Muslims. From the inception of their community until 1848, Sikhs fought and defended themselves against Muslims; relationships between Muslim and Sikh were, and are, regarded as those of persecutor to persecuted. Over this period Sikhs became distinct through sharing in an historical experience which they saw as unique to themselves. They were one in the light of their shared historical memory. The Sikh tradition in the Punjab was that they had fought and died for their community. The Sikh heritage was a past of 400 years of Muslim persecution;[3] and these 400 years were packed with legends of brave actions. Sikh mythology was therefore not that of the Ramayana and Mahabharata; it consisted of accounts and tales of ancestors and heroes who in a very recent past fought and died for 'community'.

A Sikh did not necessarily learn of the historical tradition of his community from the history taught at school or from his family—he daily repeated it at sunset and sunrise in the Ardas (the Sikh prayer). Community and past were sanctified in the Ardas. First, the Ardas was a record of the historical experience of the Sikh community since its inception: any event regarded as significant would be added to the Ardas. The famous couplet reminded the Sikhs of their goal:

> *Raj karega Khalsa yaqi rahe na koe*
> *Kwar hoe sabh milenge bache sarn jo hoe.*

> (The Khalsa shall reign supreme and
> none shall be kept in subjection.
> Those who seek protection shall be saved.)

Second, the Ardas was a prayer to God said for and on behalf of the community. The community considered itself to be placed under God's special care, and any victory was considered to be a victory of God.

Community and past were sanctified temporally in the gurudwara, the temple. All the major Sikh temples were built to commemorate important events in the history of the community. They were under the control of a central governing body known as the SGPC (Shiromani Gurudwara Parbandhak Committee). This was a body of 160 members, 140 of whom were elected at five-year intervals by voting open to all Sikhs wearing the five symbols and over the age of twenty-one; Punjab was divided into a special set of constituencies for this purpose. The gurudwaras were held to be sacred, as were the spots over which they were built. Seven hundred historical gurudwaras dispersed throughout the United Punjab made it for the Sikhs a holy land.

The gurudwara was inviolable by any other authority. It was a place of refuge. In the gurudwara the Granth or Sikh Holy Book was kept. Inside its precincts there was also a free kitchen and a free rest house. For the gurudwara was not simply a place of worship. It was in the temple that holy food, pershad (a mixture of equal parts of sugar, flour and clarified butter), was distributed. All Sikhs visiting the gurudwara received this holy food out of the same vessel, a custom originally intended to achieve social communion as eating together implied social equality. The gurudwara also gave free food and shelter to the poor and strangers. The free community kitchen was known as 'langar'. Just as the institution of pershad was symbolic of the fact that in ideological Sikhism there was supposed to be no caste, the institution of langar was materially expressive of the meaning placed on the value of service in the community ideology. In the 'free kitchen' Sikhs could voluntarily serve one another, by cooking food for others, by distributing food to others and by cleaning the utensils of others. But in the course of history the gurudwaras have become richly endowed; attached to some there are estates and these often aid in the maintenance not only of the 'free kitchen' but also of schools and dispensaries.

Service, then, was principally service for the community. A Sikh could not attain salvation without serving his community. This was held to be his duty. The food in the langar was cooked in a large vessel known as 'degh'. Degh was the meaningful symbol of service to the community's poor and to strangers. The correlative concept was 'tegh', a sword, emblematic of the virtue of defending community and sacrificing one's life for it. Sacrifice of one's life for the community as well as service to it were means to personal salvation. God was the rewarder. Death was therefore not to be feared and was spoken of by Sikhs as an expedition into the next world. Community was conceived of as being the medium through which a man ought to practise service and sacrifice, and there was a plea for the victory of both virtues in the Ardas in the form of a plea for the victory of that in which they were symbolized, namely '*Degh Tegh Fateh* (victory to the cooking pot and the sword)'. Materially, in this life, it was the practice of service to the needy and oppressed through patronage, and through sacrifices rendered to the community in the destruction of its enemies, that made a man influential,[4] while, spiritually, the practice of service and sacrifice led to realization. One may say Sikh ideology showed a preoccupation with the achievement of dominance both in the temporal and spiritual spheres. Consequent on this, indifference to pain and the development of qualities of endurance were two further virtues that were much prized. God and comfort were never found together in the beliefs and ideology of the Jats.

These, in brief, were the ideas and religious practices that appeared to be visibly meaningful to Sikhs: they were ideas and practices that emphasized community solidarity. All Sikhs had originally been Hindu, and there remain still ties of kinship between the two communities. Almost every refugee Hindu family from West Punjab was affinally connected to a Sikh family, because Sikh trading classes accepted Hindu girls in marriage. Also, Muslims had for centuries been the common enemy of both Sikhs and Hindus, and a feeling of solidarity had developed between the two communities, the Hindus looking upon the Sikhs as protectors in this situation. In West Punjab many Hindus had a tradition of making either their eldest or youngest son a Sikh.

In the post-partition years certain political leaders of the Sikh community feared that the Sikhs, free from the menace of threatened extermination, would readily re-absorb into the fold of Hinduism. This led to a further emphasis on a development that had been proceeding since the latter quarter of the nineteenth century, namely that of stressing the distinctively Sikh institutions and values and, above all, the Sikh symbols,[5] in order to establish difference and exclusiveness and to preserve the community from assimilation. Sikhs were relatively few in number, then eight million—that is, not quite 2 per cent of the population of India at that time. Especially in the five years immediately following partition, the common feeling in the community was that democracy was suitable only within homogeneous societies, while in a heterogeneous society it was ruinous for minority groups, who could be made helpless before the majority. It became the specific policy of one political party— Akali Dal—to campaign for an area where Sikhs would be in a numerical majority and could therefore protect their identity through exercising effective political power. Not all Sikhs were behind this specific political demand, but all Sikhs did value what they conceived to be their very special cultural identity. They conceived that this could be preserved and its transmission ensured to future generations only by the achievement of Sikh dominance in the Punjab. The vociferousness of Sikh community aspirations was a regular feature of the province's political life both prior and subsequent to partition. To this I now turn.

The historical trend towards separatism

(*i*) *Before partition*[6]

Under the Government of India Act, 1935, the various provinces of India achieved some autonomy. In Punjab, a Muslim-dominated ministry was elected.[7] Sikhs claimed that under this government, Punjabi, in which their scriptures were written, was suppressed and discouraged, that the administration of the gurudwaras was being interfered with, and that their proper share in the administrative services was being denied to them. In 1940 the Muslim League passed a resolution outlining its plan for Pakistan in the northwest of India. In 1942, when Britain rejected this demand, the Sikhs presented a demand for the constitution of a new province in which Sikhs would be in the majority. The Allahabad Session of the Indian National Congress, held in the same year, tried to encompass both demands by envisaging a federal union for India, with no unit being compelled to remain in the union against its wishes. But by 1944 the situation had changed and the partition formula had been evolved whereby Muslim aspirations for Pakistan were to be accommodated by separating areas where Muslims were in the majority from areas where others were in the majority. Sikh leaders saw that if there was a division of Punjab the Sikh community would also be divided into two—between a Muslim Pakistan and a Hindu India. In the same year, Master Tara S., the Sikh leader, made a demand for a Sikh state should Pakistan be established. The demand for a Sikh state was a countermove to the demand for Pakistan: there were bitter memories of Sikh–Muslim enmity over the preceding three centuries. The area claimed was a compact piece of territory in the Central Punjab: the tract lying between the Chenab and Sutlej rivers. It was an area agriculturally developed by the Sikhs; its

landowners and property owners were Sikhs; and 80 per cent of the
total Sikh population of the then united province was in that area.
Its history for the past three centuries had been the history of the
Sikhs, and it was studded with innumerable gurudwaras commemora-
ting events in that history.

On 21 March 1946 Jinnah, the leader of the Muslim League, had
issued a statement:

> Today I met the President and Secretary of the All-India Sikh
> Students' Federation and had a discussion with them. I made it
> clear to them that the Sikhs as a nation are entitled to a state of
> their own. I am not opposed to it as such provided they show me
> where it can be created. . . .

This statement was to have formed a basis for a meeting between
him and Master Tara S. Master Tara S., however, backed out, under
the influence, it is said, of S. Baldev S.,[8] subsequently Defence
Minister in the Interim Coalition Government formed in August
1946, and Pandit Nehru. The difference between Jinnah and Master
Tara S. had been solely on the point of secession—Jinnah was not
prepared to give the Sikhs a right to secede. Jinnah repeated his
offer to the Maharajah of Patiala in 1947, that he was prepared to
give the Sikhs whatever status they wanted provided they stayed
within Pakistan. The Maharajah turned it down.

Congress was also courting the Sikhs. In April 1946 Pandit
Nehru issued the following statement: 'I stand for semi-autonomous
units . . . If the Sikhs desire to function as a unit I should like them
to have a semi-autonomous unit within the province so that they
may have a sense of freedom. . . .'

It is said also that the British made offers to the Sikhs of the area
from Ambala–Karnal to the River Ravi whether they wanted to
stay in Pakistan or not.[9]

In March 1947 there was a planned massacre of Sikhs in the
Muslim-majority areas of Rawalpindi and Multan (later part of
Pakistan), where Sikhs formed only 4·98 per cent of the population
before the massacre. This attack was a retaliatory one against
Master Tara S., who had led a procession in Lahore and raised the
slogan of non-partition. It was subsequent to this that Sikhs began
to flee West Punjab in large numbers. The ferocity of the Muslim
attacks fell principally on them, and not on the Hindus, as they

MAP 1 *The Punjab before partition, 1947*

were, on account of economic and religious interests, the principal
opponents of partition.[10]

There were also attacks on the Sikhs in Amritsar city. And on 6
March, Patel (later Deputy Prime Minister, Government of India)
spoke to Bhargava (then an MLA and later to become CM of divided
Punjab) at Lahore, asking: 'Who is being killed more?' The answer
was that Hindus and Sikhs are being murdered more. Patel replied:
'Whenever I receive news it is only this.'[11] He requested Baldev S.
to hint to police officers to supply arms. The Akali Dal also instructed persons to try to obtain licensed fire arms wherever they
could. The organization managed to secure some arms through an
Italian woman married to a Jat subsequent to the Muslim attacks on
Sikhs in Amritsar. A few industrialists supplied money for purchase
of weapons. By the beginning of the summer of 1947 a factory for
arms manufacture had been set up on the farm of a Patiala landlord.
Sikh retaliation for Muslim atrocities was, however, at this stage
still on a very small scale. After the Rawalpindi riots Sikhs had
repaid in kind only in the areas surrounding two *chowks* (small
squares in the bazaar area). One reason for this was the shortage of
arms. The fact that the police force was mainly Muslim was another.
General the Lord Ismay notes the increasing tendency among the
police to support their own community.[12] The Nagokes (see p. 117),
who earlier in the same year had been given an assignment to kill
the Pathans in Rupar district as a retaliatory measure for what was
happening to Sikhs in West Punjab, did not do so for fear of the
police. Moreover, Sikhs were aware of how partition would damage
their interest and an effort was made initially to let disturbances be
handled by due process of law. For example, in March when Muslims
had attacked Sikhs and Hindus, collective punitive measures in the
form of fines had been imposed by the Additional District Magistrate
on the villages concerned in April. When, however, towards the end
of May these were suspended by the District Sessions Judge, Sikhs
attacked Muslim property in Amritsar. A fine was similarly imposed
by the ADM to be subsequently invalidated by the District Session
Judge. By this time it was the first week of August, police had been
disarmed and the only concern that remained was to include within
the Indian Union any area which had a sizeable Sikh population.[13]

The Sikh wish was for a separate autonomous state in those areas
of the Central Punjab where they were in a majority. The Muslim
League and the Congress could not agree on a plan of partition that

was acceptable to the Sikhs and so the community's immediate plan on the eve of the massacres of August 1947 was to at least save half of the Punjab. The responsibility for the extension as far as possible of the area to include all areas where there was a sizeable Sikh minority, for the mobilization of the Sikhs, and for the raising of a volunteer army for purposes of self-defence, was assumed by Master Tara S. in co-operation with the then General Secretary of the SGPC, Mohan S. Nagoke, office bearers of the All-India Sikh Students' Federation and the then President and General Secretary of an organization known as the Shahidi Dal (army of protectors who are prepared to martyr themselves for the community)—respectively Udham S. Nagoke and Ishar S. Majhail. They arranged that Muslims should leave certain districts, for example, district Amritsar where, before the arrival of Sikh refugees from West Punjab, the Sikh percentage was not above 38 and the Muslim was 44, while the Hindu was 17. In this situation both the Hindu and Sikh populations had to be forcibly kept up so that the non-Muslim section of the population would remain in the majority, while the Muslim minority had to be reduced in size. A place was thereby created for the incoming Sikh refugees; moreover, the lift in morale achieved by driving out the Muslims contributed to the feeling of security that the whole Amritsar district would remain within India and that therefore Sikhs and Hindus of that area would not need to flee from their homes.[14] Similar plans were organized in other districts of the Punjab.

It is said by some Akali Dal leaders now that the exodus for which the Nagokes were responsible in district Amritsar was done for personal prestige alone: to outdo one Amarjeet S. in the district of Hoshiarpur who had already managed to get rid of that area's Muslims. The Nagokes were also, as were others in the community, sensitive to chiding that they were standing by while their own people were being killed and, it is said, eager to cover up their earlier cowardice. Whatever the motives—personal vengeance for loss of one's own relatives and family, personal rivalries or, as in the case of some of the individuals mentioned in chapter 11, private profit— such actions, except when for personal defence or in collective defence of the community, were discouraged by the Akali Dal. The allegation by the Government of Pakistan that massacres were pre-planned at an official level is without foundation.[15] Through all this community discord many individuals remained faithful to their friendships rather than their communities. An instance of one Akali Dal leader, who got an ICS officer to take the mother of a prominent Muslim Leaguer in his car to the border, is now well known. On account of this act of mercy he is known as their 'sixteenth child'. There were many such acts on both sides.

In the partition, 40 per cent of the Sikh community was displaced and it suffered a loss of 70 per cent of its land. The fleeing Sikh population went to the areas where it had relatives and to the Sikh states.[16] The result was a concentration of the Sikhs in the Central Punjab, a fact that was to have significant political implications. The partition experience had strengthened the determination of the Sikhs never to be a minority again, since minorities were defenceless. The ensuing attempt to create a Sikh majority area in the part of the Punjab which eventually went to India was born of that determination.

(*ii*) *After partition*

The aspirations of a large number of Sikhs in the period after partition centred on the attempted formation of a Punjabi-speaking province out of the then existing state of Punjab. Punjabi had never been the language of the entire Punjab but was principally spoken in the areas between the Ravi, Beas and Sutlej rivers. Specifically, Punjabi was the language of the Sikhs, since it had been founded by their second religious prophet and since their sacred scriptures were written in Punjabi in the Gurumukhi script. In the Punjab of pre-British days the court language had been Persian, and Punjabi had almost invariable been written in the Persian script, though also in Gurumukhi and Devanagari. During British rule Urdu had been introduced under the pressure of the Muslim majority as the language of the courts and administration, in addition to English. Hindus, as a reaction, laid emphasis on Hindi in the Devanagari script and Sikhs on Punjabi in the Gurumukhi script. Language thus became a communal matter, a means for the establishment of differences between religious communities, to be utilized for political purposes. Thus after partition, when the Congress proceeded apace with the formation of provinces on a linguistic basis in other parts of India, but failed to act similarly in the case of Punjab and declared the continuance of Punjab as a bilingual state, the Akali Dal[17] made political propaganda out of the issue.

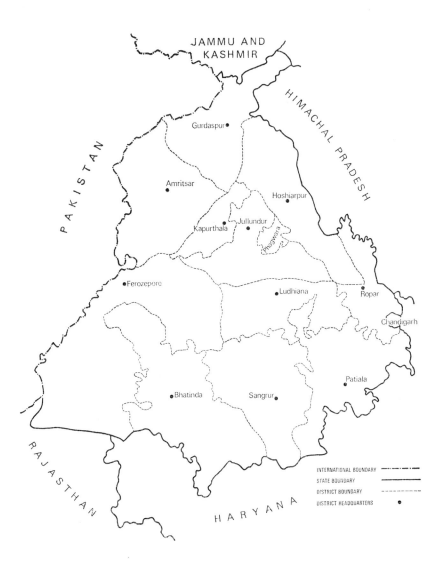

MAP 2 *The Punjab after November 1966*

The Akali Dal had been formed in 1920, out of a struggle for control of the Sikh gurudwaras. Jathas—groups of a hundred— were enlisted and sent to seize the gurudwaras. Many died martyrs' deaths. It was the Akalis who organized the Muslim exodus from East Punjab. They had around them a halo of heroism. It was also the Akalis who had been committed to the idea of a Sikh state and, subsequent to partition, it was they who were associated with the campaign for the creation of a Punjabi-speaking province within the Indian Union.

The two major political parties in the Punjab were Congress and the Akali Dal. Sikhs dominated the leadership and organization of both. In the twenty years after independence, when the Akali Dal was in opposition, support for the party specifically took the form of mass demonstrations (*morchas*) against government; large numbers of small farmers or owner-occupiers, notably from the southern districts of the Punjab and from Amritsar district, would participate. At general elections, however, voting behaviour, as I shall show later, was determined primarily by personal loyalties and antagonisms, and by loyalty to a faction.

The more continuous support for the Akali Dal came, in speeches and in writing, from the Sikh educated class in the towns and in money from prosperous Sikh businessmen in Delhi, Bombay and Calcutta. Sikhs in the Congress party were not necessarily anti-Akali; many of them were ex-Akalis who had joined the Congress for reasons of political careerism or who thought that they would benefit their community more from within the Congress party. Nevertheless, many of those who were associated with the Congress party disliked the central government, claiming that the latter was careful not to permit the development of industrial projects in the Punjab that would make the state able to sustain an independent industrial growth. Many of these educated Sikhs, who in other circumstances might not have felt sympathetic to the Akali Dal, felt considerable resentment at the central government's distrust of the Sikhs, more especially so since the sacrifices Sikhs had made in the freedom movement and for the defence of India were totally disproportionate to their numbers. Hindu leaders, also, were constantly stressing that Sikhism was a branch of Hinduism and that Sikhs were Hindus. In this situation the Akali Dal capitalized on the distrust felt by the Sikhs for the central government and for the Hindus and on its own prestige in freeing the gurudwaras, to aid its political fortunes. Moreover, the idea of Sikh rule in the Punjab, whatever disagreement there might be within the community over the exact area to be included within the political unit of the Punjab, represented an emotional tie of the Sikhs with their past. In the heads of most Sikhs there was the idea of Sikh rule in the Punjab not as a plot but as a romantic yearning for the fulfilment of their history. The Akali Dal merely used the cultural heritage of the Sikhs in the service of the notion that a political unit was needed to guarantee the preservation of the Sikh nation.

The only segment of the Sikh population that was consistently anti-Akali was the non-landowning scheduled castes. Otherwise the majority of Sikhs, if not politically aligned to the Akali Dal, were certainly, up until the early years of Kairon's rule, emotionally aligned and sympathetic to its aims; and it was for this reason that the central government branded the party as communal, i.e., because it drew its support solely from the Sikh community. Likewise, the demand to carve out an area where Punjabi was spoken was labelled a communal demand, since only Sikhs were campaigning for it. And, since, in the proposed Punjabi-speaking province, Sikhs would numerically dominate Hindus, it was seen as a step in the direction of secession.

Not only did the central government fear and distrust the Sikhs but so also did a section of Punjab's Hindu population. In the villages Hindus belonged to the menial class, but in the cities they were the traders, the moneylenders, the shopkeepers, and after Independence they formed the class of rising merchants and industrialists. The institutions where the rich among them were educated were mainly controlled by a reformist sect of Hinduism known as the Arya Samaj, which claimed the allegiance of 6 per cent of Punjab's Hindu population. The latter emphasized Hindi in the Devanagari script as the language of Hindu culture. It was also a proselytizing body and it was in this capacity that feelings of enmity between Sikhs and Arya Samajist Hindus had developed. Many Sikhs, especially from the trading classes, had fallen back into Hinduism at the instance of the Samaj in the early twentieth century. It was also the Samaj that had effectively put a stop to the custom by which certain Hindu families made their eldest or youngest son Sikh. They were also both in competition for converts from the scheduled castes.

The main opposition to the demand for a Punjabi-speaking

province came from a section of urban Hindu businessmen from the Punjabi-speaking region of the then existent province.[18] They felt that such a province would be controlled by the Sikhs, and that Hindus being a minority, although a very sizeable one, they would not find themselves safe nor would their interests be secure. They claimed that Sikhs had little respect for law and order, seemingly echoing a view of Justice Rattigan of the Punjab High Court thirty years ago, but conveniently applying it to Sikhs alone. The learned Justice had said, 'Punjabis are fit only for the field or the front. Otherwise it is better they are behind the prison bars.' The Hindu bias against Punjabi became symptomatic of the determination not to put themselves under Sikh rule. During the 1951 census, leading Hindu politicians of the Punjab carried on a vigorous propaganda in which they called upon their co-religionists to declare their mother tongue as Hindi, although as a matter of fact they spoke Punjabi, a fact admitted by the then Home Minister:[19]

> A section of Hindus have been asking people to return Hindi as their mother tongue instead of Punjabi. This has caused resentment among the Sikhs, with the consequence that in public speeches in Punjab strong statements and counter statements have been made on this issue.

Bitterness was rife between the two communities, and Sikhs believed that the persistent rejection of the demand for Punjabi Suba was because it was opposed by the Hindus of Punjab. The leaders of the latter propagated the analogy of the creation of Pakistan, conjuring up images of the repetition of the murder of hundreds of thousands and the subsequent homelessness of millions, to create fear in the masses. Sikhs were advised not to press this demand, as it would result in their eviction from other states of the Union. It is alleged[20] that Nehru and other national leaders went as far as holding out the threat of persecution of Sikhs by Hindus outside the Punjab if the former insisted on Punjabi Suba.

The persistent Sikh pressure for a Punjabi-speaking province was, at any one moment in the struggle, supported by innumerable grievances,[21] some real, others imaginary.

First, Sikhs objected that the government did not continue the British practice of enforcing the requirements of standard Sikh religious discipline among the Sikh personnel in the defence forces.[22] It was said that Sikh officers in the army were encouraged to cut their hair, and that some complied because they knew that otherwise they would certainly not be promoted.

Second, it was only after a struggle undertaken by the Akali Dal that Sikh scheduled castes were legally provided, in 1953, with the same privileges as were Hindu scheduled castes. But before this legal provision was made many scheduled castes are alleged to have left the fold of Sikhism.[23]

Third, another issue widely propagated by the Akali Dal was the eviction of Sikhs from the Terai. The Terai area is a strip of territory, rising in height from 500 to 3,000 feet, which covers the foothills of the Himalayan ranges for a distance of eighty miles in the state of Uttar Pradesh (UP). It has a humid climate and until recently was swampy, ridden with malaria and infested by wild animals, all adverse to human habitation and agriculture. Following partition 200,000 Sikh refugees—principally Jat—were invited to settle in the area by the UP government. To this end they were allotted holdings and asked to cultivate the land. It became an area colonized by Sikhs, and the UP government took rent for land and taxes and other government dues from the settlers over a period of ten years. In 1959 the UP Legislative Assembly passed a law—the UP Land Eviction and Recovery of Rent Damages Bill—with the object of evicting a large proportion of the Sikh population of the area. Sampurnanand, the then CM of Uttar Pradesh, claimed that many of the Sikhs had no right to be there; in his speech he used many emotionally charged terms, such as 'infiltrators' and 'trespassers'. He said that since UP itself had a large landless population, these Sikhs would have to be evicted. The Sikhs had converted jungle into cultivable land and now that land was capable of giving return they felt that their labour had been secured only to do the dangerous work of clearing the jungle, and that the government had never intended giving them security of tenure in return. The Sikh community as a whole became full of resentment over this issue, feeling that all were being exploited, and that to submit to such acts was not consonant with their dignity. It gave emotional content and meaning to the Akali demand as a demand arising specifically as a protest against failure on the part of the central government to implement its professed policy of secularism. The Revenue Minister of UP had called the Sikhs who had come to settle in the state 'criminals'. On an objection to being sent this statement by S. Hukman S., Deputy Speaker of the Lower House of Parliament in Delhi,[24] the CM replied that the Revenue Minister was not referring to all Sikhs but only to those Jats who had migrated from West Punjab. He claimed that it was not meant to cast any reflection on the Sikh community as a whole. Jats, however, formed over 50 per cent of the Sikh community.[25]

A fourth instance of what any Sikh branded as the communalism of the majority was that when a Hindu, Sachar, became CM of the Punjab in 1954, he had Arya Samaj rituals performed, whereas in a complementary situation it was said that if a Sikh had had an Akhand Path (continuous reading of the Granth Sahib) he would have been accused of being communal; the feeling was that it was always the minority that had to prove itself non-communal, never the majority.

All these feelings contributed to a mass upsurge of feeling among Sikhs against the Congress government as Hindu Raj, while, on the latter's part, their discriminatory acts symbolized fear and distrust of the Sikhs. Although there were many Sikhs in the Congress party, there was a tendency on the part of certain persons in central government to equate 'Akali' with 'Sikh' and to use the two terms interchangeably. This fear and distrust of the Sikhs expressed itself in the political sphere in the recurrent interference of the central government in the affairs of Punjab.[26] In 1954 Sachar, a Hindu and an Arya Samajist, had been made CM of the state, despite the fact that most of the power lay in the hands of Partap S. Kairon, a Sikh Jat from Amritsar district. As president of the Punjab Provincial Congress Committee in 1949–52 Kairon had been in charge of the total Congress party organization of the state, and he chose most of the candidates for the 1952 general election. As Rehabilitation Minister he had taken the initiative in settling many agriculturist refugees on evacuee lands, and to large numbers of those with an urban background he had given permits for operating as carriers of goods. As Development Minister after 1952 he had begun the process of land consolidation and the establishment of measures for security of tenure for tenants. By 1954 his popularity in the rural areas was on the rise, while he had the largest following in the legislature. In view of the fact that Punjab was a state with a Hindu majority, Nehru formally chose Sachar as CM. The Akalis put out propaganda that Partap S. Kairon had not been made CM simply because he was Sikh.[27] But it was said to me[28] by a senior Sikh cabinet minister that Nehru had given a positive directive to Sachar that no policy decision was to be taken without Kairon's approval.

On 10 May 1955 a *morcha* (mass demonstration) was launched by the Akali Dal to protest against the government's ban on the raising of the slogan '*Punjabi Suba Zindabad*' ('Victory for a Punjabi-speaking province'). During the agitation Kairon contrived to engineer Sachar's resignation. A contingent of police entered the Golden Temple, the central Sikh shrine, whose precincts were sacred, and fired on the assembling crowds. Many now say that the officer in charge acted on Kairon's instructions.[29] Kairon advised Sachar to apologize to the Sikhs for this outrage, and he himself resigned from the Sachar cabinet.[30] But by arrangements with his supporters, telegrams were sent and deputations complained to Pandit Nehru to emphasize that Sachar's act of apology was that of a weak man who could not control the state.[31] The Akali agitation culminated in what was known as the 'regional formula', whereby, for the transaction of government business with regard to certain specified matters, the state was to be divided into two regions, one Hindi-speaking and the other Punjabi-speaking, and for each region there was to be a regional committee consisting of members of the Assembly belonging to the region.[32]

This, briefly, was the background to communal enmities in Punjab before Kairon took over as CM of the state. For Nehru, preoccupied with the unity of the province and the effect that its division might have on the integration of the various minority communities throughout India, the regional formula had been a defeat. He became dedicated to sponsoring inside the Congress party strong Sikh leadership that would destroy the influence of Master Tara S. and combat the demand for a linguistic state. Nehru chose Kairon as CM against the background of Akali agitations in the state. It was with reference to Sikh aspirations as these were expressed in agitations that the province's relationships with the central government had been ordered and were to be ordered; and it was in the situation resulting from Sikh pursuit of these aspirations, the consequent reaction of Arya Samaj Hindus, and the resultant communal tension, that Partap S. Kairon came to power. It was Nehru who was responsible for Kairon becoming CM in January 1956; Kairon was made CM because of an expected ability to control a Sikh demand which the central government regarded as being so damaging to the integration of India.

Nehru had personal experience of the CM's strength. The attachment between the Prime Minister and Kairon was, indeed, a historical one. In 1937, Kairon had fought against Congress on the Akali ticket.[33] Nehru went twice to address meetings against him and also put up a renowned Sikh as candidate against him. Kairon won. Nehru had always remained grateful to those who helped him at crucial moments in the struggle for India's independence. In 1946, when both the Muslim League and the Akali Dal had objected to proposals for the setting up of an Interim Coalition Government, Nehru had requested Kairon to see what he could do to lift the Akali boycott and to assure Master Tara S. and Baldev S. on his behalf that the previous promises to the Sikhs would be kept. The boycott was duly lifted and the Akali Dal agreed to get their members elected. It is said that Nehru could never forget this favour done to him in a time of adversity. Then, too, when Subhas Chandra Bose was flirting for Akali support, Kairon again brought the Akali Dal in behind the Congress.

Kairon rules[34]

The programme outlined by Kairon laid especial emphasis on the promotion of communal harmony and the suppression of those elements likely to create dissension between the two communities of Sikhs and Hindus. On 30 May 1957 the Arya Samaj raised the slogan 'Hindi in danger' and launched an agitation lasting until December of the same year to press for a uniform language formula for the whole of Punjab. In fact the slogan was a bogus one, since Hindi was India's national language. The agitation was directed against Punjabi, which was being used as a symbol of the Sikh community's ambition. The majority of those who were behind the agitation belonged to the Punjabi-speaking region and spoke that language at home and at work,[35] but they claimed that the language was being used as a basis for the Sikhs to gain political power in the formation of a Punjabi-speaking province. Master Tara S. retaliated in a statement to the press: 'What is really at the back of the mind of those who wish to oust Punjabi or Gurumukhi script is to make the Sikhs feel that they are inferior people.'[36] All the elements of communal bitterness were again brought to the surface. Each agitation could only further embitter relationships between the two communities.

The Hindi agitation was therefore ruthlessly suppressed by the CM. But Kairon did not implement the regional formula, implying as it did too much devolution of power, and he began undermining the influence of Akali Dal. To appeal to the Sikh masses he kept up consistent propaganda that the Dal was misusing Sikh temple funds for personal purposes. He interfered in the SGPC elections in 1960 by nominating forty-eight members loyal to him for the newly added PEPSU region, in order to maintain a group on the committee against Master Tara S. In January 1960 the elections to the SGPC were held on the issue of Punjabi Suba, but out of the 140 seats the Akali Dal captured 137 and those sponsored by the Congress party only three. In May 1960 the Akalis launched a mass demonstration against the government in which 57,000 Akalis went to jail and which only ended seven months and ten days later. Besides the usual sanctions against those taking part, i.e., loss of job and property, other key factors which eventually allowed the CM to gain control of the situation were the rivalries and dissensions within the Akali leadership and the Criminal Investigation Department's widespread network in the state. Divisions in the Akali Dal were successfully exploited by the CM, who also, through spies, knew in advance of all the moves the Akali Dal was going to take.[37]

Nehru was consistent in his demand for the unity of, and peace within, the province no matter which community was threatening the *status quo*.[38] No state in India had been created at the demand of a particular communal group and it was inconceivable, to Nehru at least, that a state should come into being for such a reason—the same principle that had led to the creation of Pakistan. His conception of Punjab as a battleground of communal forces was very important, since it determined his choice of its leader and the maintenance of that leader in office; the Congress party at the centre always defended its support of Kairon on the grounds that he was both stamping out communalism and bringing a measure of economic progress to Punjab. Kairon, for his part, was aware of Nehru's fear that the Sikhs would try to become independent and he fully exploited this fear at the opportune moment. In May 1960, for example, principally with Nehru in mind but also the Sikh masses, he accused Master Tara S. of entering into a secret arrangement with President Ayub of Pakistan to train Akalis in guerilla warfare. To keep his position as CM of the state, Kairon's propagation of policies acceptable to Nehru and his fight against certain divisive elements and tendencies in the province were necessary, since he knew he could retain his political power only with Nehru's agreement.

But in addition he himself was unequivocally committed to those policies. He was dedicated to the Punjab and very much involved in its future, and therefore he was against the further partition of the state. The irreconcilable fight he put up against communalism was partly because, in the conditions of insecurity which it bred, private capital fled to industrial centres outside the province. He also regarded the particular way in which his own community sought to realize its aspirations as reactionary and a hindrance to its economic progress. He aimed particularly at securing the mass support of Sikh farmers. As a means of associating the Jat section of the community with himself, and indirectly with the Congress, he would say, 'I am the first Jat to have brought power to Jats in Punjab since Maharajah Ranjit S.', and he would associate Master Tara S.'s Akali Dal with 'vested interests from Rawalpindi' (in Pakistan) playing on the Jat dislike of the trading classes of this area, who were synonymous with moneygrabbing at the farmers' expense. The majority of the development plans initiated by Kairon were immediately of benefit, or would ultimately be of benefit, to the Jats.[39] I enumerate these.

First, there were the innumerable acquisitions of land for seed farms which he took up on becoming CM in 1956 and which were not part of the five-year plan.[40] Second, there was the enormous emphasis placed on the construction of metalled roads, the consolidation of landholdings, the provision of an electricity supply to villages[41] and the giving of loans to cultivators for the construction of tube wells. Third, it was during Kairon's period of tenure in the office of CM that poultry farming and grape cultivation were introduced into Punjab; he supplied the funds out of the state budget. Fourth, Kairon played a major role in the establishment and development of the Agricultural University in Ludhiana.[42] Fifth, the attempt to implement strictly the government of India's policy on a limitation of the standard acres one man could own was used as an opportunity to encourage enterprising farmers to move into the towns to start up machine tool workshops, for which Kairon made provision for loans from the state. Agriculturalists would complain to him about the limit of thirty standard acres, that on this amount of land they were unable to educate their children and that in two generations they would only have one acre each. Kairon would argue with them that if, in addition, they had the smallest shop, they would have sufficient money. The limit imposed on landholdings was part of a plan to industrialize the Punjab, the ultimate aim being to divert one-third of the total population from agriculture to industry.

Kairon was concentrating on wooing the farmers away from the Akali Dal. After each agitation he would painstakingly point out the cost of the disturbance in terms of the reduction it would mean in the government's expenditure on roadbuilding or in the installation of tube wells and the building of schools. For Kairon, rampant communalism and economic backwardness were inevitably associated:[43]

Punjab, which was once a prosperous state, was relegated to a backward place by partition, and the protagonists of further division of this border state are now playing with fire; trying as they are to create the same conditions of insecurity and lawlessness. . . . These are eventful times when all the States of India are vying with each other to achieve economic prosperity. Our State, which is supposed to take a lead, almost every year unfortunately is made to disrupt its progress on account of the irresponsible behaviour of some of its leaders. . . . Punjab whose peasantry . . . traders, industrialists . . . are expecting considerable help for improving their economic conditions and who have to face difficulties like the shortage of raw materials, electricity . . . and the menace of waterlogging etc., needs time and energy for putting in voluntary efforts and securing government assistance for mitigating these difficulties. Such ill-advised agitations, like the ones launched by Masterji, mar the chances of any improvement in our economic prosperity. Any further division of the state . . . will reduce its economic viability. . . . Gigantic undertakings are possible only in larger units of administration. Had the entire expenditure of the projects like the Bhakra Nangal dam been made through taxation on the inhabitants of one region alone, nobody could have afforded to bear such an enormous burden, and consequently the projects would have been abandoned altogether. . . . Slogans, agitations and morchas hold no answer to any problem of real nature confronting the State and its people. We have to provide food, clothing and shelter for every person in the state and no morcha can ever secure these things for the people. We have to fight out shortage, ignorance, disease and superstition, and no resort to agitation will enable us to conquer these enemies. We have to emancipate our State from the menace of waterlogging and no slogans of separation will ever give us the energies in any other direction except those reinforcing economic development and collective progress. Let us work to keep Punjab as the strong 'Sword Arm' and 'Granary of India' instead of converting it into a land of morchas and agitations.[44]

A second, and certainly not negligible, factor which made the promotion of peaceful relationships between Hindus and Sikhs an ideal, and the disturbance of order a cardinal sin, was that Punjab was a border state,[45] and Kairon propounded that Pakistan might easily take advantage of the communal disturbances resulting from state reorganization.[46]

> Punjab is a border province. Its security, its stability and its peace are essential not only for its own citizens but for the whole country. When enemies on its borders are already threatening, any fissiparous or separatist tendencies creating ill-will between the two sister communities are nothing but suicidal. After centuries of struggle and after sacrificing millions of our people, we have been able to achieve our country's freedom; how dare we endanger it so easily?

Most Sikhs, irrespective of political affiliation, believed in the 'rightness' of Sikh dominance in the Punjab. Yet Kairon came to power and retained that power on a basis of the predicted suppression of Sikh aspirations, as expressed in the political claims of the Akali Dal. The attempt to control the Akalis was one of his means to gain power with the central government's blessing; yet he used that power to work for Sikhs. In successive agitations in the post-partition period the Akali Dal had been using the Sikhs' ideological conception of their community as a slogan to carve out of the Punjab as it then was, an area where Sikhs would be numerically dominant. For the Akalis the notion of Sikh dominance was that of Sikh political power in a smaller definite area, i.e., that area where the population was predominantly Sikh. It was not expansionist. Kairon believed the Sikhs would not only survive in an open system but also that a larger area offered wider opportunities for domination. He sincerely believed that the agitations of the Akalis would not secure for the Sikh community as a whole the kind of power that would ultimately be useful for it. Kairon's conception of Sikh power was essentially less limited. He believed in a higher percentage of Sikhs joining the Indian army,[47] the extension of the landholdings of the Jats into adjoining areas of the province of Rajasthan[48] and a reduction of the population pressure on the land by the development of small-scale industries in the town.[49] His conception of Sikh dominance was thus quite different from that of the Akali's, as were the methods he used to try and attain that dominance. Communal harmony and economic progress were both goals and slogans of the CM. As slogans, they were useful in the competition of the Congress with the Akali party for votes. They served as counter-rallying points, to maintain the power of the Congress in Punjab, and to keep Kairon himself in the high estimation of the Prime Minister so that he could retain his position. But Kairon considered that economic progress and development as a slogan was justified by economic progress and development as a goal contributing to advancing the interests of his own, the Sikh, community. At one level communal harmony and economic progress represented a personal commitment; on another level they were strategies based on an appreciation of the relationship of power between a state government and the Union, and of the relationships between the Congress party and other parties in the state, the most vocal among which was the Akalis.

Kairon's friendship with Nehru, similarly, was genuine, even while it involved strategic considerations. He had known Nehru since 1936, and Nehru was drawn to him by his resourcefulness and his dynamism in tackling problems. As persons, both were brave, and tenacious with respect to their friendships. Nehru believed that it was Kairon who kept Punjab united, and he admired the way in which Kairon withstood the communalism of both Sikhs and Hindus. The Punjab and its CM were publicly praised by the Prime Minister and set up as examples for other states to emulate:[50]

> I do not wish to compare one part of India with another, but the example of Punjab and its people is a source of strength and inspiration to the rest of us . . . his [Kairon's] chief qualities, if I may emphasise them, are his fearlessness and his close contacts with the people of Punjab. . . . Under his guiding care Punjab has made great progress. In some ways Punjab is a symbol of progress for other States in India. Because of its dynamism it has sometimes fallen into wrong courses, but S. Partap S. Kairon has helped to put it on the right path.

Nehru is said often to have remarked in private: 'I love this man.'
Kairon, on his side, was strongly loyal to Nehru. They were directly
in contact, with nobody acting as go-between. Thus Kairon's
opponents at state level rarely approached Nehru to air their
grievances; instead they recited them to those in the central leadership who were jealous of Kairon's close relationship with the Prime
Minister and therefore antipathetic to Kairon.

It was Nehru who intervened decisively in the Punjab's affairs
whenever Kairon was in danger of being unseated. By his successful
control of the Punjab during agitations, Kairon convinced Nehru
that he was indispensable,[51] and thereafter Nehru sustained him
in power. In 1958, charges were brought against Kairon, alleging
irregularities in his administration of the state and insinuating
corruption and the misuse of power in the interest of family and
friends. A report was made by the then General Secretary of the All-
India Congress Committee in May 1958.[52] It came to the conclusion
that there was no basis at all for any allegation of corruption, but
'that in some of the charges relating to his family members or others
associated with him, certain improprieties were committed'. The
report continued: 'While S. Partap S. Kairon might not have been
personally aware of these, a person in his position must be deemed
to be constructively responsible and that there were certain procedural irregularities in administrative matters.' Thereupon Kairon
offered to resign. The Central Parliamentary Board refused either to
accept or to reject this offer of resignation but asked the Congress
party in the legislature to 'indicate in the normal way whether they
have confidence in him as CM or not'. In the ensuing meeting of
Punjab's Congress MLAs on 5 June, it was Nehru who secured, at
the last minute, the support of the then President of the Punjab
Provincial Congress Committee and of many MLAs, as a result of
which Kairon was not ousted.

Eventually, however, the opposition to Kairon from within the
Punjab became so persistent that Nehru decided that a judicial
commission of inquiry should be held. Despite this, Kairon remained in Nehru's confidence, and in the latter's note to the President on 20 October 1963, in which he recommended an inquiry
into certain allegations that had been made against Kairon, he
remarked:

It would be undesirable, I think, in the inquiry that is being suggested by me that the CM of the Punjab Sardar Partap Singh Kairon be asked to resign. . . . His resignation would not, I think be in the public interest.

In 1963, when the Supreme Court had passed strictures on Kairon, Nehru had similarly and unequivocally supported him. At a meeting of the Congress Parliamentary party he had observed:[53]

. . . So far as I am concerned, I want to say it openly; in terms of patriotism, initiative and public spirit, in my considered judgment, in the whole of India there is not another man who can measure up to S. Partap S. Kairon.

In fact the bulk of the judicial commission's report is a catalogue of the alleged misdeeds of Kairon's sons. There is only one very minor instance in which it mentions the CM himself as having abused his influence. However, the judgment of the report stands in contradiction to this. Neither the spate of slander gathered together and placed in various documents by opposing political leaders in the months before the CM's resignation nor the Das Commission report itself correctly gives weight to the situation and environment which caused everyone in the state, except the CM's most loyal supporters, to turn a blind eye, firstly, to the character of those who crystallized the opposition to Partap S. Kairon. With few exceptions they were disreputable.[54] Secondly, the essential social fact that it is quite common for Punjab government ministers to mix with smugglers (complicity in gold smuggling was one of the more serious accusations that his opponents levelled at the CM) in a variety of capacities and that many ministers, unlike Kairon personally, were involved in smuggling for their own private gain was conveniently neglected. The situation within the Punjab which did not lead to more people rallying around a most gifted and able CM was that of annoyance that traditional values were being trampled upon by the sons of the powerful and that the izzat of too many families had thereby been affected. In addition, the CM himself showed a certain disregard for tradition in his eagerness to see the Punjab strong. In the process he encroached on the private areas of power of too many persons. The existence of such an environment at the time meant that no one asked publicly whether a CM could penalize his own children and his own family for acting, in every sense, only according to their cultural tradition. One wonders, for example, what is the relevance of the sons and relatives of the CM exploiting his position 'to get undue favours or advantages from government officials'[55] for business purposes, within the cultural context of the rural Punjab. Only after his death did political leaders, free once again from the fear that they would lose their standing, feel safe enough to remark that Kairon had done a lot for the development of the province and, 'after all', as one congressman remarked, 'Kapur and Garewal were not good men, you know', agreeing with the CM's treatment of them.

Nehru died in May 1964, and the very direct association of Kairon with the former Prime Minister, which, while supporting him, had made him disliked by other central leaders, became a significant factor in his downfall. It is alleged that the concluding part of the judicial commission's report was altered on instructions from the Home Ministry. In August 1964, three months after Nehru's death, Partap S. Kairon resigned from the office of the Chief Minister. No longer in office, however, he remained a figure of considerable power. He was expected to become Union Minister for Agriculture. But in February 1965 he was assassinated.

Kairon was murdered in typical Sikh Jat fashion: his killing was an act of private vengeance. Typical to the Punjab political scene was also the fact that the particular private enmity of his killer found collusion and support from those who were politically antagonistic to the CM.[56]

8 The relationships of the Chief Minister at state level

> I've not only read Machiavelli, I've mastered him.
>
> *Partap S. Kairon*

In the preceding chapter I have shown that Nehru's patronage of Kairon could not be understood without reference to the need to promote policies that were conducive to national unity in India. Kairon had to show Nehru that his hold on power at state level was complete. Nehru wanted a strong CM to control the Sikhs, and Kairon laboured under the pressure of proving that he was indispensable in this respect. The demands of the CM's vertical relationship with the Prime Minister affected the intensity of his political rivalries at state level; and the pressures from this relationship affected relationships of power inside the province. *Vis-à-vis* his rivals at state level, Kairon was fighting to keep a tight control of the instruments of power that would allow him to consolidate his position. The concentration by him of political power in his own person was in one respect a consequence of the necessity he attached to retaining Nehru's confidence and fulfilling the latter's demands regarding the interrelated problems of law and order, communal harmony and economic development. Kairon also needed to retain the attachment of Nehru because he was forcing the pace of centralization. It was a principle of the CM's that there should be as little devolution of power as possible. He had been an admirer and follower of Patel[1] and he believed, like Patel, that in a newly independent and economically backward country with no democratic tradition the opposition had to be rooted out before it was possible to govern.[2] The continuance of Nehru's support provided Kairon with the necessary sanction for the centralization of state political power in his own person.[3]

Kairon's attempt to use and control factions in the rural areas was part of the process of centralization. Factional support was

one of the instruments of power used by the CM to attack political
rivals and competitors. In addition, Kairon sought to gain control
over other centres of power in the state, notably the judiciary, the
civil and police administration, Congress members of the legislature
and certain industrialists. The quality of Kairon's relationships at
state level was thus characterized by a struggle to control the
province's entire political resources. In order to intervene effectively
he had to have cores of supporters in all key institutions. In so far
as a detailing of his activities in these spheres may provide a wider
context and setting to certain incidents I shall be describing later
when discussing factions in a specific local area of the province, I
comment initially on Kairon's attempt to control these institutions.
Since, however, my prime task with reference to the faction is to
focus on the links connecting leaders at different levels of the
political system, I will go into the nature of the horizontal relationships of these leaders only when these appear to be relevant to the
particular factions I discuss in this study. I purposely restrict data
which does not depict horizontal relationships inside these two
factions.

Kairon's attempt to control centres of power other than the faction

(i) The judiciary and process at law

Kairon frequently intervened in court cases involving his political
supporters at district and high court level. Also, his main mode of
dealing with actual or potential opponents, whether they were in the
police, the civil administration or political life, was to institute
cases against them.

Thus the judiciary, not only at district level, but also at high court
level, was not at all free from political influence. This was indicated
in the sometimes successful pressurizing of judges,[4] and in the
various petitions for revision of sentences imposed not only by the
district courts but also by the high court.[5] Nowhere was the lack of
impartiality of the judiciary and its lack of freedom from political
influence more evident than in the Karnal murder case, instituted
in November 1958. The SP Karnal district, D. S. Garewal, was
accused of murdering certain criminals known to the CM. Kairon
was interested in securing the conviction of Garewal (for reasons
which are irrelevant here) and I quote below two extracts from the

judgment on the case, which was tried outside the Punjab, in Delhi, by a special sessions judge—S. D. Singh[6]—from Uttar Pradesh:

> It is a matter of some regret that the Magistrates . . . played into the hands of the police and went through . . . part of their magisterial work with some amount of indecent haste. . . . The course of justice was to some extent subordinated to expediency, the expediency itself being judged from the point of view of investigation rather than the administration of justice [at p. 184].

The judgment spoke of influence and pressure being put on the various police officers and magistrates acting as witnesses and accused them of forging and concocting evidence of every type possible (at p. 591). It also made this comment:

> Having regard to all the circumstances, I have not the least hesitation in coming to the conclusion that high as the rank of the witnesses . . . happens to be . . . they have unhesitatingly indulged in naked lies either just to feed their grudge against the accused . . . or maybe at the command of one who has been and maybe is in a position to dictate [at p. 452].

There are allegations that Kairon to some extent succeeded in exercising influence in the appointment of high court judges. So long as he remained in power two well-known judges were not confirmed in their appointments and at least one other judge did not receive the further extension of his period of appointment.[7] It was, however, more especially his intervention in appointments at district level that was deemed to be successful, the judiciary being still under the control of the executive during his period of tenure in the office of CM, with the DC controlling the district magistrates. Only in the latter part of 1964, after Kairon's resignation, was control of all judicial magistrates finally transferred to the high court.

(ii) The administration

Kairon's attempt to control the administration has to be considered in two contexts: first, in terms of the CM's deep emotional attachment to the rural community and to his own personal vision as to how the rural areas could be developed; second, in terms of the situation he faced on assuming office where an urban-dominated administration dealt with the problems of a predominantly rural population

in terms of its own set of stereotypes. The bulk of the rural population were thought of as rude, ignorant and uneducated, good only
for defending the country and ploughing the land to produce a
wheat surplus. The few Jats who were accepted as rising above this
level were primarily seen in their respective roles of landowner and
military officer. To possess an intellectual perspective of the economic
and political problems facing the province was not expected of a
Jat. It seems as if at least part of the resistance Kairon encountered
from the administration owed its origin to the fact that he was a Jat
CM determined to push through, on his own initiative, policies that
would benefit the rural areas.

Owing to a lack of co-operation on the administration's part, it
became necessary for the CM to create his own personal network of
links inside the administration.

Control over the administration was crucial. From the administration Kairon required personal loyalty to himself. He did not want
the administration acting as an independent base of power, but
wished it to function under his supervision for the implementation
of certain policies, economic and developmental, and political.
Coupled with this, he was interested in its efficiency. His view of the
administration was that it legalized inhumanity under the mask of
repeated delays and sticking to rules.[8] Both these interests combined
to induce him, in many instances, to override the rules to allow the
able and talented of his own choosing to be promoted over others.[9]
His attitude to the innumerable irregular promotions that he made
was that he had often worked with the persons concerned for years
and was therefore in a better position to judge their capabilities
than were, for example, members of the Public Services Commission
who interviewed them for a short period of time.

Many administrative officers gave their loyalty on the basis that
he was the CM, i.e., they were loyal civil servants. Still others were
loyal out of hero-worship. Others were subservient in fear of transfer
to an unfavourable posting, of demotion or of suspension,[10] and in
the desire to be in his favour by obliging him and his relatives.[11] Those
loyal to him demonstrated that loyalty unscrupulously. Patronage
was used to gain the administration's support but it was given with
the clear knowledge, on the recipient's side, that its acceptance would
be turned into a stigma were the return of a consistent support ever
to falter. Kairon sought, chiefly with the rural electorate in mind,
to undermine the glamorous image of the administration, with its

high status. To this end, he often humiliated officers in front of crowds of small farmers. He put forcibly across to the rural electorate that it was the power of election that counted and not the rules. Thus Kairon sought to impress upon the small farmers that they were the principal basis of power in the state and that he could and would override the rules in their service. He is reported to have told administrative officers reluctant to oblige him, 'Don't you bother about the rules. Do as I say. I shall change the rules when and as I wish. The Assembly is with me.'[12]

Selected officers were singled out from the police and civil administration by the CM and blackmailed. When a complaint was made against an officer, a lenient view would be taken by the CM if the officer had otherwise proved loyal; but the officer would be warned that the CM could do him harm at any juncture. When more serious offences by an officer were discovered, no immediate action might be taken, but the officer would be harassed and the case would be kept pending precisely in order to extort as many favourable actions as possible. What was important was not always the actual content of the charge, but the precise moment when the officer was charged with it; this was usually after he had been insubordinate or disloyal.

The job of keeping a watch on the administration with respect to these matters was the special province of the Vigilance Department, which collected information on those matters which gave a man a bad reputation in the Punjab—'womanizing' and 'corruption'. Details on mistresses kept, and bribes taken and accepted, by prominent politicians and members of the administrative cadre would all be recorded in the dossiers of Vigilance. Certain officers of the CID loyally served the CM in this capacity. In a society where male dominance was unquestioned and whose political system operated on a patronage basis the focus on 'womanizing' and 'corruption' as 'bad' seems contradictory.

Helping each other when possible in a relationship of friendship or of patronage led to continuance of the relationship; refusing to help broke the relationship and led to future hostility. It was a cultural expectancy that a man would help his relatives and his friends; to do so was approved as moral. What might be termed 'corruption' in another system was considered 'reciprocity' in the Punjab. According to the culture, reciprocity of this kind is an obligation, and not a moral fault.

Although a man, whether it be Kairon or an administrative

officer, acted according to some of his own cultural norms in favouring friends and browbeating enemies, his political opponents judged him by a set of entirely different standards, arising from a general feeling in administrative and political circles that some time, in a future carefully unspecified, a depersonalized bureaucratic machinery functioning according to rules should be set up. 'Corrupt' was merely a convenient tag to pin on to someone one had already decided to discriminate against or oppose on some other basis. As an example, Kairon's opponents used the term freely in their endeavour to besmirch the public reputation of the CM. Charges of corruption were, in effect, levelled against the CM on account of faction rivalries in the Congress party of Punjab. They were levelled merely whenever the opposition had gathered together enough power and resources to try to throw him out of office. They were indications of the opposition's strength at that time. It may be said, also, that likewise Kairon had no independent concern with the rooting out of that which, according to other standards, was called corruption; but rather he also attempted to use the so-called corrupt to get work done for himself.[13]

The levelling of charges of 'womanizing' was similarly incongruous in a society where male dominance was enshrined unless these charges were seen as being related to and part of the struggle for the elimination of political opponents and competitors. The businessman, for example, could keep as many women as he pleased; but once he entered the political arena his actions came under surveillance and his entire past was then of interest to his political opponents. There they used a standard from a different world, namely the ideal of the loyal monogamist—because it was in their interest.

Control of the district police, who dealt harshly with those terrorizing the rural areas and with smugglers, many of whom were or had been politically useful to Kairon, was much more difficult than control of the civil administration. The CM's unexpected tours, often incognito, often alone, travelling into villages to inquire into grievances, the various sudden visits he paid to police stations, were attempts to show to the lower ranks of the police force that they were not outside the range of his supervision.

Such actions endeared him to the mass of small farmers, as also did the setting up of co-ordination committees at district level which were ordered to meet twice a month to review in public all complaints and accelerate the process of their disposal. Kairon frequently told the small proprietors that it was their duty to criticize and complain against officers because in this way the administration would be improved. The district co-ordination committees in which farmers could voice their grievances were part of this scheme. At least once a month a minister was required to attend the co-ordination committee meetings in each district. According to the CM:[14] 'the whole point of this highly unorthodox system of public audience was that the element of fear be eschewed from the dealings of the people with the administration' and 'the departmental officers should feel they are answerable to the public . . . the unreal gulf between the administrator and the administered had to be bridged so as to ensure a complete identification of interests'. The fear, in fact, had been transferred onto the officers, for Kairon judged an officer from the results achieved and the goodwill he promoted: 'Since taking over the portfolio of Agriculture I have decided that the merit of an officer will be judged by the increased production he can show.'[15]

The setting up of the district co-ordination committees was part of the attempt to diminish the self-importance of members of the IAS. Thus also many PCS officers were brought into the IAS.[16] New administrative bases of power were created for patronage purposes. Such was the Subordinate Services Selection Board, a body started on the initiative of the CM. It dealt with recruitment to jobs up to 150 rupees per month—mainly teachers, bus conductors and clerks. On the Public Services Commission, as on the Subordinate Services Selection Board, Kairon usually placed those whom he trusted or wanted to reward in some way for their services to him.[17] But the commission could never fully be relied upon to comply with the CM's requests on every occasion when he intervened. And it was because of its unreliability here that Kairon had rules passed in the legislature in 1957, first to remove the necessity for local bodies to consult the Public Services Commission about appointments by promotion and transfers within the administrative service; and second, to provide that certain posts be removed from the purview of the Public Services Commission. Thus, for example, the post of BDO was taken out of the jurisdiction of the commission and placed under the Punjab government. A percentage of the posts of BDO were to be reserved for political sufferers, i.e., for persons who had been imprisoned by the British and whose property had been confiscated. Fifty per cent of BDO's were recruited from among such political sufferers, and thus covered Akalis and Communists as well as Congressmen; this left half the BDO posts for persons who would and might oblige him. The post of BDO was one form of patronage, and many were promoted from being BDOs into posts in the regular administrative service. The post of BDO was very important in rural areas until 1962. The BDO would oblige people with loans for improvement of land, by the purchase of fertilizer or the sinking of a tube well; the loan was returnable in easy instalments. He could also see that they got their due quotas of sugar and fertilizer. In return he would ask them to vote Congress. BDOs also brought ministers along to the village to address meetings and open schools. The BDOs were active Congress party propagandists.

Kairon's control of the administration and the police served both economic and political ends. It was economically helpful because if he had an actively loyal DC and SP in a district, it was possible to decide upon and to acquire land quickly for industrial development,[18] and to make sudden raids on black marketeers in order to keep prices steady. Politically, suppression of agitations was possible only if the CM had the full co-operation of the DC and SP. In 1962, also, huge sums of money were collected for the National Defence Fund to resist Chinese aggression only because certain DCs were zealous in supporting Kairon's appeals. The DC, moreover, was responsible for such crucial people as the District Food Controller and the industries officers. The former regulated the supply of controlled commodities such as foodstuffs, cement, kerosene and oil, etc., as specified from time to time by the state government. The industries officers sanctioned loans for industries and were responsible for acquiring land to set up these industries, and for allotting it to applicants. Export and import licences for articles required for production were also granted on the recommendation of the industries officers. This placed a large amount of patronage at the disposal of the CM if he controlled the DC, as Kairon usually did. Politically, also, control of the administration was a means of recruiting new support; and it was Kairon's control over administrative personnel that enabled him to sustain the power of his faction in the various local areas of the province whenever he wished.

(iii) *Congress members of the legislature*

It was important that the CM's men should form a majority in the

Vidhan Sabha (Punjab Assembly) so that he could pass his legislative measures. In 1957–64, in fact, more than half of the Congress MLAs depended directly on Kairon. If Kairon considered that the financial position of a legislator who was loyal to him was weak, he would give him such financial help as a permit for running a lorry.

He dealt harshly with those in the Congress party who opposed him in the legislature. Thus he tried to prevent the re-election of the MLA for Karnal, Ram Piara, in 1962, and thereafter suspended him from the Congress legislative party because he was using the Assembly to complain vociferously about alleged acts of corruption and maladministration on the part of the CM. In 1963, Ram Piara was beaten up by Kairon's men in his own constituency of Karnal city.

(iv) Industrialists and transport companies

The industrialists of Ludhiana and Amritsar, truck operators and bus company owners were important to the CM in that they donated large sums of money to Congress party funds, thereby indirectly financing the buying up of, and the neutralizing of, the political opposition. It was obviously not possible for Kairon to play 'patron' to his supporters without resources, and the donors of these resources were principally urban Hindus who owned large factories and who supported Kairon on the grounds that there would be no danger to their property so long as he remained the CM of the state. Loans, quotas, permits and import licences were given by Kairon to a number of industrialists in the city of Ludhiana who set up industries under government patronage.[19] (It may be noted that it was in the time of Kairon that large exports of hosiery and bicycles began.) In return, they provided the Congress party with money to fight elections and brought pressure on their employees to vote for Congress.[20] The large industrialists whom Kairon benefited could also themselves benefit many smaller industrialists and traders. One industrialist particularly was a major beneficiary in this respect: the brokers selling his products in the markets would sell them at cheaper rates to certain small shopkeepers. Bus companies and transport companies gave money to the CM for the same purposes, under threat of nationalization of their concerns; the threat was real, since 50 per cent of the transport in Punjab was already owned by the state.

*   *   *

This, briefly, was the pattern of Kairon's control over other major centres of power in the state. His success as CM of the Punjab for eight years was due to the fact that despite a university education in America he remained in every sense a Jat, and understood and reacted to the Jats as Jats and not in their varying capacities as administrative and army officers. There were, however, several centres of opposition to him. First, the Press, which was controlled by urban people, was antagonistic to him because he supported rural interests. Second, the administration was antagonistic because it disliked his repeated interventions. Third, the CM had innumerable bitter political enemies from all political parties as well as enemies inside the ranks of the Congress itself. Fourth, there were all those industrialists who had not received permits. All these combined solely to oust him. In so far as it was united, this opposition did not have an ideological basis, and its members seemed to have nothing in common but their dislike of Kairon. Common enmities and little else similarly characterized the faction in rural areas, though to a lesser degree. The Kairon faction at state level, consisting of the CM's supporters in the institutions just described, formed a mutual aid society which, when directed by the CM, also protected his men in the various rural areas of the state. Faction was the means employed by the CM to stretch out to a particular local area, in order to form a base of power there: he did this by utilizing already existing opposition against the local support of a political opponent who was a temporary threat to him in his position as CM of the state. I now turn to these processes in the particular local area in which I did much of my fieldwork, describing first, in chapter 9, the content of the rivalry between Kairon and Rarewala as it affected the Doraha –Payal–Sirhind area. Subsequently, in chapter 11, and then in chapter 13, I discuss the opposition and alignments of the local area leaders and of ordinary village participants in the factionalism, indicating with respect to a series of cases the background of mutual enmities and interests that promoted their respective alliances with political leaders or their local area lieutenants. The nature of those alliances is discussed in chapters 12 and 14.

9   The Kairon–Rarewala rivalry

Factionalism in the Doraha–Payal–Sirhind area at state level principally involved Partap S. Kairon, the CM of Punjab from January 1956 until August 1964, and Gian S. Rarewala, a former leader of the Congress Assembly party in opposition and previously the Irrigation Minister in the Kairon cabinet. The Doraha–Payal–Sirhind area was the area where Rarewala had influence and it was therefore the area where Kairon attempted to build up support against Rarewala. It was thus a key area for recruiting to their respective factions. I first sketch in the background to the rivalry between Kairon and Rarewala.

In 1947, as has been noted, Punjab had been divided on the basis of religious differences between Hindus and Muslims. Sikhs belonged to neither category, and they were the main opponents of the partition, since it involved the loss of a substantial part of their home and economic assets. Of those Sikh refugees who fled from West Punjab and settled in PEPSU—approximately a quarter of a million (that is, a quarter of the total refugee population from West Punjab)—the majority were under the influence of the Akali Dal. In the early months of 1952 Gian S. Rarewala, a Jat, and also maternal uncle of the Maharajah of Patiala, the premier Sikh prince, won the assembly seat of Doraha and formed a ministry in which the Akali party predominated. Rarewala's United Front Ministry in effect constituted a wing of Master Tara S.'s Akali Dal in PEPSU.[1] In the elections, leading political personalities had come to campaign against Rarewala on the grounds that as Punjab was a border state a non-Congress government in even one part of it would jeopardize national security. Partap S. Kairon, also Jat, who was at the time president of the Punjab Provincial Congress Committee, had spent several days in Doraha constituency, at the suggestion of Nehru, to organize the opposition against Rarewala. It is from this time that their rivalry may be said to date.

115

MAP 3   *The Punjab: parliamentary and Vidhan Sabha constituencies,*
1967

The combined opposition did not manage to secure more than one third of the votes, and Rarewala's government became the only non-Congress government in the whole of India. After eleven months in office, however, it was dissolved by the National Congress Ministry on the allegation that law and order were in peril;[2] Governor's rule was proclaimed. Presumably it was because the Akali Dal dominated Rarewala's government. Many non-Congressmen were then removed from the administration, including very many supporters of Rarewala. Congress funds were placed at the disposal of small owner occupiers inside the Akali Dal in PEPSU, and a number of their leaders moved over to the Congress. The image that the Congress presented at this stage was therefore a very radical one.

When Partap S. Kairon became CM of the Punjab in 1956 he advocated the merger of PEPSU with Punjab. It is said that he did so in order that the Sikh percentage of votes, which in PEPSU went principally to the Akalis, would be reduced: the Sikh percentage would then have been only one third of the total population of the then united Punjab after partition, while it approached 60 per cent in PEPSU. Provision for the merger of PEPSU with Punjab also had an anti-Rarewala aspect in that it was a response to an upsurge of feeling among PEPSU's smallholders, many of whom were still tenants, against the feudal landlords with whom Rarewala was associated. There was thus also an economic side to the CM's antipathy to Rarewala. Kairon had always been associated, from the beginning of his political career, with small landholders. On the other hand, although Rarewala only had two hundred acres of land, as the maternal uncle of the Maharajah of Patiala he was connected, at least in the minds of the mass of the rural populace, with the feudal rulers of the former Patiala state.

Kairon was dedicated to breaking the power of the large landlords[3] and from 1952 had been responsible for attempting to implement various land reform measures. This was one basis for his antagonism against Rarewala. But in addition their associations and the activities in which they had respectively engaged during the independence struggle had pulled them into polar opposition. Kairon was associated with the Nagokes, Udham S. and Mohan S. (see chapter 11). The latter were the veteran leaders of the jathas who, in the early 1920s, had fought against the British to gain control of the Sikh temples. All of them were from Majha, from district Amritsar. When Kairon returned from the United States after obtaining an MA in political science at Michigan University, it was the Nagokes who, in 1933, brought him into politics. Throughout the 1940s, with them, he participated in the freedom movement against the British, and he was imprisoned in the 'Quit India' movement of 1942. During the same period, however, the Maharajah of Patiala, with Master Tara S., was co-operating with the British to get more Sikhs enlisted into the army. Kairon especially utilized this contradiction between his own associations and those of Rarewala. Their respective records were thrown before an electorate that was likely to listen, since large numbers of PEPSU smallholders, many of whom were tenants, had participated in the Quit India movement, in the course of which they had been shot at not only by the British but also by the Patiala police. The rulers of Patiala state had, indeed, a long tradition of co-operation with the British. They had entered into an alliance with the latter against Maharajah Ranjit S. and played a decisive role in putting down the Indian Mutiny in 1857. Kairon exploited this traditional co-operation of the house of Patiala with alien rulers to lower Rarewala's reputation.

Shortly after the merger of PEPSU with Punjab, Rarewala, in April 1956, entered the Congress party on the promise of a ministry, and the rivalry between him and the CM was thereafter rivalry inside the Congress party itself. That Rarewala joined the Congress party did not imply that he was ideologically uncommitted. In fact his ideological commitment was and remained Akali. But seemingly he felt he could reconcile this with his personal interest, which was to join the ruling party, for once inside the Congress he campaigned for Akali demands.[4] This was a further theme which Kairon exploited to recruit neutral support: he argued that Rarewala was communal-minded, an associate of the Akalis, and feudal-minded, and in these respects unfaithful to Congress principles.

Rarewala did threaten Kairon's position as leader in the Doraha–Payal–Sirhind area. In the series of ministerial posts he had held in PEPSU and as Rehabilitation Minister, his position was unrivalled. During his periods of office as Financial Commissioner (1948–51), Chief Minister (April 1952–March 1953), and then Leader of the Opposition, large numbers of people from the area had been re-cruited by him into the administration of that state. Whether he was in or out of office, his contacts in the administration remained throughout the whole area. When PEPSU joined Punjab in March 1956, therefore, Kairon's primary task was to throw out its old-established leaders and build up new ones who owed their allegiance to himself alone. In 1957 Doraha was therefore declared a 'reserved constituency'—that is, a constituency which can be contested only by members of the scheduled castes—in order to cut Rarewala off from his principal source of localized support. But by virtue of his old links and associations Rarewala won in Sirhind, though his majority was greatly reduced.

Initially, Rarewala had been a rival to the CM because of his contacts with the Akali leadership and because, in his capacity as a state minister, he had links to national leaders. Moreover, as long as the threat remained that agitations by the Akali party would continue and the centre might therefore view it as prudent to have a Sikh permanently in the office of CM, Kairon feared that Rarewala might be considered as a suitable successor to him. In the Hindi agitation of 1957 Rarewala's approach was more moderate than that of the CM, and the latter suspected that Rarewala was trying to obtain the support of Hindus in order to challenge his power and replace him.

The CM, then, wanted so to diminish the influence of Rarewala that the latter could never again compete for the chief ministership. His associates in the enterprise at state level were General Mohan S. and Captain Rattan S.,[5] both formerly of the INA (Indian National Army). It was specifically General Mohan S., who had a farm some miles from Doraha, who acted as a filter for the information that reached the CM about what was going on in the Doraha–Payal–Sirhind area. Co-operation between the General and the CM was especially close from October 1962, with the setting up of what was known as the Raksha Dal—an organization for civil defence purposes—to beat the Chinese aggression. Political opponents spread doubts about Kairon's loyalty and Rarewala complained to certain national leaders that the Raksha Dal could be used as a private army. Kairon also had the temporary support at state level of a Hindu associate interested in the factionalism of the Doraha–Payal–Sirhind area—one Brish Bhan. He had been associated with the Congress party in PEPSU and Kairon had supported him as a candidate for the office of CM in PEPSU before its amalgamation with Punjab proper.

The local area in which Rarewala had extensive influence was, as stated, the present-day Assembly constituencies of Payal, Khanna, Sirhind and Amloh. The villages of this area were a recruiting ground for his faction and that of Kairon. The area had its own deep-seated rivalries based on personal enmities and antagonisms which were unresolved when Partap S. Kairon came to power in 1956. These were, however, located inside each separate village unit, and the enmity inside each village had not spread into the district so as to affect all the villages over a given area. Kairon's entry attached these local disputes to the rivalry at state level between himself and Rarewala.

I now pass on to consider the general nature of faction rivalries in rural areas, prior to discussing, in chapter 12, the particular enmities that influenced prominent personalities in the local area to align with Kairon or with Rarewala.

10   The general nature of factional rivalries in rural areas

Actual influence and status among the Jats was measured in two ways: first, by the fear a man generated in others, either through his use of force in the settlement of issues, since this use, if it went un-checked, implied political links and the support of a faction; second, by having others indebted to him by virtue of being a large landlord and thereby controlling credit relationships. Possession of a large holding of land was necessary to enable a man to control other men.

Factions in rural areas were therefore competing primarily over land and political links as the most important resources. The average holding of cultivated land per owner in the area where I worked was four acres.[1] Land was fertile, with very little fluctuation in the harvest from year to year, since it was well watered by tube well and canal. As quoted, yields—especially of wheat and maize—were among the highest in the province. But the system of inheritance whereby all sons received an equal share of the land split up many a viable unit into several unviable ones. Hence in larger families with small acreages of land the acquisition of more land was essential.

The area where I worked had also received a large influx of refugees from the Sialkot district of West Punjab. This was an area of very small landholdings, and because of the application of graded cuts[2] on the landholdings of all refugees coming from West Punjab, these holdings were still further reduced in size. This situation led to more competition.

Punjab was India's richest state, agriculturally, and Ludhiana was its most prosperous district. Land was competed for because it was an essential economic resource and a rich source of profit. Also, attached to the holding of land was a way of life which had izzat, i.e., which was 'honourable'. Factional coalitions helped to protect the right of each of their individual members to remain in unchallenged

121

possession of their land and to challenge the rights in land of those in the opposing faction. As well as being economically profitable it was a matter of honour to win a dispute over land in court.

The factions in the local area also competed for positions on the many elective institutions and for the limited amount of patronage at the disposal of political leaders at state level. Membership of institutions meant control of the sources of patronage, while the election to the position of sarpanc in a village implied a control over men. For the local leaders of the faction, as well as for the ordinary village participants, the faction was also a means of winning personal vendettas. Each man wanted defence against his opponents, and aimed to gain some economic and political advantage over them; if a man's opponents were attached to one faction, he automatically joined the other. Relationships of enmity or of friendship in many instances thus affected the choice of vertical links.

It was in the interest of the general population to be aligned with some faction. The Congress government, which was in power in the state until February 1967, controlled the quota and permit distribution of so many basic essentials[3] that it was useful to be aligned with it. The political links of leaders of the faction in the local area guaranteed them a certain amount of defence and protection in their private quarrels, and guaranteed them a certain amount of economic aggrandizement. The ordinary village participants used their links with the local area leaders to obtain such things as a job, an arms licence,[4] support in the election to the sarpancship of a village. Although, in a large number of instances, specifically personal enmities were given as a reason for joining a paarti, this particularized enmity was thereafter superseded by enmity to all members of the opposing paarti, since all members of a paarti aided one another. The ties between leaders of the faction in the local area and their supporters in the villages would tighten on such occasions as litigation, elections and attempts to defame and slander the political leader of the opposing faction.

Both the support which Kairon drew on in the Doraha–Payal–Sirhind area after 1956, and the support which Rarewala brought with him from his period of tenure in various official positions in PEPSU, were based largely on persons whom Punjabis term *dacoits*. There is no adequate English equivalent of the word. Here I intend it to convey a picture of a person with a particular style of life: a landowner, a middle-class farmer or, more rarely, a small proprietor who operates with the daring traditionally ascribed to the bandit—only one who does not live in a series of hideouts, but in a defended farm, guarded by a double gate, two dogs, his own gun and, if he is rich enough, a few bodyguards. Each dacoit usually also has a small number of men under his control. Irrespective of the position he occupies, he is prone to use violence in the settlement of issues.[5]

In the local area under consideration, this was the type of person offering allegiance to political leaders. For Kairon, patronage of the dacoit element in rural areas was merely a means of dealing with, utilizing and enlisting the support of the wilder elements of the society. A former private secretary of a former minister told me, 'No politician can control the Punjab without the help of bad characters. If Kairon had not roped the dacoit element into his group some other politician would have done so.' That is, the support would have gone to an opposing faction and been lost to him. Kairon understood the Jat character particularly well—that the only sanction which could be brought to bear on it was force or the threat of force. The Jats often quote a proverb to explain why they openly, but not covertly, succumb to whoever is in power over them: '*Rab nehre ke ghason nehre* (God is further away from you than the blows that are likely to fall on your head here and now).' Dacoits were useful to political leaders because as large landlords and as the sarpancs of villages they had control over others, and they could approach other leaders who had such control. It was frequently said of the area in which I worked that all its sarpancs were *das nambar*, i.e., they were all jailbirds. Small farmers, tenants and labourers could rarely go against their wishes.

Dacoits had a very obvious function to perform in the social situation as it existed in Punjab at the time of partition. In the implementation of certain social reform measures, such as land consolidation, the breaking up of large estates, and the legal provision for the giving of land to the tenants, the influence of those powerful in rural areas was invariably felt. In the state as a whole the dacoit element, recruited into factions, was in most instances used to keep a watch on the administration and to see that it acted according to the CM's directives. In one such instance, where the local supporter of the CM was also head of the urban Amritsar District Congress Committee, he boasted that he and not the DC effectively controlled the district: 'When I speak, the DC and SP know that S. Partap S.

Kairon is speaking.' Dacoits held sway in rural areas. They certainly feared the police, but others could not rely for protection on the police, as they were frequently bribed. Moreover, many policemen were dacoits themselves. There was no faith in the judiciary, for, as the Chief Public Prosecutor, District Courts Patiala, told me in March 1966—'People take their own vengeance because they believe the courts cannot give them justice.' Litigation was used as a means permanently to harm one's opponents and help one's supporters, since both the police and judiciary were subordinated to personal enmities and loyalties. Litigation therefore deepened the conflict between the factions.

11 Factional participants in the local area

The good old rule, the simple plan
That they should take who have the power
And they should keep who can.

In this chapter I outline the nature of the ties between the members of each faction and the nature of their hostilities with persons of the opposing faction in the local area. These allegiances and hostilities provided in each instance the context for a vertical alignment with either the CM or Rarewala. The data given in this chapter richly illustrate the comment of Gallin[1] that the membership of political factions 'is recruited primarily on the basis of interpersonal relations' and local antagonisms.

The Rarewala faction

As noted in chapter 7, in 1947 the entire Sikh community of West Punjab had been uprooted. As from March 1947, in the Muslim majority areas of the West Punjab, members of the Muslim League had systematically carried through a series of attacks on the lives, property and honour of members of the minority communities. Those who successfully fled to the safety of East Punjab brought with them memories of a mother or sister abducted or dishonoured, brothers killed or forcibly converted and property looted and burned.[2] It is therefore partly in this context that those who were subsequently to form the core of Rarewala's political support in the Doraha area combined in a band to drive out of PEPSU as many of its Muslim inhabitants as possible in order to create room for incoming Sikh refugees.

The initial ties between members of Rarewala's faction in the local area were thus forged at the time of the communal riots between Sikhs and Muslims. In the general climate of political disturbance and under the imperative of reclaiming the lost honour of their community, those individuals who co-operated with influential leaders and politicians to achieve the exodus of Muslims from PEPSU were thought by the general public to have rendered a valuable service to the Sikh community.

Until his assassination by the opposing faction in 1964, Rarewala's chief supporter in the Doraha area was Hardev S., a refugee from West Punjab; he and one Baljinder S., who was a medical doctor in Doraha but who was in the opposing faction, were married to two sisters in Doraha. The sisters belonged to a family that had many connexions, by association and marriage, with Sikh political leaders.

TABLE 1 *Local leaders of the Rarewala faction*

Balwant S., Tejinder S. and Manjeet S., of Lassowal	Wealthy transporters; Rarewala's chief financial supporters.
Gurbachan S.	An affine and business partner of the above; eighty acres of land; sarpanc of a village near Rara.
Ajmer S.	An affine of Gurbachan S.; owner of a small factory; sixty to eighty acres of land.
Hardev S.	Rarewala's chief lieutenant in the Doraha–Payal–Sirhind area; member of the SGPC.
Sham S.	Member of block samiti; lorry owner; a one-time director of the Central Co-operative Bank, Ludhiana.
Mihan S. Gill	Non-Jat; member of the SGPC and ex-MLA.

Ajmer S. was another prominent member of the faction in the local area. He was a one-time vice-president of Doraha's municipal committee and chairman of the local Khalsa high school. He had a machine tools factory, a number of trucks, four brick kilns and between sixty and eighty acres of land in a village near Payal. In the 1967 general elections he had managed Rarewala's election campaign.

Ajmer S. and Hardev S. had not been on good terms.[3] They had originally been partners in a brick kiln but Ajmer S. alleged that Hardev S. had embezzled the money from the business. In 1960 he expelled him from the business. Hardev S. used to gossip to Rarewala that Ajmer S. was visiting Kairon. Once, also, when a friend of the leader of the opposing faction had approached Ajmer S. to mediate between the two factions, Hardev S. complained against him to Rarewala. Indeed Ajmer S. seemed to dislike Hardev S. intensely and when he was drunk it was common knowledge that he used to ask an affine of the leader of the opposing faction: 'When are they [i.e., the opposing faction] going to murder him?'

Another member of the Rarewala faction, also from a village near Doraha, was one Sham S. He had been the terror of the area until finally he had fled from the Punjab out of fear that he would be killed by the leader of the opposing faction. He had been a BA student at Lahore and a one-time member of Doraha block samiti and a director of the Central Co-operative Bank, Ludhiana. At the time of my fieldwork he was resident in Bihar, where he was a truckowner.

In the period 1957–62 the Rarewala faction was represented in the State Assembly by one Mihan S. Gill, a non-Jat, also from a village near Doraha (Rajgarh). He was chairman of the Federation of Scheduled Castes in PEPSU 1953, and a former Labour Minister in PEPSU. In 1957 the Congress party allocated to Rarewala a number of candidates for his supporters; he gave one to Mihan S. The latter won the seat of Doraha in 1957 but he lost it in the two subsequent general elections. At the time of my fieldwork visit he was running a cycle repair shop in Doraha and was a tenant on government land. He had no other resources.

Mihan S., it is said, did not get on well with either Hardev S. or Ajmer S. As far back as 1952 Hardev S. had had posters stuck up on the eve of elections to say that Mihan S. was not standing in the elections at all. This led to a split between them which had widened over the years, with Hardev S. continuing to undermine Mihan S.'s capacity to win at elections. But after the death of Hardev S., Mihan S. took steps to organize the case concerning his murder in court; he was pressed by the other members of the faction on the grounds that otherwise the Rarewala faction would be demoralized. Mihan was similarly not on very good terms with Ajmer S.: he alleged that if Ajmer S. had supported him as the Akali Dal candidate in Doraha in the 1962 general elections he would have won. Instead Ajmer S. was campaigning for Rarewala himself in Sirhind constituency. These quarrels appeared to have been resolved in 1967, when Ajmer S.

pointed out to me that one of Mihan S.'s brothers was a district welfare officer and the other was a station house officer[4] and that they were 'of good family'.

The wealthiest members of the Rarewala faction were undoubtedly Balwant S. and Tejinder S., of the village of Lassowal near Khanna, a grain market between Doraha and Gobindgarh. Together with their brother-in-law Manjeet S., with Gurbacban S., whose sister was married to Manjeet S.'s son, and with Malkeet S., the paternal uncle of Gurbachan S., they led in supporting Rarewala after Hardev's assassination in 1964. They were the owners of a fleet of lorries and buses and were reputed to be multi-millionaires.[5] Gurbachan S. was sarpanc of a village close to the village of Rara, Rarewala's home village. He had eighty acres of inherited land there. Ajmer S., it may be remarked here, was also a relative of Gurbachan S. and hence also of Balwant S. This group of affines formed a 'visiting group' and the contacts which factional alliances consolidated gave rise to ties through subsequent marriages.

But even among this group of affines there were quarrels. In the court case relating to the murder of the leading member of the opposite faction, for example, Balwant S. is alleged to have become involved in, on a conservative estimate, an expenditure of £2,381 (50,000 rupees). As a result of this, both Gurbachan S. and Malkeet S. took their shares out of the transport company. But if there were indeed such quarrels, it was not openly admitted. When I asked Gurbachan S. about the matter he merely said that he had taken out his share of the property and formed a new company because he had two grown-up sons and he wanted to have a compact economic concern free from the interference of others. He claimed that he otherwise still shared the enmities of Balwant S. and that the family who led the opposing faction were a 'criminal type of people'.

Thus internally there were quarrels and a struggle for influence among members of the Rarewala faction in the local area, but extension of these quarrels into public expression was rare. All members of the faction had received favours from Rarewala, who had become their political patron. Since 1947 they had tried to oblige him, in the expectation of further favours. But they were not only connected to one another because of their loyalty to Rarewala. Ajmer S., Sham S. and Hardev S. had initially co-operated in a truck union at Doraha and, for a time, Ajmer S. and Hardev S. ran jointly a brick kiln. When they collected support in the villages for

Rarewala they complemented one another in that they each had different areas of influence,[6] though these overlapped. Hardev S. tended to attract those who had virulent enmities against members of the opposing faction, and he exploited these for Rarewala's benefit; Ajmer S. would do most of the routine tasks of trying to get jobs for those who approached him and interviews with ministers when required. The Lassowal family provided much of the finance not only for Rarewala himself to conduct his election campaigns but also to do the necessary bribing of the police and judiciary at crucial moments.[7]

But Sham S., Mihan S., Balwant S. and Tejinder S. of Lassowal, and Hardev S., were primarily the persons who always formed an alliance to harass the opposing faction and to compete for the disposal of available patronage.

They lived fairly near one another. Sham S. and Mihan S. came from villages close to Doraha, while Ajmer S. and Hardev S. lived in Doraha itself. Only Balwant S. lived twenty-two miles away, in Sirhind, while his place of employment was seventeen miles distant, though the family's ancestral land was in the village of Lassowal, which was only nine miles from Doraha. Distance was never a problem, as the network of roads in the area was good and most of them had some form of private transport.

The Kairon faction

All members of the Kairon faction in the local area had previously been members of the Rarewala faction. The Kairon faction's unity was based on persons who were aggrieved against certain persons of the Rarewala faction for one reason or another.

The core of the Kairon faction in the local area was a family of six brothers: Kulwant S., Jagmohan S., Santokh S., Narinder S., Gurdial S. and Jagmail S., from the village of Dhanipur near Payal. They were the sons of the late Avtar S. As a family they cultivated 130 acres of inherited land and 115 acres of acquired land[8] and they used three tube wells for its irrigation. As a family they were not only one of the largest landlords in the eastern half of Ludhiana district but they were also among the area's most progressive farmers. They worked the land with three tractors, employing six labourers on a yearly basis and a large number of daily labourers. They also owned various agricultural implements such as a threshing machine, a wheat-sowing machine and a fodder-cutting machine. Their other assets included a car, a partnership in transport by trucks at Gobindgarh and two brick kilns. The sarpancship of the village had been hereditary in their family for at least two generations, their father, Avtar S., on his death having been succeeded as sarpanc of the village by his eldest son, Kulwant S. In 1962 Kulwant S. became a member of Doraha block samiti, and his brother, Narinder S., took over as sarpanc.

TABLE 2   *Local leaders of the Kairon faction*

Satnam S.	Supporter of Kairon since 1952; holder of a share in a steel rolling mill; forty acres of land.
Kulwant S., Santokh S., Jagmohan S. and Jagmail S.	Owners of over a hundred acres of land in Punjab and partners in a small lorry business; leaders of the Kairon faction in local area; Kulwant S. a member of Doraha block samiti (1962–5).
Dr Baljinder S.	Member of Doraha block samiti (1962–5).
Kamiikar S.	Member of Doraha block samiti (1965); sarpanc of a village near Payal; fifty acres of land.
Lieutenant Bhag S.	Non-Jat; member of the INA; MLA for Amloh until defeated in February 1969 mid-term elections; former MLA for Doraha.
Beant S.	Former president of Doraha block samiti and present member; candidate for Payal constituency in the 1967 general elections; MLA for Payal constituency from February 1969.

Narinder S. was not involved in the factionalism. This may have been because he owned, independently, between forty and fifty acres of land near Payal which he cultivated himself. (The only other member of the family possessing independent land resources was Kulwant S.'s wife; she had sixty acres.) Gurdial S. did not participate in the factionalism either, because he was an alcoholic.[9] Kulwant S. was assassinated in December 1965, and his brother

Jagmohan S. was imprisoned a few months later. Thus the *de facto* head of the household for most of my fieldwork visit was Santokh S.

The brothers had the necessary foundation for prestige among the Jats. First, they were several in number and, with the exception of Jagmohan S., represented the Punjabi ideal of good looks, i.e., they were tall and fair-skinned. Their appearance was also such as to inspire fear. Second, they had a large holding of land. They were the richest members of the Kairon faction in the local area specified.

Since 1950 the family of Avtar S. had been enemies of the family of Kartar S., of the same village. Both families had initially shared a common well. However, Kartar S. had begun to quarrel with Avtar S., father of Kulwant S., when Kulwant S. put a diesel engine on the tube well. Kartar S. said that it would break the tube well. I was told by members of both factions that Kartar S.'s reason for acting thus was that he could not bear to see the family of Avtar S. prospering. He alleged that he could not get water from the pump when the diesel engine was working, so he decided to obtain some land near a second well, and he used to threaten to kill Kulwant S. and return to his land at the first well. On a certain day in 1950, when Kartar S. and some associates were drunk, they came to the house of Avtar S. and shouted some rude and insulting remarks. In the ensuing brawl, Kulwant S. and his brother Jagmohan S. were accused of having fractured the arms and legs of Kartar S., who later died in hospital of his injuries. Kulwant S. and Jagmohan S. were charged and sentenced in the lower courts but were acquitted in the high court. They were acquitted by S. Gurnam S.,[10] who was later to become CM of the Punjab in November 1967 and who was then a judge of the Patiala High Court.

Dhanipur was a very small village of only fifty to fifty-five families, and Kulwant S.'s family, as the largest owners of land, and as monopolizers of the sarpancship, controlled it. After his acquittal in 1952 Kulwant S. therefore began to seek influence over a wider area. As he had now been involved in one criminal case, he had learned how useful it was to have links with powerful outsiders. He began to associate with and to prove his usefulness to Dr Baljinder S. of Doraha: in fact he took Baljinder S. under his protection. Baljinder S. wanted an ally to help him in his own rivalry with his wife's sister's husband, Hardev S. of Rarewala faction. The two men were involved in a family quarrel concerning the financial resources of their father-in-law's mill in Doraha of which Hardev S. had been the manager. Hardev S. was jealous of Baljinder S. because the latter had two brothers who were officers in the army. As Hardev S. was linked with the notorious Sham S., it was therefore initially to protect himself that Baljinder S. became an ally of Kulwant S.

Another prominent member of the Kairon faction in the local area was Kamiikar S., the sarpanc of a village near Payal. He had been friendly with Kulwant S. for some fifteen to twenty years. Kamiikar S. had fifty acres of land and owned one truck in Kulwant S.'s combine. In 1967, he was also a member of Doraha block samiti. He had previously been sentenced to twenty years' imprisonment but had not completed the sentence. He had joined the Kairon faction on the occasion of a death of a friend who had been a supporter of the Rarewala faction. He made the excuse that Hardev S. was neither a good man nor reliable. But Kamiikar S. came from the village in which Ajmer S.'s family had land, and his immediate reason for joining was that he was not on good terms with other members of the Rarewala faction who had supported Ajmer S.'s paternal cousin as a candidate in the pancayat elections in 1957. Since 1965, when both Kairon, the leader of the faction at state level, and Kulwant S., the leader of the faction in this local area, were both assassinated, Kamiikar S. and Santokh S., brother of Kulwant S., have become increasingly estranged. The faction lacks a powerful political patron; and Kamiikar S., who had, with his sons, previously been very active in the Kairon faction and close to Kulwant S.'s family, drifted away from it out of fear for the lives of his sons. He no longer morally supports the faction. During the general elections in 1967 he did not campaign for Beant S., candidate of the Kairon faction in Payal constituency—and since then he has made many approaches to the opposing faction to get his truck included in their combine. There seemed to be two conditions that influenced a local leader when he was considering changing sides. One was the actual fact that his faction had lost power; the other was whether his enmities with persons in the faction he had formerly opposed would decrease sufficiently for him to join it. In Kamiikar S.'s case, Gurbachan S. had said that the Rarewala faction was not ready to include Kamiikar S. because 'he's criminal', and he said that they had rejected his approaches. Kamiikar S. is, so to speak, in limbo.

The representative of the Kairon faction in the State Assembly was Bhag S., the present Congress MLA for Amloh constituency and an ex-MLA for Doraha. He had been a lieutenant in General Mohan

S.'s Indian National Army. He was not a Jat but belonged to the scheduled castes; he had originally been a refugee from West Punjab, and after partition he worked initially as a typist in the land revenue officer's court at Payal. It was he who had removed Mihan S. Gill of the Rarewala faction from his post as chairman of the Federation of Scheduled Castes in PEPSU. In 1957, however, he had been defeated by Mihan S. Gill in the general elections. It was at this time he had joined the Kairon faction, primarily as a protection against Mihan S.

Beant S., who was the Kairon faction's candidate for Payal constituency in the general election of 1967,[11] was also originally a refugee from West Punjab. Both his brothers were officers in the army and his family had a good holding of land, seventy-five acres. He was a former president of Doraha block samiti but had left the Rarewala faction as late as 1960, it is said because Rarewala was showing favouritism to another prominent landlord in the village where he himself owned land. He felt, too, that Ajmer S. and Hardev S., as he put it, 'surrounded Rarewala' and let no one else near him. In other words, he thought that the Kairon faction offered him more chances of rising into a prominent position.

From 1951 Kulwant S. had been acquainted with a Satnam S., originally from the district of Amritsar, who, to escape responsibility for a murder, had shifted to the district of Gujranwala (now in Pakistan) prior to partition, where it is said he made a profit out of reporting the activities of the local people to the British. Satnam S. and Hardev S. had known each other for some time, as they had together been followers of the Nagokes. They had been friends, but Satnam S. had quarrelled with Hardev S. over some trees which Rarewala had allotted to Satnam S. in Doraha. In 1952, when he sold these, Hardev S. demanded a share in the money. Satnam S. was also on bad terms with Ajmer S. He had originally come to Doraha with a letter of introduction to Ajmer S. from Ishar S. Majhail (who has already been mentioned in chapter 7 as a political associate of the Nagokes). Ajmer S. alleged that Satnam S. had embezzled money from him. Thus in the same year that Satnam S. quarrelled with Hardev S. over the trees, he allied himself with Baljinder S. and Kulwant S. simply because they were hostile to Hardev S. At the instance of Partap S. Kairon, he gathered together a working group to publicize the weaknesses, personal and other-wise, of Rarewala to the electorate in the mid-term elections. It was, in fact, through Satnam S. that Kulwant S. came in contact with

Kairon. In 1956 Satnam S. approached Kairon, and suggested to him that Kulwant S. had strong support in the Doraha–Payal area which could be useful to him. Kulwant S., however, thought of Satnam S. as a coward, and used to sneer and laugh sarcastically at the mere mention of his name. He used to relate an incident of how, after the murder of Hardev S., Satnam S. had induced someone by paying him 500 rupees to go down in a taxi to Amloh merely to find out if his name had been included in the initial police report. During the course of the association Satnam S. also began to dislike Kulwant S., one reason seeming to be that Kulwant S. had a powerful friend and associate at state level in the person of General Mohan S. These feelings of rivalry with Kulwant S. were such that he also became antipathetic to General Mohan S.; privately he used to make such remarks as, 'Over a half of the quarrels in the Congress party organization of the state are due to General Mohan S.' His attitude to Kulwant S. when I met him (which was after the latter's murder) was rather ambivalent. On the one hand he appeared grudgingly to admire him, as when he said, 'Kulwant S. rose to power individually. He did not need Kairon. Soon he would have become an MLA,' but on the other hand he was clearly trying to throw all blame for the violence in the Doraha–Payal area on to the family of Kulwant S.

Those attached to a faction often used it as a protection for smuggling activities. Similarly under the mask of factional rivalry individuals would attempt to benefit themselves economically and financially ruin their competitors. In the Kairon faction in the local area, every major participant in both the factions became richer as the dispute proceeded. But for both Dr Baljinder S. and Satnam S. the faction was primarily a means of economic aggrandizement and therefore when it lost its powerful political patron in 1965 they no longer saw it as able to continue to serve them in this respect. Satnam S.'s loyalty to the faction, however, was unwavering until the assassination of Kairon himself in 1965. After Kairon's death he left the district and did not maintain any connexion at all with other members of the faction in the local area. Out of the factionalism he had gained substantially. By 1965 he had a quarter share in a steel rolling mill in Gobindgarh and forty acres of land. Dr Baljinder S.'s loyalty had wavered two years earlier. Supported by the Kairon faction, he had been elected to the zilla parishad in 1962. In 1963, however, he openly started supporting Rarewala. The occasion for his defection from the Kairon faction and his open support for Rarewala was Kulwant S.'s action in getting the son of Hardev S. falsely implicated in a charge of murder in August 1963. Baljinder S. made this change of loyalties evident by thereafter helping Hardev S. Through his brother, a major-general in the army, he used to approach on Hardev S.'s behalf a certain inspector general of police[12] who was also Rarewala's personal friend.

It may thus seem as if Baljinder S.'s disagreements with Hardev S. belonged to a period when there was no danger to the lives of either Hardev S. or his son, who were, of course, his affines. It is, however, more likely that Baljinder S. merely used them as an excuse to change sides. After the death of Hardev S., Baljinder S. again switched his allegiance back to the Kairon faction. His changing allegiances need not necessarily be explained in terms of loyalty to affines. In 1962 Kairon, for reasons I shall explain later, dealt a decisive blow to the rising power of his own faction by imprisoning Kulwant S. In 1963 the first attempt was made on Kulwant S.'s life by the opposing faction. Baljinder S., who had made a considerable amount of money out of his factional allegiance, perhaps thought it unlikely at the time that he was going to gain more. He became situationally a part of the faction again only at the time of the 1967 elections, when the political candidate of the Kairon faction, fighting on the Akali ticket, happened to be his friend. His support for the Kairon faction at this time was undoubtedly facilitated by both the murder of his affine (Hardev S.) and the murder of Kulwant S. It is important to note that it in no way implied any notion of a tie with Kulwant S.'s brother, Santokh S., who was then the dominant personality of the faction in the Doraha–Payal–Sirhind area. Baljinder S. had, in fact, considerable personal enmity against Santokh S.; and Santokh S. viewed himself as vulnerable at Baljinder S.'s hands, making such remarks as, 'We may belong to one faction and be together supporting the same political candidate, but as individuals we are against each other.'

I now want to examine in more detail the reasons why Kulwant S. was a member of a faction. I have already hinted at these reasons. He perceived the usefulness of outside links, initially to protect a holding of land seized by force, and wished to see his influence and prestige expand over the Doraha–Payal–Sirhind area. These were the dominating motives influencing his decision to set up a truck combine in 1962 when he was offered two truck permits by the CM.

The local small shopkeepers were searching for a person who would set up a truck combine to rival that of Balwant S. of the Rarewala faction, since Balwant S. had a monopoly, in order to lower the rates of transport. Kulwant S. saw in this a source of influence. In addition, Kulwant S. himself had the experience of high transport charges for the bricks manufactured at his kilns. There was evident also an element of personal rivalry with Balwant S. Kulwant S. wanted to progress in life. He was ambitious.[13] And he thought that if Balwant S., who was only a bus driver in 1944 and who had very little land, could rise, so could he. The family was large enough anyway to spare some of its members from cultivation. Eventually, also, as a result of the innumerable cases in which he and his family became involved, the profits from operating the trucks were needed as a financial resource additional to the land. The family was large and, with the exception of Narinder S., who held his land separately in Payal, it was undivided. Expenses on their lawsuits were estimated by their lawyer at 10,000 to 20,000 rupees per case, while their income (in 1966) was 80,000 rupees from their acquired land and roughly an equivalent amount from their own ancestral land. And they also had to take into account such contingencies as the wrecking of their tube well engines by the police.

Kulwant S., then, became and remained a member of a faction in order to seal an illegal acquisition of land with political protection. He was not pulling on the outside alliances that he henceforth established principally to bolster his position inside his own village, but he was using these links to try to enter politics at state level. He used the faction to attain a position of dominance in the Doraha–Payal–Sirhind area, and his connexions with the faction's representatives at state level particularly achieved the purpose of securing help in acquittals on charges in court, and, for a time, protection against assassination.

In the period 1957–65 members of the Kairon faction in the local area were associated with two cases of murder, two cases of attempted murder, with many cases of damage to the person and property of members of the opposite faction, and with involving them in very many fabricated minor cases. The murders and attempted murders were on the persons of those who challenged the dominance of the leading family of that faction by testifying against them in court, who supported their enemies, organized witnesses against them and who betrayed them. They considered it a dishonour, an insult, that they should be so threatened and not to have retaliated would hence have ruined their reputation and suggested weakness. Court cases were thus instigated and murders or assaults planned in order to show that they had power to protect themselves against those threatening the security of their lives and possessions. They were able to threaten, abuse and insult because all these actions could be committed with a certain impunity so long as their political patron remained in the office of CM and did not openly disown them.

This does not exclude the fact that their murders and other attacks were in accordance with izzat. Acting according to izzat favourably influenced the retention of economic resources and was intimately connected with security in their possession. Acting according to 'honour' achieved security through the display of power and through the elimination and terrorizing of enemies. It was a demonstration and reinforcement of a family's security. The more a man was judged to be a person who would defend his honour the more he was feared and the less it was likely that someone would threaten his position. Not defending one's honour made one vulnerable to the predatory acts of one's neighbours. It demonstrated weakness. Strength derived from political patronage was usually attained before a man acted according to izzat, more especially when this involved him in acts of murder. Acting according to izzat was, in these instances, therefore, an index of political links. Law as laid down by the central government contradicted the moral code of the Jats. Therefore in a situation where a man was without political links, the act of performing izzat, where so doing involved another's death, was temporarily suspended.

After the death of Kairon, Kulwant S.'s family was left without a secure political patron. The pressure on his brother Santokh S. to act according to izzat remained.[14] The opposing faction—responsible for the murder of Kulwant S.—assumed that Santokh S. would take revenge for the murder when he could and was therefore making plans to eliminate all his brothers before this eventuality overtook them. Santokh S. had every intention of acting according to izzat: the family honour would be lost if izzat was not fulfilled, the opposing faction would brand him as a coward, and his reputation would fall within his own faction. The situation would then be propitious for the original owners to seize back the land forcibly taken from them by the group of brothers when these had the power to dictate terms to others. Santokh S.'s pursuit of secure political patronage therefore continued. He was visibly a very frustrated person. He was acutely conscious that he and his faction could only do what they had the power to do.

The set of values which the ideology of izzat sanctioned perpetuated murders and counter-murders; and the relationships of power at particular times only explained why and when a particular person was murdered. Favourable relationships with the powerful enabled a man to act according to izzat. In the Punjab the Jats are the sole owners of that aspect of the philosophy of izzat enjoining murder in revenge for murder. Law as defined and imposed by the central government prohibited such acts. To this extent the 'ought' of the law was therefore not an 'ought' the Jats recognized or respected. To this situation Santokh S. (among others) responded by choosing those occasions when he would perform izzat so that they coincided with a period when he had political patronage. His attitude was that he was doing the right thing: why should he be penalized for it?

The faction in many respects provided the political context in which the value of izzat could be achieved, since factional alignments enjoined aid to friends and undying opposition to enemies. The faction protected its members when they acted according to izzat. This was one reason why many ordinary folk joined a faction in the first place. But otherwise the context for faction membership in local areas lay mainly in the expectation of deriving from it economic security and political influence. It was because of this that tendencies towards the break-up of the faction in the local area did not develop independently of events at state level. Break-ups occurred, as in 1965 after Kairon's assassination, when the image of the faction as such, to its own members, became one of weakness: that is, when the faction leaders in the local area ceased to be supported by a political leader at state level. It was then thought by some of its members that attachment no longer could protect them or advance their interests. People like Kamiikar S., as I have mentioned, then tried to change their allegiance, out of fear, or to opt out completely as Satnam S. did.

Out of the original core of local area members dating back to the early 1950s only Lieutenant Bhag S. and the remaining active brothers of the family of Kulwant S.—Santokh S., Jagmail S. and Jagmohan S.—were members of the faction in 1967. In many respects Bhag S. and Santokh S. were dependent on each other. The former needed the money which people like Santokh S. could gather through their resources in lorries, in land and in affines who were money-lenders; while Santokh S. needed Bhag S. in his capacity as an MLA and as one who, with the other MLAs associated with the former CM, Kairon, could support his interests before the appropriate minister or official. Both Santokh S. and Bhag S. were also associated with General Mohan S., though for different reasons,[15] and the General seemed to have an interest in having them continue to co-operate. When Rarewala was elected leader of the Congress Party in 1967 Dr Baljinder S., Beant S., and Santokh S. each separately pressed Bhag S. to move out of the Congress Party. The United Front (the major opposition party comprising Akalis and Communists) had offered Bhag S. cabinet ministership. The reason Bhag S. gave me for not doing so was that he would, with his friends, be more effective inside than outside the Congress, and that after vilifying the Akalis in the recent election he could not switch so soon without attracting too much adverse criticism from the electorate.[16] Bhag S., however, must not have found the political setting very conducive to the decision he made. There was much swapping of allegiance between the Akali and Congress parties during this period. The Akalis were temporarily in power, however, and Santokh S. thought that, as a minister, Bhag S. could extract more benefits for the faction were he to accept the offer. Also, Santokh S. in the course of the election had aligned himself to the new CM and to the Speaker of the Assembly, both of whom were Akalis. Bhag S. was in a dilemma, but it would appear that the influence of General Mohan S. was decisive at this time, as Bhag S. did not leave the Congress Party. General Mohan S. no doubt wanted to retain Bhag S. as part of a following to support him in his attempt to become a minister, and perhaps even the CM of Punjab.

Both factions had members in institutions such as the block samiti, the Central Co-operative Bank and the zilla parishad. Both factions also had a member in the Vidhan Sabha. Likewise, both factions possessed a truck combine. About one hundred trucks were affiliated to Kulwant S.'s combine, which meant roughly that the combine sustained in employment slightly more than two hundred persons. The families of these persons were also usually associated with the Kairon faction. To have members on the block samiti and zilla parishad was important in that certain government allocations went to those institutions, and they were therefore local sources of patronage which could be used to assist followers. Being in a position of a patron or a protector did not necessarily mean a man had to be visible to whomever he protected. What was meant by a protector was one who could dispense small benefits to his followers, or who had influence with the local police and judiciary; and he was a patron to whom a man demonstrated attachment so that those with whom he was at enmity would not touch his property. Within each core the more dominating personalities were those who could offer such protection, i.e., they were those having upward links with a political leader or reliable links in the police and administration, and who might also have a secure economic position through having resources in land and transport. Thus the most important members of the Kairon faction in the local area were Satnam S., Kulwant S. and his brothers, and Lieutenant Bhag S. The most important persons within the Rarewala faction were the Lassowals and Hardev S. To a larger extent Rarewala was associated with all his lieutenants in the local area and not just with three of them, as was Kairon, the CM. Thus all members of the Rarewala faction were important from the point of view of their direct connexion to their political patron.

It was a characteristic of both factions in the local area that they had a relatively unvarying and consistent membership. All members of Rarewala's faction in the local area knew him personally and seemed to be in a very close relationship with him, this being a major factor in keeping the faction cohesive, as he mediated in their disputes. Clear and distinct reciprocal loyalties operated between Rarewala and the individual members of his faction in the local area. In the Kairon faction, however, not all its individual members in the local area had a link with the CM. With the exception of Kulwant S., Satnam S. and Lieutenant Bhag S., none in the Kairon faction was in close relationship with the CM, while Kulwant S.'s family was the only family in the faction that directly received any favours from the CM. But the range of enmities of persons in the Kairon faction, as has been seen, was coincidentally the same for all (and did not become so through association, though the intensity of these enmities was definitely increased by it). Relationships of enmity with *Rarewale di paarti* (Rarewala's faction) had been responsible for the formation of *Kairon di paarti* (Kairon's faction) in the local area and the fact that all members of the paarti had this common set of enmities was a significant factor in its continuance. As rivalry developed with the opposing paarti, all these members co-operated in (i) involving members of that paarti in court cases, (ii) organizing active opposition to it by intervening in village disputes and in pancayat elections favouring those opposed to Rarewala, (iii) sharing in the broadcasting of slander about Rarewala's family, and (iv) seeking protection for its own members where they had been properly or falsely involved in court cases. This was the range of their common interest. The Kairon paarti in the local area appeared as a coalition of individuals, the underlying principle of whose unity was the realization that the ties which they had with one another and which a few of their number had with a political leader were necessary were their paarti to win in elections and on committees and hence obtain a larger proportion of rewards available, both political and economic. Except on the occasion I mentioned above, they seldom acted in concert. There seemed to be, at times, a certain ignorance about what one's fellow members of the faction were actually doing, unless they were also one's close friends or relatives. For example, Bhag S., MLA, once asked me, in my capacity as Santokh S.'s affine, 'Who are they going to murder now?' Each faction leader in the local area would go independently and approach the various leaders at state level favourable to their faction; all the faction leaders would not go together.

The members of the Kairon faction would often characterize the Rarewala faction as being different in terms of the pattern of associations and ties of its leading members, as, for example, Rarewala had connexions with the owner of a large transport firm, Balwant S., and with a feudal landlord, the Maharajah of Patiala. In fact, however, it was only Rarewala who throughout most of his life had had such connexions, and most members of both factions in the local area had risen to what they were in their lifetime.

The six brothers of the Kairon faction were marked by their rustic habits and their direct and straightforward manner. They had not educated their children beyond the school-leaving age, and the son of Jagmohan S. was working on a truck. Only one son of Kulwant S. (a boy of twelve) could speak English. Although by 1967 Santokh S. had begun building a modern bungalow in the state capital of Chandigarh, he remained close to the soil, a *kacchha* man.[17] The family house in the village of Dhanipur always seemed as if it were under siege. To see this mode of life as reflecting in any way the personalities who stayed there would be wrong. Kulwant S., living in the Jat rural areas, ambitious and yet at the same time not having

from birth a set of links useful to him, had to depend on force and
violence in order to become sufficiently powerful to attract such
links.[18] It is useful, in this one instance, to compare his position
with that of another landowner, Rarewala himself. Rarewala was
related to the Maharajah of Patiala, he had had 'a good education'
and 'he had been taken into IAS service', as I was frequently told. He
had a long-standing association with all prominent persons in the
Congress and the Akali Dal. It was these links that made the position
of Rarewala very different from that of Kulwant S. There was also
another difference. Compared with Rarewala, it was less easy for
Kulwant S. to maintain his upward links. Their respective families,
although then cultivating an equivalent amount of land, each
practised a different type of farming. Rarewala's land was farmed by
tenants, under the supervision of one of his three sons, and Rarewala himself was, of course, most of the time away from his land.
In the family of Kulwant S., four brothers farmed the land with the
help of labourers, while by 1962 the acquisition of two brick kilns
and a truck combine meant that it was even less likely that the
family would move out of the particular set of social relationships
in which they were embedded. Absentee farming was associated with
a more established access to outside links. These links continuously
involved the absentee landlord in a social circle which was clearly
useful to him.

I mentioned at the beginning of the last chapter that I had de-
limited the Doraha–Payal–Sirhind area as being the area over which
the factions operated. In so doing I did not intend to give the
impression that recruitment was entirely from this one local area
exclusively; in this respect the area was unbounded. But recruitment
from outside the Doraha–Payal–Sirhind area was of a situational
nature. I will give examples of this. In 1959 Balwant S. of Lassowal
had attempted to break the monopoly of a very large transporter in
loading trucks at two other important markets for goods carriers.
The transporter, a Congress MLA (and a supporter of the CM),
resented this, and with the support of the local shopkeepers and
merchants of Gobindgarh, and Kulwant S., he attempted to start a
combine in competition with that of Balwant S. (The attempt
failed owing to the Lassowals arranging for their own trucks to
collide with the new combine's truck.) A second instance is that in
early March 1966 the sarpanc of a village completely out of the area

affected by the factions had offered twenty thousand rupees to Jagmohan S. as a contribution towards the assassination of the Lassowal family. The sarpanc's buses were in competition with those of Balwant S.'s on a particular route, and he would have been very happy to see the ruination of Balwant S.'s family.

TABLE 3   *Dates of key events*

1947	The partition of the Punjab.
1952	Kulwant S. and his brother acquitted for the murder of Kartar S. of Dhanipur.
1952 April– 1953 March	Rarewala rules in PEPSU.
1956 January	Kairon becomes CM of the Punjab.
March	Regional formula. PEPSU joins Punjab.
April	Rarewala joins the Congress party. Land consolidation.
1957 February	Third general election.
August	Kulwant S. seizes the land of Ashok Ram. Ashok Ram lodges an appeal.
December	Two cases of assault on various relatives of Harnam S. by members of the Kairon faction.
1958 March	Murder of Harnam S.
October	Court case regarding the murder of Harnam S. opened.
1959	Second elections for pancayats. Sham S.'s Mauser case. Beating up of the servant of Gian S. of Jhabbowal village. Kulwant S. given licences for two brick kilns by Kairon. Abduction of Gian S. of Jhabbowal village.
1960 January	SGPC elections. Rarewala tube well case. Dilbagh S. joins the first attempt to set up a truck combine in competition with the Lassowal family.
1961 September	The beating up of Karam S.
1962	Third pancayat elections and first block samiti and zilla parishad elections.
1962 February	General elections. Kulwant S. becomes a member of Doraha block samiti, is given two permits for trucks by the CM, and starts a truck combine.
August	Court case about the beating up of Karam S.
September	Kulwant S.'s conviction in the above case.
November	The Chinese invasion of India.

1963	August	Kulwant S. shot at Khanna.
		Two cases registered against Karam S.'s son by members of Kairon faction.
1964	January	Murder of Kardev S.
	August	Kulwant S. shot at in Ludhiana.
	November	Court case regarding Hardev S.'s murder begins.
1965	February	Murder of Kairon.
		Members of Kulwant S.'s family acquitted of the murder of Hardev S.
	August	*Fieldwork commences.*
	December	Murder of Kulwant S.
1966	March	Imprisonment of Jagmohan S., Kulwant S.'s brother.
1967	February	General elections.
		Rarewala heads the Congress opposition to the United Front Ministry.
	June	*Fieldwork ends.*

12 Vertical links between leaders of the faction in the local area and those at state level

The two factions in the Doraha–Payal–Sirhind area were competing for control of the area's economic and political resources. In this chapter I outline the nature of the relationship established for that purpose between state level political leaders and their local area supporters.

The Rarewala faction[1]

Rarewala's relationship with his local area supporters in the local area was developed partly in the situation in PEPSU in 1947. At that time there was a large amount of land vacated by Muslims and available for settlement by Sikhs. Not all of this, in fact, was, allocated to refugees but much was seized by those who were influential and their supporters. This situation was not special to the Doraha area, as is noted by Rai. As she points out,[2] resources acquired during this period of lawlessness were not readily given up, despite orders to that effect; members of what was subsequently to be known as the Rarewala faction were no exception to the general rule. Had they not had the protection of certain political leaders it is doubtful if they could have retained all they had acquired. This was especially so of the period prior to and preceding governor's rule in PEPSU, when those with grievances developed during the period of Rarewala's tenure in the office of CM in PEPSU were continually pointing out the origin of his supporters' acquisitions. A prominent member of the Kairon faction described Rarewala's supporters as '1947 models' since, according to him, it was in that year that they had established the beginning of their rise to affluence. Once peace had returned to the Punjab and members of the Rarewala faction had become respected and influential members of the local community, the opposing faction endeavoured to defame them with

145

reference to their activities during the partition period. This the following letter shows:

> They were the chief actors in the 1947 riots. They ... looted property worth lakhs ... It is an open secret there that the loot, property and ammunition have not been recovered from them with his [i.e., Rarewala's] connivance. [Part of a letter addressed to the SP Fatehgarh district (dated 11 February 1953).]

If we are to take the above letter as revealing a true state of affairs[3] then it would seem that Rarewala's protection became vital to these men, particularly in the immediate post-partition years. Certainly they were to be seen helping him in the 1952 elections and in subsequent elections.

In the early fifties Rarewala's supporters were, for a variety of reasons, continually in need of protection. Particularly this was true of Sham S., Hardev S. and the Lassowal family. When Muslim refugees were fleeing to Pakistan the Lassowal family made a profit out of transporting them. They began their financial accumulation during this period. Later they were to receive many of their truck permits and licences in gratitude for political support. The case with Gurbachan S. was similar. Among the Jats it is quite customary to exploit such periods of lawlessness for the benefit of one's family and to settle private vengeances.

Rarewala was the patron of his supporters as was every Punjab political leader. In that capacity he dispensed the usual small favours to them as did all politicians: granting licences for the running of trucks and for firearms, arranging promotions and transfers in the lower ranks of the administrative service and intervening with the police at the local level when necessary. This was the routine for every political leader who wished to remain a leader. In the case of Rarewala the dependence between him and his supporters was a more reciprocal one than the relationship between Kairon and his local area supporters. Rarewala was particularly dependent financially on Balwant S. of Lassowal. The latter was the main financial support of the Rarewala faction and in this respect frequently helped the faction in its relations with the police and judiciary. Such an instance of this occurred subsequent to the murder of Kulwant S. In a sessions court report, Santokh S. is noted as claiming that the police were conniving with the Lassowal family because of the latter's wealth and connexions and were helping those accused of his brother's murder. He said the evidence of this was that the police said those whom he named as assailants had been falsely implicated and that the inspector who was investigating the case was not going to put in a warrant for the arrest of the guilty members of the Lassowal family because he'd been bribed.

Ajmer S., whose specific function was to get members of the Rarewala faction on to important committees, managed Rarewala's election campaign in 1967. Over the years, in return for his loyalty, he also had been rewarded with licences for brick kilns and with permits for trucks.

Hardev S. stirred up enmities in the villages and ensured that the Rarewala faction had a core of supporters in each village unit. In return he also received licences for brick kilns, as well as an extra allotment of land. Rarewala became increasingly dependent on both Hardev S. and Ajmer S. to gather support; he had no mass appeal and portrayed a very visible lack of ease in his dealings with farmers. Mutual reliance, rather than control, dominated Rarewala's relationship with his followers in the local area.

Rarewala took his obligations to his supporters seriously. This is illustrated in the prompt action he took after the abduction of one Gian S. of Jhabbowal village in 1959: he immediately arranged that the SP Patiala conduct a search for Gian S., who was merely an ordinary participant in the factionalism.

The permanence, closeness and lack of variability of Rarewala's connexion with his faction in the local area can be contrasted with that of the variable connexions Kairon maintained with his faction at the same level. Of necessity, Kairon could not be in as continuous connexion with his supporters in the Doraha–Payal–Sirhind area, as they formed only a single core of persons in a system of such cores covering most local areas of the state, with all of which he had to maintain active relationships. Kairon had to see the total picture of the state. The range of Rarewala's interests was significantly narrower and their degree of correspondence with the interests of his supporters thus greater. It was by virtue of his own rivalry with Kairon that Rarewala would protect his paarti men. The occasions for acting out his own enmities with the CM were also the occasions for stressing his solidarity with his supporters in the local area. In 1958 and 1964, for example, on the respective occasions of the murder of Harnam S. and Hardev S., he went to see the Union Home Minister to complain that there was no rule of law in the Punjab. It was only with respect to Rarewala's ties in a wider system of political and administrative relationships, independently inaccessible to his supporters in the local area, that he exercised his role of patron. By consistently acting in concert with his supporters and protecting them, he was much more a part of his faction than was Kairon. The difference stemmed from the fact that Rarewala's major role was that of a faction leader, whereas Kairon's major role was that of cm.

The Kairon faction

The occasion for the establishment of an alignment between the cm and those who came to be known as his paarti men was a series of incidents that took place in the Doraha–Payal area in the period 1957–65. I will concentrate particularly on the relationship of Kulwant S., who dominated the faction in the local area, with the Chief Minister, Partap S. Kairon, as it developed over these nine years.

The alignment came into the open in 1957. At the time of land consolidation, a certain inspector of consolidation accused Ashok Ram, a *mahant*, or priest, who possessed 115 acres of land near Payal, of making incorrect adjustments with his land, but assured him that this would be put right if he signed a letter admitting that it was an error. Ashok Ram, being illiterate, was subsequently deceived into signing a deed of lease accepting Kulwant S. and his brothers as tenants on his land. When he found that the latter were ploughing the land he approached the station house officer—the police officer in charge of a subdivision of a district—at Payal, who then proceeded to communicate the news to Hardev S., the chief lieutenant of Gian S. Rarewala. Hardev S. decided to intervene against Kulwant S., since he himself wanted a share of the land.[4] Also, by that time Kairon had given Kulwant S. and Satnam S. the task of undermining the influence of Rarewala in the Doraha–Payal–Sirhind area. Hardev S. informed the sho that he would arrange for men to plough the land, and in due course truckloads of men were sent by Balwant S. and Tejinder S. of Lassowal, the owners of Patiala Bus Service, to take over the land. At this crucial juncture, however, the sp district Ludhiana intervened and sent a contingent of police to prevent a re-seizure of the land by the opposing faction. On the basis that it was illegal to claim land before the crops were harvested, Kulwant S. obtained a court order staying the suit. The land had been seized on his own initiative but it was said by everyone I encountered, that

Kairon gave the impression that the brothers would be allowed to retain possession. Since Hardev S. was the principal protester against Kulwant S.'s action in his capacity as Rarewala's chief lieutenant, Kairon had found an occasion for expressing his own opposition to Rarewala by demonstrating support for Kulwant S. Kulwant S. and Kairon had in Rarewala a common enemy, and Kairon knew that if Kulwant S. could be made more hostile to Rarewala, he and his followers would support Kairon. The oft quoted proverb, '*dushman da dushman dost*'—'an enemy's enemy is your friend'— explains very well the motives behind their alliance. Kairon transferred the SHO to a different district because of his attempted opposition, though he simultaneously promoted him, presumably to make his own partisanship more acceptable. (A similar instance is recorded in n. 11 of this chapter.)

This land seizure and the tacit patronage the act had received from the CM quickly affected the whole area. Divisions within each village, on the basis of personal enmities, were given a common political meaning: that is, if a person with whom a man had enmity had affiliations with the Rarewala paarti, his opponent would automatically join the Kairon paarti. The existing divisions within the villages of the area became significant on a wider scale. Hostile feelings and inimical actions were no longer confined to the village, manifested only against members of the opposite paarti within it, but were extended to all members of the opposing paarti in the local area. Enmities inside each village were exploited, but each village ceased to be isolated and free from outside interference: now one faction within a village could easily invite in powerful outside supporters to fight its opponents. Political intervention on the one side had made it inevitable that there would be a crystallization of allegiance on the other. Kulwant S. and his brothers came to be known as the 'Kairon of the ilaaqa',[5] the 'Kairon of the area'; and to gather support and influence they used to describe themselves as Kairon's men. On the strength of this one act of the CM's, people would come to ask them for favours, believing them to be very close to Kairon. Persons who were inimical to others in their village would invite Kulwant S. to protect them, and this would strengthen the allegiances of the paarti, because these others would then attach themselves to the opposing paarti, and each set of people would subsequently believe that they had to cling to the paarti to ensure their safety.

In the succeeding years the prosecution witnesses against Kulwant S. and his family in the case over the seizure of land, as well as other opponents, were beaten up, and two of them were killed. Chief among those who were attacked were Harnam S., a refugee who had joined with Hardev S. on condition that he got a share of Ashok Ram's land, and Karam S., headman of the village of Singhpura, also a refugee, and an associate of Harnam S. In 1958 Harnam S. was murdered by members of the Kairon faction,[6] in September 1961 an attempt was made on the life of Karam S.,[7] as it was he who had had a charge instituted against Kulwant S. for this murder. Kulwant S. was convicted and sentenced to two years in prison. In 1959, also, Gian S. of Jhabbowal village, who had been a friend of Kulwant S., was abducted and badly beaten.[8]

In January 1964, after an attempt on Kulwant S.'s life in August 1963, Jagmail S., the younger brother of Kulwant S., murdered Hardev S. But in February 1965 Partap S. Kairon himself, the CM, was assassinated and with his death there was a major shift of power. Ten months after Kairon's death—that is, in December 1965—Kulwant S. was shot and killed by persons associated with the Rarewala faction. What happened at the level of the local area therefore reflected what was happening at state level. Everywhere in the state, after Kairon's death, whether at state level or in the rural areas, his men were removed from their positions of power and entangled in law cases. Developments since the CM's death have revealed the total dependence of the faction at local level on a political leader at state level for the preservation not only of its power but even of the elementary legal rights of its members. For example, when the hearing into the murder of Kulwant S. began, the magistrate did not even issue the summons necessary for Santokh S., his brother, to appear as a witness.[9]

Vertical links in operation

Whether or not the CM supported the leaders of his faction in the local area in all these incidents was determined primarily by the situational content of his relationship with Rarewala and, latterly, by the need to contain the growing power of Kulwant S. in the Doraha–Payal area. Kairon felt obliged to help Kulwant S. only so long as he could be used effectively as a tool in ruining Rarewala's reputation. The CM had also to give the appearance of acting lawfully, and this was another variable affecting his support for his faction in the local area.

In the period 1957–60 Kairon gave his faction much moral encouragement in so far as he gave them the impression that if they showed enmity towards certain persons of the Rarewala faction they would be protected. He had acquiesced in Kulwant S.'s seizure of the land and transferred officials unfavourable to the family. The land, which remains still in the possession of Kulwant S.'s family, could not have been retained by them over such a long period of time without his help.

Kulwant S. received in patronage two brick kiln licences from the CM in 1959 and, in 1960, he received some mosummie (small oranges) plants that had originally been destined for a high official of the Agriculture Department.

Kairon also helped his faction in the local area in 1959 by imprisoning Hardev S., of the opposite faction, and by instituting a case against Sham S. and attempting to secure his conviction on a charge of possessing an unlicensed pistol.

Also in 1959 a prominent political associate of the CM is said to have been instrumental in influencing the police to get Kulwant S.'s name taken out of the initial police report in the court case regarding the abduction of Gian S. At the time of Gian S.'s abduction General Mohan S., who was still on good terms with the Lassowal family of the opposite faction, was able to help those members of Kulwant S.'s family responsible for the abduction; the abduction had been witnessed by one of Balwant S.'s busmen and on this occasion the General approached Balwant S. and suggested that this man should not give his evidence in court.[10] When these two loyal associates of the CM at state level helped their supporters in the local area they were presumably sure that the CM would not disapprove. If at this early stage the CM had not given the impression that he intended to back his men, all opposition to Rarewala in the area would have crumbled.

In the period 1957–60, therefore, the Kairon faction became more powerful by virtue of the CM's association with it. His patronage reinforced Kulwant S.'s already existing power over local officials such as the SHO, the land revenue officer and the petty officials beneath him, such as the patwari.

Even throughout this period, however, Kairon's support of his local area faction was not consistent. The CM, for example, did not help his supporters on those occasions when they had been involved in an unfavourable light with those who had direct access to Nehru. After the murder of Harnam S., in 1958, a certain high-ranking police officer had made a very brutal raid on the village of Kulwant S. Kairon transferred the said officer out of the district and into a post which kept him away from the public.[11] He also deputed a certain high official of the CID to file a charge against a subordinate of the said officer because Kulwant S.'s son had been put in prison on the very day that he was to sit his matriculation examination, and let out immediately afterwards. The man was convicted. It was explained to me by a CID officer that this was as much as Kairon could do, being aware of the officer's access to the Prime Minister.

Most ministers who had been in the Kairon cabinets testified that the CM carefully watched over his own links and those of his opponents with persons in the central government. These links were an inhibiting factor in the free use of his power in favour of supporters.

The CM also had to put on a face of acting legally. Thus in 1958, after the murder of Harnam S., Rarewala went to the then Union Home Minister and implicated Kulwant S. in the murder by informing the minister that he feared that if Kulwant S. remained at large he (Rarewala) would be murdered.[12] At this stage Kulwant S. was arrested, it is alleged, on Kairon's orders, though shortly afterwards it is said the CM had a CID report drawn up which proved that Kulwant S. had taken no part in the murder. Kulwant was then released.

A state-level political leader's support of his local area faction, especially if that leader happened to be the CM, was thus very selective, and any help given was given in the context of the wider situation of provincial politics as seen from his own viewpoint. This was most clearly evidenced when Kairon suspended support for his faction in the local area in 1960 in order to support Rarewala, whose activities were fitting in with his wider plans to defeat the Akali Dal. Some of Rarewala's moves were helpful to Kairon. Rarewala had built up an organization in order to mobilize his supporters to fight for seats to the SGPC, the central governing body of the Sikh gurudwaras. But as this organization was also competing for seats on the committee, which previously had always been controlled by the Akali party, the CM endeavoured to use him to divide the Akali vote and get a number of Congressmen onto the committee.[13] After the elections to the committee Kairon succeeded in making Rare-wala's organization ineffective.

It was at this point in time that proceedings were begun against Rarewala in what was known as the Rarewala tube well case. This case concerned the sale of a tube well by Rarewala when he was Minister of Irrigation. According to Rarewala,[14] his tube well had a capacity to irrigate 600 acres, whereas he himself possessed only 200 acres. On the suggestion of the chief engineer he therefore thought he would sell it. Rarewala is said to have made a profit on the transaction, nobody being agreed on exactly how much. As he was Minister of Irrigation at the time, the CM contended he should not have done so. A Kairon MLA asked in the State Assembly whether Rarewala had sold the tube well at a price higher than its real value. Ostensibly on the basis of this suspicion, the CM took away the Irrigation portfolio from Rarewala and ordered an inquiry in order to harass him and defame him in the eyes of the centre. In this inquiry Kulwant S. and Satnam S. were key prosecution witnesses, providing innumerable instances of 'corruption' on the part of Rarewala. Kairon's great concern for Rarewala's conviction was revealed by the manner in which the inquiry as a whole was staged, i.e., all the supporters of the CM, not only in his faction in the Doraha–Payal area but also in the legislature and the administration, combined to discredit Rarewala. On the commission appointed to re-assess the value of the tube well there were two superintending engineers, one Jaswant S. Klaire and one Jagman S., who were good friends. They disagreed over the valuation. Klaire said that the tube well had not been over-valued; he refused to oblige his friend, who was very pro-Kairon, and agree to write a joint report condemning Rarewala. A senior CID officer is then alleged to have approached Klaire and to have given the message that 'Sirdar Sahib [i.e., Kairon] said that this should be your report' and proceeded to dictate. Klaire again refused. When he went to his office on the following day his file had been stolen. Thus when the same officer came and asked for the file Klaire could not produce it, whereupon the former said either that he was to do what the CM wanted or, since he had lost the file, he would be arrested, as there were government papers inside and they could have been sold to anyone.[15] Klaire shot himself the next morning.[16] This incident, as well as illustrating the usefulness of leaders of the faction at local area level to the CM, also illustrates the point I made earlier—that the faction was merely one of

the instruments of power the CM used to crush political rivals
and competitors, and that it was part of a wider set of relations
maintained by the CM with his supporters in the administration and
legislature.

That Kairon could not and would not support his faction in the
local area beyond a certain point was again evidenced in 1961. The
enmity of Kulwant S. towards one Milkha S., who was an ordinary
participant of the opposing faction from Kulwant S.'s own village,[17]
was being exploited by Hardev S. of Rarewala's faction. Shortly
before the death of Pant, the Union Home Minister, in March 1961,
Kulwant S. had made a complaint that Milkha S. should be arrested,
as he presented a danger to his life, and that Balwant S. of Lassowal
be also arrested for harbouring him. Two months passed, and no
action had been taken on Kulwant S.'s complaint. Meanwhile a
letter of Milkha S.'s to his parents fell into Kulwant S.'s hands. In
the letter Milkha S. asked for his clothes and related how he stayed
with 'Sirhindwala Sirdar (the Sirdar of Sirhind)', for ten days and
that he was now staying in *Chandigarh wallah sardar di naii kothi*
(the Sirdar of Chandigarh's new house)'.[18] General Mohan S.
brought the letter to the CM and they both went together to the
inspector general of police. The inspector general said the letter was
faked, but when the handwriting was checked with Milkha S.'s
exercise book, at the general's request, it was found to be genuine.
Milkha S., however, was never arrested. According to General
Mohan S. the inspector general had served as an officer in PEPSU at
one stage of his career and had family connexions with Rarewala.
He was also credited with having very close relations with Pandit
Pant, who was the Union Home Minister and who had not seen
eye to eye with Kairon's ruthless administration of the state except
when this ruthlessness was directed towards suppressing the Akali
party. Kairon, therefore, did not want to alienate the inspector
general, and in this instance curtailed the use of his power in favour
of his faction because again the officer concerned had an important
link in the centre. It was said, however, that otherwise, concerning
the administration of the state, Kairon was very dependent on the
inspector general and therefore could not afford to antagonize him
over a matter which in terms of state interests was of minor importance. If, however, the political situation in the state allowed him,
Kairon associated himself with his faction in the local area. On those
occasions when he visited the constituency he would be seen many

times in the company of Kulwant S. and Satnam S., and he openly told the electorate that they were to contact Kulwant S. and Satnam S. 'if you want anything from me'.

The year 1962 saw the CM both overtly helping and overtly hindering Kulwant S. In that year Kulwant S. received two truck permits from the CM and started a truck combine at Gobindgarh. The use to which these permits were put by Kulwant S. was, therefore, a reflection of his enmities and jealousies with Balwant S. of Lassowal. His action had the effect of widening still further the area of conflict with the Rarewala faction in so far as the new union threatened Balwant S.'s monopoly in charging whatever he liked in transport costs. The truck union was opened by General Mohan S.; and a former Home Minister presided, and is said to have issued a warning in a formal speech that anyone could open a transport company and that any interference with its functioning would not be tolerated.

It was also, however, in 1962 that Kairon initiated attempts at compromise between the two factions at local level, and this coincided with the false implication of Kulwant S. in the court case concerning the attempt on the life of Karam S. Kulwant S.'s imprisonment must be seen in the light of the fact that by 1962 the power of the Kairon faction was established, while Rarewala's political influence had faded: Kairon could therefore afford a *rapprochement*. It was at this time—i.e., while Kulwant S. was in prison—that Ajmer S. says Surinder S. Kairon, the CM's son, visited his house on a number of occasions and 'tried to neutralize our opposition'. Kairon did not want Kulwant S. to emerge from dependent status and become a leader himself. He did not want his faction in the local area to establish so clear an ascendancy over its rival as would inhibit him from forming links with and drawing support from the opposite faction at certain times. He wanted a balance of power in the area. In March 1962 Rarewala had supported Kairon in his election as leader of the Punjab Assembly Congress party, and the imprisonment of Kulwant S. was part of Kairon's technique further to appease him for a time. Kulwant S. certainly did not serve even half the full two-year sentence. Moreover 1962 was the year of the Chinese invasion, and Kairon took advantage of the situation to correct the impression of his complete identification with one faction by patronizing the other and, by so doing, attempting to mitigate their hostility temporarily. Thus he gave Balwant S. four truck permits for the route to Simla, the value of one such permit being 85,000 rupees. The attempt to minimize the factional rivalries in the area was, however, undoubtedly part of the huge effort Kairon made to mobilize all sections of society in Punjab for the purpose of collecting money and gold for the National Defence Fund. It would not have been appropriate for the CM to have been seen to patronize specific sections of that society when he was, on a public platform, appealing to all political parties in the state to sink their differences and work unitedly. It was at one such meeting in Khanna, at the height of the Chinese invasion, that Balwant S. personally presented the CM with 75,000 rupees for the National Defence Fund on behalf of his transport company.[19] For this fund Punjab collected a larger amount than any other state of the Union, running to over 50 million rupees.[20]

However, because the CM, on any one occasion, did not find it prudent to identify himself overtly with the interests of his faction in the local area, it must not be assumed he had ceased undermining Rarewala's sources of support in the Doraha–Payal–Sirhind area. He merely did so without their help.[21]

It may be noted that the solidarity of interest between the two levels of the faction related particularly to their relationships with the police and judiciary. A high-ranking police officer from the CID was frequently sent to Doraha to prevent police brutality on the part of subordinates to members of Kairon's faction and to hush cases up.[22] And a one-time Home Minister of Punjab belonging to the CM's faction at state level helped the Kairon faction to obtain revolver licences, which was sometimes difficult because the factionalism extended into the police and the SHO gave recommendations for arms to be supplied only to members of the faction to which he himself belonged.[23] But the mutuality of interest between Kairon and his lieutenants in the local area was never so permanent as to constitute a definite and expected commitment on his part. Even the granting of revolver licences was conditional on the situation: for example in 1962 the SP Patiala got Kulwant S.'s revolver licence cancelled[24] and Kairon did not interfere to get the licence restored, although Kulwant S. had petitioned him to do so. Only on occasion was the 'coincidence of interest' between the CM and his local area supporters complete. Such a situation had occurred in 1957 and again in 1964. In January 1964, Kulwant S.'s brother—Jagmail S.—had murdered Hardev S. Though this arose from the enmity of the family of

Kulwant S. towards Hardev S., it has been said that the murder was politically useful to the CM.[25] When Jagmail S. was captured shortly after the murder, the CM's son, Surinder S. Kairon, is said to have secured his release[26] and the local police did not prosecute their investigation into the case vigorously until pressure came from the centre.

What I think is interesting is the degree to which the relationship between Kairon and Rarewala influenced the dynamics of faction rivalry. The extent to which Kairon needed to maintain his commitments of patronage to Kulwant S. depended on the balance of power at state level between himself and his rivals. Similarly, at the level of the local area the words one heard constantly on the lips of Kulwant S. were *meri dushmani, apni khlaaf*—'my enmities', 'our opposing party'. Leaders at each level, in other words, tended to be moved by their own interests, and their links tightened only when these interests coincided. The determination of whether they in fact did coincide or not was left with the political leader at state level. In the Kairon faction I have therefore stressed the vertical link as a one-way downward link from the CM to the leader at local level. Even the kinds of service with which Kulwant S. reciprocated Kairon's help were determined by the latter. For example, Kulwant S. used to provide vehicles and free petrol so that Congress candidates could disseminate propaganda at election time, and it is said that 5 per cent of the truck combine's money was kept for elections. Kulwant S.'s allegations against Rarewala himself, regarding financial corruption, and against members of his family, alleging sexual immorality, and the institution of cases against supporters of the Rarewala faction, were such as would ultimately benefit the CM, and their form and pattern were very similar to those made elsewhere by the CM's supporters against their opponents. The leader at local level strove to keep up political links so as to retain resources and benefits that had initially come from or been kept with the help of these links, and he therefore retained even his association with the faction after the death of the leader at state level. He also retained the connexion in the hope of obtaining more patronage. For example, Captain Rattan S., a former minister of state for agriculture and animal husbandry, is said to have helped Santokh S., who had become the dominant personality in the faction on Kulwant S.'s death, by getting Phagwara mills to accept their sugar in November 1966.[27]

In the Kairon faction the focus was always on the political leader at state level. The link of the leader at state level with the leader in the local area, was the weakest in the faction because of the fluidity of the state leader's enmities. The quality of the relationships of key participants at the local level, with their associations of murder, etc., was, in the case of the Kairon faction, an inhibiting factor in the successful development of vertical relationships within his faction. This was because the Rarewala faction used the quality content of these vertical relationships to lower the prestige of the CM with the administration, the legislators, and above all, the central government, using them as focal points around which an already existing opposition in these institutions could gather and crystallize. This presented a very real and evident threat to Kairon. During his period of tenure in the office of CM there had been three inquiries into his government of the state on charges of corruption and misrule. It was, therefore, in the context of Kairon's own relationships at state level that he operated the vertical relationship of help and protection to his men. The CM never helped them, for example, on those occasions when he needed to mobilize the support of the opposite faction; he never helped them if they had been involved in an unfavourable manner with those who had a direct link to Nehru. His aim was to use them as much as possible but to minimize his returns, as the connexion was used to taint his image with associations of murder and lawlessness.

Vertical relationships were, however, important for faction leaders at local level in that they drew their strength from these and each faction had only as much power as its leader was willing and able to give it; for example, it has been previously noted that Kulwant S. was imprisoned in Karam S.'s case of 1962 and that this gave the impression that his potential support from Kairon was much less than had been supposed. Revenge for the murder of Kulwant S. has not as yet been taken by his brothers for want of the open, definite and committed support of a powerful political patron at state level. A leader at local level had to keep up his connexion with a political leader at state level to retain his prestige and influence both with his associates and with the large number of ordinary participants in the faction. A leader at local level could effectively threaten members of the opposing faction only when he had a powerful outside link, for the reputation of having such a link retained the fervent support of men who would come forward to give evidence in favour of members of their own paarti and who would threaten prosecution witnesses. Once he lost this outside link he no longer could command a position of prestige in the area, and the power of his faction correspondingly declined: the lack of violence in the period following the death of Kairon and Kulwant S. was associated with such a decline. Above all, the Kairon faction in the local area had to work within the framework of the policy defined by the CM if its members were to continue to obtain or retain any benefits for themselves; for example, certain members of the Kairon faction were able to treat officials offhandedly only because that was Kairon's policy too—to lessen the esteem in which the administrative class was held.[28]

This was how links were operating in the faction during the period of tenure in the office of the Chief Minister of Partap S. Kairon. The latter did or did not interfere, as suited his wider purpose, in factional disputes in the local area, and this meant, in effect, that the tone of the factionalism was set by him. Thus between the political leader at state level and his lieutenants in the local area, in the case of the Kairon faction, the relationship was a very variable one. Kulwant S., while admitting that General Mohan S. was a good friend, thought that the CM never gave help at the moment it was needed and clearly did not place him in the category of a friend. He often talked of how, after an attempt on his life in October 1964 in the main bazaar of Ludhiana, he had approached the CM. The latter he said, had certainly contacted the Home Minister to make arrangements for his security but he said that he himself, by that time, refused to believe that formal protection would help him.[29] The feeling of emotional commitment and involvement seemed to supersede the feeling of distrust that normally persisted between leaders at state level and leaders in the local area in the Kairon faction only when the two men on different levels happened also to be friends.

There was a reluctant acceptance that ties with political leaders were necessary. The feeling of the ordinary small proprietors and of local leaders such as Santokh S. was that political leaders at state level were crooks and that they were to be used and exploited simply for what they could immediately offer. There was a continuous expectation of support from higher political levels. Various local leaders would visit the secretariat in Chandigarh, the state capital, in the attempt to pressurize a state political leader into courses of action favourable to them. The appreciation of the need for political support and political links was constant in view of the greater political flexibility at state level. This was particularly in evidence in the Kairon faction after the CM's death. In February 1967, after the general elections, a coalition government comprising Akalis, Independents and Communists was formed, and Rarewala was elected Leader of the Opposition in the State Assembly. If, however, prior to his being elected to this position, he had entered the United Front,[30] he would presumably have been offered a high cabinet post, and it would have been impossible for Santokh S.— who had become head of the family of Kulwant S. after the death of his brother—to obtain police or CID protection and impossible for the family to hold on to its acquired land. The Kairon faction at local level therefore continued to remain interested in political changes at state level. Santokh S. alleged that at a meeting of Congressmen at the beginning of March 1967, when the former Union Foreign Minister and Rarewala met with others to decide on the leadership of the Punjab Parliamentary Congress party, that General Mohan S. had told the Foreign Minister that he did not want Rarewala to be made the leader of the party, since he had had a hand in the murder of Kulwant S. However, in April 1967 a compromise was reached between the General and Rarewala. Congress was weak in opposition and it had to ensure that it would regain ascendancy over the other political parties. The firm basis for the compromise was that the general was to get a ministership were Rarewala ever to form the ministry. According to Santokh S., 'General Sahib', as he called him, rationalized his action by saying that if Rarewala did not become CM he would not become a minister and therefore could be of no help in offering adequate protection or in helping them to seek revenge, adding as an afterthought, 'through the courts, of course'. These attempts at compromise illustrate the fact that factional divisions were not so persistent at state level. Compromise for leaders at state level was merely a political bargain. But the leaders at local area level regarded it as a disgrace. In the general elections of February 1967, Rarewala and General Mohan S. reached a compromise to restrain and reduce enmities. The General discouraged Santokh S. 'from operating too much'[31] because he did not wish to see factional rivalries inflamed. The compromise perhaps worked because the competition was unequal in that the one big personality involved was Rarewala, and all major protagonists of the opposite paarti, including their political patron, were either dead or not participating.

After the general elections, in February 1967, Santokh S. did not rely solely on General Mohan S. He also attached himself to S. Gurnam S., the then CM, whom he tended to trust since the latter had been responsible for the acquittal of his brother, Jagmohan S., in the case over the murder of Kartar S. to which I have referred earlier. The context for the renewal of the association was purely fortuitous: Santokh S. had been supporting the Akali candidate in Payal—Beant S.—in the 1967 elections while Gurnam S. had been fighting on the Akali ticket for his own constituency of Raikot. When the latter came to Payal constituency to speak in favour of Beant S., Santokh S. took the opportunity to offer his services to him during the election campaign. It was specifically S. Gurnam S. who helped Santokh S. in April 1970 by directing the SPs of four districts to alert their police for a man intending to murder Santokh S. at Balwant S.'s behest.

With the calculated motives of putting himself in a stronger position at a later date, Santokh S. had also, during the 1967 elections, campaigned for S. Joginder S. Maan,[32] who later became the Speaker of the Assembly in Gurnam S.'s government. Joginder S.'s brother, fighting on the Congress ticket for the same constituency, had been supported by Balwant S. of Lassowal. Santokh S.'s support of Joginder S. himself was therefore automatic in terms of the existing faction rivalry. Perhaps it was also not a coincidence that Santokh S. was granted an order in the high court staying action over the land of Ashok Ram. This was expected to be the last decisive order of this type. The family had been cultivating the land for ten years, technically as tenants, though for all other purposes as owners, and according to law any tenant cultivating a piece of land for ten years gained legal ownership of that land. Practically, however, the tenancy could not be converted into ownership, since the moment it was relinquished the opposing paarti would claim possession of the land in court.

Such was the history of relationships between leaders at local level and leaders at state level subsequent to the assassination of Kairon in February 1965. His faction continued to have the name 'Kairon' attached to it even though Kairon was by that time fully two years dead.

For all levels, the wider scene in which the factionalism was set was that of a situation in which the government had considerable control over the administration and where the patronage controlled by government in the form of jobs and in the form of quotas for controlled commodities, loans, permits and licences was great. The context for the civil and police administration's support of the CM has already been indicated in chapter 8. Broadly, it may be repeated here that, aside from the persons attracted to the CM by his personal dynamism, the reason for an officer's support was either fear or ambition. Regarding the latter motive, a Persian saying—that 'if the king desires an apple, his servants spoil the entire orchard to procure the apple for him'—would seem to have been particularly appropriate to the support given to Kairon by many officers. An individual's factional contacts had also to be seen in the context of government control of quota distribution for such commodities as iron, steel and glass, over import and export licences, and over the supply of cement and paraffin, as well as its major role as a supplier of secure jobs. Often, by giving employment in the administration or police force to a man, the government would thereby take over the allegiance of his whole family. That the government, indeed, treated a man and his family as one when it suited its interests can be seen by referring to notes 4 and 6 of chapter 8. This attitude and policy could also be noted in the government's treatment of the 1960 Akali mass demonstration, mentioned in chapter 7, when leaders and participants in the movement had their licences and permits confiscated and those connected with them were not employed in government service.

What has emerged as very central in Kairon's patronage of his faction was that it was his powers of suspension, demotion, promotion and transfer of officials in the police and civil administration that enabled him to sustain its power in the local area whenever he wished. He effectively used his control over certain persons in these positions to intervene in favour of political supporters and to institute court cases against important political opponents, as in the Rarewala tube-well case. Leaders of the faction in the local area, in several local areas, cabinet ministers and certain civil servants, formed the CM's faction in the state; the solidarity of the faction behind the CM has been seen not only in the Rarewala tube-well case but also in all court cases in which supporters were involved.[33]

A similar situation can be noted in the Rarewala faction during the period 1948 to early 1953, when Rarewala was a ruling influence in PEPSU, i.e., the activities of his supporters were both condoned and overlooked with the help of chosen administrative officials. These connexions provided ammunition for the growing opposition to, and attacks on, Rarewala, which came mainly from the class of tenants and smallholders and from the poorer class of Hindus in the market towns; they focused their attacks on the corruption of the civil service. The attacks were made particularly when PEPSU came under governor's rule, ostensibly so that law and order could be restored. I provide some examples:

> S. Gian S. Rarewala on coming into power has appointed such officials in this district who always have overlooked all the high-handedness and wrong doing of this gang [referring specifically to Sham S., Ajmer S. and Hardev S.]. The DC in particular is a tool in their hands and takes his orders from the leader of this gang at the instance of Rarewala. [Letter to the Adviser dated 21 September 1953.]

> The DC Fatehgarh Sahib paid a visit to Doraha on 24 April 1953 and it is said here that he had come to inquire into the law and order situation in this town and to find out the real cause of this lawlessness in Doraha Mandi. A couple of days earlier a deputation waited upon your good self at Bassi and explained in detail the true state of affairs regarding *goondaism* in Doraha and it is presumed that the DC was ordered to make a thorough inquiry and to submit a detailed report to your honour. The DC never made any attempt to contact the deputationists and what he really did was to find all sorts of means for the defence of the alleged guilty persons. . . . In fact he had his tea at the resthouse Doraha with the very men who are supposed to be at the back of the lawless element. . . . We will respectfully suggest that as a first step district officials from the DC to the sub-inspector police Payal may be transferred to other places. [Letter to the Adviser, dated 29 April 1953].

> We, the citizens of Doraha, beg to draw your attention to a brutal attack made by *goondas* armed with naked kirpans and sticks on a 'peaceful procession in Doraha' on the night of 2 February 1952. . . . The SP Fatehgarh Sahib took no effective steps to safeguard the public order although he was informed of the situation a day earlier. [A letter dated 15 February 1952 addressed to the Chief

Secretary, PEPSU, Patiala, referring to the procession celebrating the success of the Congress nominee for the CM of PEPSU.]

If a faction had control over the relevant officials it could retain for an indefinite period the resources it had given its members. For example, when Sikh refugees came to PEPSU following the 1947 riots, Rarewala's chief supporter in the Doraha–Payal area, Hardev S., had got

> some temporary stalls pitched up in the front of the regular shops for these people on the clear understanding that this was a temporary measure and that these stalls would be moved to other sites as soon as possible. A period of six years has elapsed since then and these people are not willing to move from their present positions. . . . The local small town committee has been repeatedly requested to move into the matter and they have served notices on them several times to move these stalls. The DC has been approached several times but powerful communal elements have always gained the upper hand. . . . The director of local bodies had selected a site for them and asked the town committee to shift them there and keep the road clear of all encroachment. The town committee has again gone into deep slumber over the matter [due to pressure put on it by Hardev S. and Rarewala faction to take no action]. [Undated letter addressed to the Adviser.]

Co-operation of the Rarewala faction, particularly with the police and judiciary, subsequent to the death of Kairon and Kulwant S. was noticeable. The members of the Kairon faction were able to point out many instances of police collaboration with the Rarewala faction due to their having been bribed. Bribes were very acceptable in the lower ranks of the police service because of the poor salaries. In August 1966, for example, one constable in the CID with a wage of 120 rupees per month became 'a protection agent' of Tejinder S. of Lassowal at a pay of 300 rupees per month.[34] He had got involved in some feuding in his village and thereafter had been imprisoned for six months. When he was released he went into Tejinder S.'s service as a bodyguard. Jagmohan S., Kulwant S.'s brother, was constantly complaining that the police were in league with Tejinder S. 'because of his wealth and consequently of his wide influence'. He said that the people whom his brother, Santokh S., had named as the assailants of Kulwant S. had then been said by the police to be falsely implicated. Instancing this, he said that a certain inspector, who had investigated Kulwant S.'s case, was not going to put in a charge against Manjeet S. and he pointed out that it was clear from this that the inspector had been bribed.

The local judiciary's co-operation with the Rarewala faction was evident from the time of Kairon's resignation as CM. Regarding the attempt to kill both Kulwant S. and Kamiikar S. in 1964, for example, the court case against the accused had been pending in the court of the magistrate, first class, at Amloh, for over two years. The following is an extract from a lawyer's report:

> Date fixed for recording of evidence was November 1964. It was then adjourned to 10 December. On 10 December one of the accused had absconded (no attempt to enforce presence of witnesses). Then to 22 December, 6 January 1965, 11 February, 11 March, 23 April, 26 April, 28 April, 4 May, 24 May, 10 June, 6 July, 7 August. On these days either the accused or the witnesses managed to disappear. Ordinarily statements of witnesses are recorded within a period of four months. The explanation of all this is that people have seen this Magistrate and his predecessor using vehicles of Balwant S./Manjeet S. The Bar Association passed a unanimous resolution against the Magistrate at Amloh, saying that he was corrupt: often found drunk in the office of the Lassowal Union, or staying with them (April 1965). Balwant S. helped in his daughter's marriage party at his own expense, providing tea and Coca-Cola for guests.

A letter written by Kulwant S. on 3 July 1964 and addressed to the Assistant Inspector General of Police at Chandigarh also implicated the above magistrate and contained accusations against the local police that they were under the influence of Rarewala's men:

> That on 27 June in the courtyard of Magistrate of Amloh . . . the police recovered from a person who is related to Mihan S., ex-MLA, an unlicensed pistol. After the recovery of this pistol the person was arrested by the police and on this enquiry he told the police that this pistol was given by Mihan S. to shoot dead the applicant.

Kulwant S. then went on to complain that after the attempt on his life at a particular village the 'SHO Payal and DSP Bassi did not take interest in the case' and that 'three months before the Khanna firing[35] Milkha S. tried to kill my nephew Baldev S., and five and a half months previous to this Shamsher S.[36] who was waiting for a bus at Payal, Harinder S. tried to shoot him dead'. He complained that though the police caught them and they were in custody the licences for their guns were never forfeited.

All these incidents which have been referred above are being done and conspirated only by the said Mihan S. Gill, ex-MLA, and Balwant S. only to kill me and my family members, as this being the fact that they are influential and rich persons and the local police is under their influence and they never taken any action upon my requests. Under the circumstances the applicant begs to submit that the enquiry of these incidents may be held and should be investigated by an officer who should not be under the influence of the said persons.

Kairon faction members felt that even the sessions judge at Patiala had been put under some pressure in February 1966 when he granted bail to Balwant S. against the advice of the public prosecutor, after he himself had dismissed this application only a month earlier.[37]

On occasions of confrontation between the factions, the relationships of the Kairon faction with the police were always looked after by the same senior police officer. The latter, who was a superintendent of police, CID, was sent a number of times to Doraha, as mentioned, to prevent police brutality and to hush up cases. It was the same CID superintendent who had a report made for Kairon in 1958 to prove the innocence of Kulwant S. in Harnam S.'s murder case and who, in the same year, brought charges against the police who in a raid on Kulwant S.'s family had ill-treated some of them. Moreover the same officer acted as an enquiry officer in the Rarewala tube-well case. For his co-operation he was later rewarded with the chairmanship of the Subordinate Services Selection Board. Thus the police and civil administration were an important element in the maintenance of support for the Kairon faction.

Administrative and police officers, however, not only acted on the instructions of political leaders in supporting particular factions but also exploited factional rivalry, and took advantage of it to further their own grudges. Thus, one of the reasons why a certain former deputy inspector general, Patiala (referred to earlier in this chapter), consistently helped the Rarewala faction and in a sense put himself at the disposal of Rarewala was that he was personally hostile to Kairon because when Kairon was CM he had not allowed him to become an inspector general of police, Punjab.

13 The factional attachments of village participants

With reference to both factions I now proceed to give a selection of representative patterns of individual allegiance to a faction from the category of ordinary village participants. The case studies are drawn from the relatively more active village followers of a local area leader, and I discuss the factors influencing their choice of alignment.

The Rarewala faction

I first discuss three cases of individual participants whose enmity towards a particular local leader was so great that they joined the faction opposed to his.

(*i*) In 1951–2 two farmers who had approximately twenty-eight acres of land in the village of Dhanipur, and who ploughed the land of Avtar S. (Kulwant S.'s father) on bathai,[1] appeared as prosecution witnesses against Kulwant S. and his brother Jagmohan S. in the trial for the alleged murder of Kartar S. of Dhanipur. Kartar S. had no children, and the two farmers alleged that as he was more closely related to them than to Kulwant S. the twenty-four acres of land which he owned in the village should have gone to them. The land was, however, taken over and cultivated by Kulwant S.'s family and as the years passed the enmity between the families increased. It manifested itself in litigation. Kulwant S., for example, appeared as a prosecution witness in a theft case against a paternal uncle of one of these farmers.[2]

Milkha S. and Harinder S., the sons of the two farmers, inherited their fathers' enmity, and sometime between 1958 and 1960 an incident happened which intensified the enmity between the two families to such a degree that Milkha S. and Harinder S. decided to side openly with the Rarewala paarti. On the day of the marriage of Milkha S.'s sister, as the bridegroom's party was arriving in the village, a member of the family of Kulwant S. shouted out: 'Oh!

You are going to marry *that* girl; we have already enjoyed her so many times!'[3] It was particularly after this incident that Milkha S., prompted, it is said, by feelings of enmity, joined the Rarewala paarti, where he began to associate with Hardev S. and became a willing tool in his hands. Hardev S. exploited the brothers' feelings of enmity for Kulwant S., taunting Milkha S. especially that he did not have enough courage to revenge his sister's dishonour. They were also befriended by Hardev S.'s son, and shortly after this Kulwant S. threatened them until they left the village in fear. He also forced them to leave the government high school, Payal, and continue their studies in Doraha and Khanna. According to Rarewala, Kulwant S. similarly terrorized the boys' fathers. One of them, he said, had been tied down to the *rehet* (Persian wheel) on one occasion and made to pull it like a bullock. The aim behind this intimidation, so Rarewala claimed, was to make the family leave the village. For a time Milkha S. and Harinder S. stayed with Hardev S. in Doraha. The latter provided them with their food and shelter and paid for their education and clothing; he made them his clients, in fact. It was subsequent to this, in August 1963, that Harinder S. and Milkha S. shot at Kulwant S. as he was standing at the Khalsa Nirbhai Transport bus stand, in the main bazaar of Khanna, and killed one of the persons accompanying him.[4] Hardev S. afterwards 'looked after' the case against Milkha S. and Harinder S., paid for their counsel, and saw that witnesses did not depose against them.[5]

(*ii*) When Kulwant S. seized the land in 1957, it was the very audacity of the act that was resented by large numbers of people, including Gian S. of Jhabbowal village, near Payal. As a supporter of the Kairon faction explained, 'It is not liked if one tries to act as a dictator.' Thus in 1957, when the factional divisions became set, Gian S., out of personal jealousy against Kulwant S.'s family, made moves to join the Rarewala paarti.

In 1952 Kulwant S. had bought a tractor jointly with the said Gian S., who had fifty acres of land. Kulwant S. acted as guarantor for Gian S., who had no money at the time, 'as he had been friendly to us'[6] in the trial for the alleged murder of Kartar S. of their village.[7] Gian S. had previously also taken money from them for the purchase of an imported engine for his tube well and in return had given Kulwant S. a half share in a bus which he had running on the Malerkotla to Khanna route. When Jagmohan S. was under trial for the alleged murder of Kartar S. of Dhanipur in 1952, Gian S. sold the bus to Balwant S. of Lassowal for 16,000 rupees and gave Kulwant S. only 5,000 of the 8,000 rupees due to him. There was no further trouble in their relationship until the winter of 1957–8, when Gian S. took away the tractor which, as has been noted, was their joint property, to lend to his sister's husband. 'He did this twice for a period of eighteen days, saying that he would return it when he felt like it.'[8] At the same time Gian S.'s servant also accused Santokh S. of not ploughing the land properly and of ruining the tractor (in fact it had not been spoilt). They quarrelled, and in the course of the quarrel the servant beat up Santokh S. A relative of Gian S. says that Gian S. instigated this:

> Gian S. was determined to teach them a lesson as he thought they were getting too big for their boots so therefore he quarrelled with them on a trifling issue. Subsequent to this, Kulwant S. made a number of approaches to Gian S. to keep him with them but the latter by his actions further deepened the enmity,

always supporting those who were inimical to Kulwant S. and helping in the collection of evidence against them.

In 1958 Gian S. was active in taking a certain police inspector, specially sent by the then deputy inspector general of police at Patiala to make enquiries into Harnam S.'s murder, to all those hide-outs of Kulwant S. with which he was acquainted. When, also, many members of Kulwant S.'s family were in custody after the said murder 'he stood and watched while Shamsher S. (Kulwant S.'s son) was being beaten by the police and did not come to his aid'.[9] This was taken by Kulwant S.'s family as a final proof that his allegiance was no longer with them.

(*iii*) After Kulwant S.'s seizure of Ashok Ram's land in 1957, Ashok Ram used to be seen twice or thrice weekly in the company of Hardev S. He aligned himself with Rarewala's faction in the hope of recovering at least part of his land. In the court case regarding the forcible seizure of Ashok Ram's land by Kulwant S.'s family,[10] Harnam S. of Payal had appeared as a witness for Ashok Ram and spoken out against Kulwant S. Harnam S. supported Ashok Ram because he, too, like Hardev S., hoped eventually to secure a share of the land. Another reason for siding with Hardev S. was that he was a tenant on some sixty acres of land owned by a friend of Kulwant S. The latter had wanted to get Harnam S. off his land, and it was Kulwant S. who had succeeded in forcing Harnam S. out of occupation. Associated with Harnam S. was another refugee from West Punjab, namely Karam S., a headman from Singhpura village, two miles distant from Payal. In the Harnam S. murder case he gave testimony against the accused of the opposing faction and, on that specific issue at least, brought the support into the Rarewala faction of a number of his affines and associates, who acted as prosecution witnesses.[11] Karam S.'s enmity was specifically against Kamiikar S., one of the local level leaders of the Kairon faction, since land belonging to a certain committee in Payal which had previously been cultivated by him had been given to Kamiikar S.

Milkha S. and Harinder S. of Dhanipur, Karam S. of Singhpura and Harnam S. of Payal, as well as Gian S. of Jhabbowal, thus had in common their enmity to key persons of the opposing paarti. Too afraid to act independently against Kulwant S., they joined the Rarewala faction, where their resistance was organized by the local area leader, Hardev S. Harnam S. and Milkha S. were members of the Rarewala faction continuously until they were murdered, in 1958 and 1965 respectively, while Gian S. was still a member of the Rarewala faction when I left in June 1967.

In the first case, faction alignment can be explained simply by the need of the family of Milkha S. and Harinder S., in their own interests, to regain some of their lost 'honour' and to recover the land they considered to be rightfully theirs, by challenging Kulwant S. They did so in company with other persons of the Rarewala faction who similarly had an interest in Kulwant S.'s downfall. In the second case, Gian S. was seeking to raise his status through opposition. When Gian S. had initially been friendly with Kulwant S., the latter had not had the same links and resources at his disposal as he had in 1957. Gian S. and Kulwant S. were then on more equal terms. By 1957 Kulwant S. had risen to prominence, and it seemed as if Gian S., to avoid being asked for the return of the debt he owed him, profited from the factious situation by joining the Rarewala faction. The other three adherents aligned themselves on the basis of a lack of security in possession of land and tenancy rights: Ashok Ram, whose land was seized by Kulwant S.'s family, placed himself under the protection of the Rarewala faction to regain part of his land; Harnam S.'s tenancy rights had been disturbed by Kulwant S.; while Karam S.'s right to cultivate a certain piece of land had been taken away by Kamiikar S. Their adherence to the Rarewala faction was consequent on this.

Rarewala had support in the area not only from persons motivated by their personal enmities and antagonisms, but also from allegiances and loyalties to him that had been established prior to partition. Those persons who had had established positions in the service of the rulers of the former Patiala state found that they gained little there if they abandoned their allegiance to those associated with that rule. One of these persons owned thirteen acres of land in the village of Jhabbowal, near Payal. He had been in the Maharajah's special guard from 1942 to 1946. His younger brother, owning eighteen acres in the same village, had spent ten years in the Patiala state forces. Both were small proprietors and both were aligned to the Rarewala faction. Their allegiance, however, was purely nominal. Although they were to be seen at most of Rarewala's election meetings in February 1967, aside from this they did not do much campaigning for him. In the 1962 elections the elder brother had gone to campaign for his sister's son, who had been standing for election on the Congress ticket in the neighbouring constituency of Raipur. In the 1967 election, however, his son, who was a teacher, went to campaign for the Maharajah of Patiala in the latter's constituency.

A second person whose support for Rarewala dated back to the pre-partition period was the sarpanc of Rampur, a village near Doraha. He cultivated twenty acres of a sixty-acre holding held by his two brothers, was in control of the village's co-operative bank and was on the executive committee of the Patiala Land Mortgage Bank. This undoubtedly meant that he had at his disposal a considerable amount of patronage and was able to secure loans at favourable rates of interest for friends. He was also a member of the SGPC and a member of the zilla parishad. His brother was a manager of the Maharajah's farm at Bahadurgarh, near Patiala, and this undoubtedly gave him an easy approach to all those connected with Rarewala. In the 1967 elections he spoke for Rarewala on many occasions in the villages.

Another associate of all the above was a major from the village of Dhamot, five miles from Payal. He had formerly been in the Patiala state army and he played host to Rarewala when the latter came to campaign in Dhamot in the 1967 elections. His was a token committal only.

The above collection of persons gave their allegiance to Rarewala on the basis of a long-standing association with his family. A third

category of persons was those who attached themselves to the
Rarewala faction after partition, in search of favours and political
protection as a result of becoming involved in the factionalism of
their own villages. One example was the son of the man who had
been Rarewala's watchman in Rara village. He was a farmer from
the village of Katari with about twenty-five acres of land, who had
at one time been a constable in the police force. He had been dismissed from his post in 1957–8 following his conviction for the
murder of a man from his own village. At about the same time, on the
occasion of the consolidation of landholdings, there was a dispute
over the common land of the village between the son of the murdered
man, who I will refer to as 'S', and the watchman's son. In the
course of the dispute the Rarewala faction managed to favour the
watchman's son. Both these incidents became the bases for factionalism in the village and in 1960 the watchman's son and 'S' were
involved in cases of injuring one another, with each suing the other;
'S's' son was convicted while the watchman's son was acquitted.

Another farmer with only fourteen acres of land from the village
of Barmalipur had been associated with the Rarewala faction from
the immediate post-partition period, when he had been a clerk in a
truck combine at Doraha of which Hardev S. had been the president.
He was illegally in possession of a rifle and was a known smuggler,
his contacts with the Rarewala faction being useful in this respect.
On one occasion he had participated in a murder near Samrala and
a relative of the murdered man was living in Barmalipur. For protection he had therefore joined up with some persons in his own
village who were associated with the brother of Sham S., and who
had together taken part in an armed robbery in village Jalhanpur in
1948–9. As Sham S. himself was firmly attached to Rarewala, these
persons, under his influence, also joined him.

The above were two cases of individuals belonging to a faction as
a protection for their activities. Others attached themselves to the
Rarewala faction in the expectation of getting favours. Such was a
former assistant sub-inspector of police from the village of Ghuddani
Kalan, near Payal, who was the vice-chairman of Doraha block
samiti at the time of my fieldwork. During land consolidation
Rarewala did indeed favour him in one instance. In the process his
interests clashed with those of a close relative, also of the same
village, who happened to be its sarpanc at the time of my fieldwork.
The difference between the two men at the time of land consolidation

had, in fact, more or less coincided with the fight between them over the sarpancship of the village in the first pancayat elections. The present sarpanc accused Rarewala's wife of interfering to support his rival.

Alignment with a paarti was in many instances designed not to obtain any special favour but simply to give expression to certain enmities and antagonisms towards others in one's village. For example, one farmer owning fifty to sixty acres of land in Jargari village, eight miles from Khanna, banked on the influence he had with Rarewala to assert his power over certain others in his own village. He got these persons entangled in a court case for setting fire to his tube well. (This in effect meant that he accused them of setting fire to some of the crops that had been gathered in and were lying around the tube well.)

All these persons not only brought their own allegiance into the Rarewala faction. The ex-guardsman brought in his maternal nephew, while the sarpanc of Rampur had built up a network of friends by virtue of his power to make loans and his membership of so many committees. In 1966 he put forward one man of his own village as a candidate for a directorship of the local branch of the Co-operative Bank. The man, supported by the Rarewala faction, did not win against the Kairon faction's candidate, but his allegiance was marked from that time onwards. Persons not only brought in their kin and their friends but sometimes also their affines. Subsequent to 1957 the sister of the vice-chairman of Doraha block samiti referred to earlier had been married to the younger brother of the sarpanc of Jhabbowal village. When this affinal connexion had been established the sarpanc used it as a reason for diverting his allegiance from the Kairon faction in his village, which he wanted to leave for other reasons, without incurring enmity.

The Kairon faction

Opposition to Rarewala and his supporters in each village of the Doraha–Payal–Sirhind area appears to have crystallized after the merger of PEPSU with Punjab in 1956, when Kairon became the CM and the political opponent of Rarewala. It was in this situation that those who felt aggrieved against the persons associated with the former ruling faction in their own villages came out openly against them and started supporting Kulwant S. Thus 'S' of village Katari remained firmly attached to the Kairon paarti because of his enmity towards the son of Rarewala's watchman. This alignment was provoked by the latter's murder of his father and by the need to get outside help. A similar situation occurred in the village of Barmalipur: as soon as Kairon became CM and began undermining Rarewala's influence, those who had previously never dared to oppose the dominant faction in the village, which was attached to Sham S. and his brother, banded together and linked themselves to Kulwant S. in order to augment their power and influence. Similarly, the person in Jargari village, whom the farmer mentioned above had involved in a court case over alleged arson, joined the Kairon faction after his acquittal.

Some supporters of the Kairon faction had no specific enmities with persons of their village but had developed grudges against Rarewala himself. One such person was Harjit S., who owned thirty-seven acres of land in the village of Jhabbowal. He had a degree in economics from Jullundur, his sister was a superintendent of Khalsa College in Ludhiana, and his father's brother was a colonel in the army. His family was connected by marriage to Rarewala, as his mother and Rarewala's mother were sisters. When Rarewala became CM of PEPSU, however, Harjit S. remarked that the two families 'became socially disconnected; that is, he never came to eat or drink with us'. Later Harjit S. married the maternal niece of Kamiikar S. and this became the affinal tie that determined his allegiance to the Kairon faction. The allegiance became further sealed when Beant S. and Lieutenant Bhag S. got his mother, originally a nurse, elected to the block samiti (1962–5).

Another person with a grudge against Rarewala was a certain farmer owning sixty acres of land in the village of Jarg, ten miles from Khanna. Together with his four brothers he left the Rarewala faction and allied himself to the Kairon faction because Rarewala did not help him to become a member of the block samiti in 1962. Beant S. also alleged that a contributory factor in the farmer's decision to leave the Rarewala faction was the fact that once he had gone to Rarewala's house and that Rarewala had not had the courtesy to come out and meet him.

As in the Rarewala faction, so also in the Kairon faction, individuals joined because of their friendships. For example, the sarpanc of Mangiwal village (eight miles from Payal), owning sixty acres of land, and also a member of the block samiti, was friendly with a man running a transport company in Sirhind. The latter was opposed to the Patiala Bus Service under Balwant S. of Lassowal because, as owner of a transport company, he resented its mono-polizing the transport of the area. Hence he was against Rarewala, and his friend, the sarpanc, also became hostile to Rarewala.

The only person who was a long-standing opponent of Rarewala in the Kairon faction was a Hindu who owned a cement, iron and steel depot in Doraha. He had belonged to, and was one of the leaders of, what was known as the Praja Mandel, a counterpart of Congress in PEPSU, which opposed Rarewala. In this connexion he had known Brish Bhan, a former CM of PEPSU and an associate of Kairon at state level, for over fifteen years.

The refugees from West Punjab who had settled in the Payal area were evenly divided between the two factions, the relatively more dis-possessed among them affiliating themselves to the Kairon faction. One Mohinder S., who was Kulwant's bodyguard, had been inimical to Harnam S. (murdered in 1958), because of a dispute over the property of a widow whose late husband was his father's real brother. The widow had been allotted thirteen acres of land at Payal and Harnam S., who had sexual relations with her, was cultivating the land for her. Mohinder S. had put pressure on the widow to get a will executed in his favour, and in this he had clashed with the sons of Harnam S., who, after the murder of their father, had begun cultivating her land.[12] It seemed that Mohinder S. had developed a friendship with Kulwant S. because of the latter's enmity towards Harnam S.'s family. Mohinder S., however, was also indebted to Kulwant S. in that the latter had let him use the common land of the village free of cost.

Another refugee, who was a relative of Kulwant S. through the wife of his brother Narinder S. and who sought his help in feuding in his own village, offered only a situational support, as his village was not in the Doraha–Payal–Sirhind area and was isolated from the factional strife.

The various participants in the factionalism from each village knew of all the members of their paarti in the other villages of the area and they knew one another at least by sight. In the large number of instances where they were not connected with each other by ties of marriage or friendship, they combined in terms of their links to the persons at higher levels of organization.

I have described different kinds of adherents to the two factions in the villages of the Doraha–Payal–Sirhind area, but not everyone in the villages of the area was firmly aligned to one of them. Every village was, certainly, divided on a factional basis, but at this level only a small core of persons committed on the bases I have already indicated were active in the factionalism. The general rural populace of the area was, nevertheless, far from indifferent. At two important meeting places—at the bus stop in Doraha, and then at the bus stop at Chawa, half-way between Doraha and Khanna, where passengers got off to catch the bus for Payal—a policeman armed with a bayoneted rifle stood guard. The 'factional situation' was obvious. Rumours about plans for assassinations would be dropped in Doraha by taxi drivers coming from Sirhind to Ludhiana, and gossip emanating from the *dhabe*—small wooden shacks by the roadside where people used to collect to drink tea—would circulate through the market towns and from there to the villages. The situation of factionalism existed; and if an individual was ambitious, and wanted to participate in public life, an allegiance was thrust on him. Individuals also became aligned by chance: maybe an accidental quarrel over the division of boundaries between their fields in the rainy season (there being no hedges or walls separating fields) would develop, and this quarrel would then take on meaning in terms of the existent factional division in the village. The effects of village exogamy and of the wide network of affinal ties meant that there was a tendency for strife to spread over into a number of villages: a quarrel could not be contained within one village and within any particular set of participants in that village. It was only to a certain extent, therefore, that a man could farm undisturbed. The in-laws of Kulwant S.'s sister had prospered without entering directly into the factionalism and supported Kulwant S.'s family only when it was in financial difficulty. This, however, did not prevent the police breaking into the life of the family and imprisoning certain of its members. Economic and social measures such as, for example, land consolidation also brought innumerable people into the factions on the basis of grievances in land settlements *vis-à-vis* others in their village. Certain institutions, such as the pancayat and the block samiti, and the competition that existed between men over member-ship of these institutions, similarly extended the factionalism; to become a member of the block samiti a man had to gain the support of one of the factions. Most of the sarpancs of the area were thus involved, as also were those fighting to oust them from the sarpanc-ship.

It is clear from the examples given of the reasons why individuals were members of factions that the faction itself was serving multiple functions. The reason given for all alignments to a paarti was enmity. Among the Jats enmity was felt for two types of person: for those who sought to establish power and for those whose power was already established, in whatever the unit, whether it was the village, the local area or the state. Those seeking to establish their power customarily encroached on the rights of all those not strong enough to defend themselves; and once their power was established, the encroachments onto the rights of others were defended by using that power to bribe the relevant officials of the administration, police and judiciary. The application of the rules was determined by the faction which held power. Thus the only limit to the expansion of a man's power and influence was the use by others of physical force. This was the sole check. Power was used to seize material goods and more power. Therefore those who sought power or who already possessed power were automatically resented and feared; and the reaction of those less powerful around was inevitably either to side with them and share in the benefits, or to associate together in opposition and thus defend themselves from predatory attacks. Accordingly, all the various motives for factional alignment on the part of individual participants—such as the desire to receive patron-age, to use faction as a means of social mobility,[13] to act out enmities and to shelter themselves from enmities—can be subsumed under the motive of seeking protection and securing protection for life and property. It was only possible for a man to benefit his family economically and increase his influence and status if he had a protector and his actions ultimately aimed at putting himself in a strong position *vis-à-vis* others. There was, however, no protection without the complete weakening of the other; the efficacy of the protection depended on the degree to which it threatened the source of livelihood of the opponent and maintained the right to owner-ship of land and expansion of existing assets in the form of supporters. The vertical linkages which ordinary participants in the factions forged with leaders in a local area and the vertical linkages which the latter forged as lieutenants of leaders at state level reinforced the arbitrariness of the political system: for the resources they attained were given the seal of full political protection only for that period of time during which the patron at state level remained in power, and for no longer. Security could be obtained and guaranteed only by dominance. There was no such thing as an established position.

14 Relationships between village participants and local area leaders

In this chapter I discuss the nature of the support for the local area leaders of the Kairon and Rarewala factions from the villages of the Doraha–Payal–Sirhind area. This support was gathered against a background of mutual rivalries and loyalties, some typical instances of which have been cited in the preceding chapter.

A number of leaders at local level and village participants in the factions were affinally connected[1] or became associated with another through ties of friendship and membership of such institutions as the block samiti, zilla parishad and SGPC. By continuing to talk in terms of levels, therefore, I do not mean to imply that there was any hierarchy in these relationships. I have separated leaders at local level from the mass of ordinary village participants primarily because they were in a different position regarding access to resources: that is, leaders in the local area were in a position to offer services to village participants by virtue of their association with a political leader. The local level leaders of the faction organized all the existing forms of opposition in villages against the rival faction, and the initiative for setting up bonds of mutual interest with people in the villages lay with them.

Key factional participants were buttressed by a small core of reliable relatives. In both Rarewala and Kairon factions in the local area, affines gave much support. To take one example, the affinal relationship between Kulwant S.'s family and the family into which their sister was married made available to Kulwant S. certain financial possibilities. Kulwant S. was deeply in debt to his sister's father-in-law and without the latter's financial help would, indeed, have found it materially ruinous to pursue the factionalism. The latter also had one truck in Kulwant S.'s combine and was feared in his own village primarily because of his association with Kulwant S. His son obtained a revolver licence on one occasion only because of the representations which Kulwant S. made on his behalf.

The opposing paarti always assumed that there was a solidarity of interest between these two affinally connected families. Moreover, the two families visited one another regularly, and were clearly seen to be friendly. Because of this the husband of Kulwant S.'s sister was thrown into prison and beaten up at the time of Harnam S.'s murder on the instigation of the opposing faction, even though he had nothing at all to do with the murder. His father was also imprisoned, though he avoided a beating by bribing the policemen concerned. The only amusing sidelight to the story was that one of the women in the family went to a magician in the nearby town of Ahmedgarh to find out which prison both of them had been taken to and when they would be released.

Affines of Kulwant S.'s family in the police service were generally favourably disposed towards them. In this connexion Santokh S. named specifically a deputy SP in the Sirhind area whom they had petitioned a Home Minister of Punjab not to transfer, shortly after the murder of Kulwant S. The police officer's brother—a sub-inspector of police—was married to the granddaughter of a sister of the maternal grandmother of Kulwant S. The police officer himself, however, bore enmity towards members of the Rarewala paarti. For example, the son of Rarewala's watchman (see p. 173) had made an attempt on his life in 1952.

Close affines usually associated themselves with their powerful relatives in a faction simply because, by so doing, they shared in some of their power. Thus the sarpanc of the village of Rano, who was Balwant S.'s wife's brother's son, had one truck in the Lassowal Union and he was one of those accused of murdering Kulwant S.

Nevertheless, all a man's close affines were not necessarily in the one paarti. For example, Narinder S.'s wife's brother—Dr Gurdarshan S., who was a retired army captain practising as a medical doctor in Doraha—supported the Rarewala faction. He did so for two reasons. First, he felt that in this way he protected the life of Narinder S. Second, he had been a friend of Sham S. since the days when they were both students in Lahore. At certain moments crucial for his affines Dr Gurdarshan S. continued to remain a Rarewala paarti member. In 1959, for example, out of loyalty to Sham S., he refused to testify in court that Sham S. possessed an unlicensed pistol when the latter was arrested and charged. When in the 1967 elections Rarewala's paarti threatened him that if he did not actively support them he would have to fear for the life of Narinder S., Gurdarshan S. succumbed.

Gurdarshan S. had lost the confidence of Kulwant S.'s family in 1959 when he refused to admit in court that Sham S. possessed an unlicensed pistol. Henceforth the family did not expect any political support from him. They did, however, trust him enough to visit his house during the 1967 elections, taking it for granted that he would not betray their presence to an enemy. Gurdarshan S., indeed, on this occasion, showed a great concern for their safety.

As well as being bound by affinal links, local level leaders and ordinary village participants became associated through membership of the same institutions. Both the sarpanc of Rampur and Mihan S. Gill were supported by the same political leaders to become members of the SGPC. The former was also secretary of Khalsa High School in Doraha, of which Ajmer S. was chairman. The ex-guardsman (see chapter 13) was said to be a close friend of Mihan S. Gill, while the son of Rarewala's watchman was friendly with both Mihan S. and Sham S. The sarpanc of village Mangiwal, belonging to the Kairon faction, was similarly close to Kulwant S. and Baljinder S., while Harjit S. was on very good terms with both Lieutenant Bhag S., MLA, and Beant S.

Between participants at village level and participants at local area level, therefore, there was not the same distance as there was between the leaders of the faction at state level and their lieutenants in the local area. As would be expected also, there was a greater frequency of meeting between local level leaders and village participants than between state level leaders and local level leaders. This was especially true of the Kairon faction.

A key factor in a state level leader's continuing support for a faction leader at local level was, obviously, that the latter be capable of retaining the faction's already existing following and winning new followers. The local level leader's base of support had to be secure to justify the patronage of the state level leader. The persons mentioned in the preceding chapter were a representative number of village participants in the factionalism with whom the local level leaders were in constant contact. With respect to both the factions I will now elaborate further on their links.

The Rarewala faction

The support for Rarewala in the Doraha–Payal–Sirhind area mainly gathered around the person of Hardev S. Immediately after the 1947 riots, when Sikh refugees had been invited, in the name of religion, to PEPSU, Hardev S. managed to allot stalls for selling goods in the market to some of the Sikhs who were given shelter at Doraha. They thenceforward became his political supporters. The transport company of Sham S., Ajmer S. and Hardev S. also gave work to a number of those, originally destitute, who were prepared to offer support to Rarewala. Hardev S. had a reputation for getting jobs for the people. One man, a Communist, of the village of Jalla, speaking of Hardev S. said:

> Hardev S. helped many people. It is not an exaggeration to say that from this ilaaqa [local area] he got at least a thousand jobs for the people. One man from our own village was got employed as a gram sewak[2] by Hardev S.

The complaint, however, often heard from ordinary people throughout the area was that a few people were controlling access to Rarewala: 'If we go to Gian S.'s [Rarewala's] house we may be told to go away because he is sleeping. Therefore we have to take with us someone who knows him; we have to pay his expenses.' Hardev S. exploited this situation to make a profit for himself, in addition to securing the allegiance of as many people as possible to the Rarewala faction. Rarewala had a reserved and retiring personality, and Hardev S. could only have been pushed out of his strategic link position between the small farmers and Rarewala had Rarewala, on his own, been prepared to come directly in contact with the small proprietors.

As I have already stressed in the previous chapter, Hardev S. drew into support of the Rarewala paarti the personal enmities of villagers against Kulwant S. and other members of the Kairon paarti. In fact after Kulwant S.'s seizure of the land the widening of the area of enmity to cover one-third of Ludhiana district and the adjoining areas of Patiala district was due to Hardev S. organizing witnesses against Kulwant S. in a number of court cases. The bases on which Hardev S. committed village participants to the Rarewala faction is apparent in each individual instance mentioned in the preceding chapter. Another local area supporter who headed a smuggling gang also committed a considerable number of persons to support the Rarewala faction. The son of Rarewala's watchman, the peasant from Barmalipur village, and two brothers from Jaipura village, close to Doraha, had some association with the gang. One brother was in jail at the time of the 1967 elections on a smuggling charge. Another reason for the alignment of both brothers to the Rarewala paarti was that their father had been on bad terms with a teacher of their village who happened to be a relative of Kulwant S. He was the teacher who had actually written out the deed of lease which Ashok Ram signed in 1957.

The Kairon faction

There were three contexts in which support for the Kairon paarti grew. First, since the early 1950s there had existed in PEPSU a large disgruntled section of the population. It consisted of those who had received no favours when Rarewala had been the ruling influence there, or who had been deprived of their positions of influence, however small,[3] or who had specific grievances against certain of his lieutenants. The gathering in of support by the Kairon faction was achieved in the context of the feeling against Rarewala current in PEPSU. The conditions described above in the villages of Barmalipur, Katari and Jargari enabled Kulwant S. to bring support into the Kairon faction by his offer to certain villagers now opposed to the Rarewala faction of an opportunity to place themselves in a stronger position. Thus he intervened in the affairs of Rarewala's own village of Rara by helping in the election of a Mazhbi sarpanc, who won against Rarewala's son. In 1957 he and Satnam S. also supported some of Rarewala's tenants in refusing payment of rent on their land. At least half the village votes now go to the Kairon faction.

Second, Kulwant S. managed to associate himself with the antipathies of the small shopkeepers of Gobindgarh against Rarewala's chief financial supporters. Until 1962 Balwant S. and Tejinder S. had been charging whatever they wished for the transport of goods. When Kulwant S. set up a truck union in competition with that of the Lassowals it gained him the reputation of the 'poor man's friend'. For two days after Kulwant S.'s murder the shopkeepers demonstrated their solidarity with him by organizing a compulsory shop close-down. I quote the president of the merchants' association, Gobindgarh: 'The king of the poor people has been killed.'

A public bhog ceremony[4] was performed at their expense in demonstration of their gratitude to Kulwant S., but it was also a demonstration of faction solidarity.

Kulwant S. thus crystallized, and was a focus for, all the forms of opposition to Rarewala and his lieutenants in the Doraha–Payal–Sirhind area.

Third, people joined the Kairon paarti and Kulwant S. because, knowing of his political connexions, they expected benefits. Kulwant S. drew many people into the Kairon faction because of his association with the then established rule in Punjab. People would vote for the Kairon MLA simply because they knew Kulwant S. was associated with him, and that the CM was the political patron of both of them: it was an attempt at obliging in the expectation of receiving a favour of some kind in the event of necessity.

A further factor in the drawing in of support to Kairon's paarti was that Kulwant S., physically a very impressive figure, also inspired a considerable amount of fear. This would draw many to approach him in the hope that they could obtain his protection, while others simply felt terrorized by him. Kulwant S. and his family exploited the feelings of the latter type of person, particularly at election time, by publicizing: 'The CM will get annoyed if you don't vote for his candidate.' Many of the villagers of the area were accustomed to 'sweating at the mere sight of them'[5] and such was the awe and fear they inspired that when they were tried in 1958 for the murder of Harnam S., witnesses would beg not to be examined in court; and when this plea was refused, as they entered the courtroom each would then touch the feet of the accused. The fear Kulwant S. had inspired around him was important; it allowed him to tamper with witnesses on some occasions and thereby to arrange an acquittal for the accused in a court case.[6] On other occasions it prevented witnesses deposing against him and his family.[7]

Finally, Kulwant S., particularly, derived much strength from doing favours for small landholders, using the CM's name to get things done for them by the land revenue officers, in the Irrigation Department, and in the Electricity Department. Satnam S. and Baljinder S. also performed such favours, but they were not so popular as Kulwant S. Satnam S. used to charge fees for carrying the appropriate recommending letters concerning what villagers wanted done to the relevant minister in the state capital, and the frequent comment was that in so doing he would 'loot the public'. Satnam S., Kulwant S. and Baljinder S. were, however, not go-betweens in the same sense as Hardev S. in the Rarewala faction. Kairon, with his reputation for hospitality to villagers, and with his complete lack of pretence at being anything at heart but an 'ordinary ruralite', prevented anyone from emerging as a regular mediator between him and the people by attracting persons with their various complaints and petitions to himself, directly.

All local level leaders, whatever their faction, were concerned with achieving control over the local magistrates, and police and administrative officials, because this meant favourable land adjustments for their supporters; it meant, too, that supporters would be absolved from their cases, or that the hearing of these cases would be delayed, and that those with whom they were on terms of enmity would be implicated, through vital evidence not being brought forward. The aim was always to weaken the political position of the opposing faction through intervening in village disputes, in pancayat elections, and, by offering protection. The associated aim was to ensure the attachment of as many people as possible to their faction. The local level leader was distinct from the ordinary participant in the faction only with respect to these functions. He was not distinct through his status. He had no distinct family traditions behind him to differentiate himself from others, nor was he the successor to a long line of local leaders. He was in a position of local prominence by virtue of his ambition, his links, and the successful use of his coercive power. So long as he maintained an effective local following he was supported, though not necessarily consistently, by a political leader at state level who sanctioned his already existing spheres of influence, and, if these were useful to him, enhanced them. So long as the local leader appeared to have this vital political patronage his support from village participants remained steady.

15 Factions in competition

The nature of the strife between the two factions was observable in certain specific types of action: in the intimidation or killing of members of the opposing faction; in litigation between members of opposed factions in court; in defamatory attacks on the political patron of the opposing faction; and in election campaigns to defeat the opposing paarti's candidates. The nature of the ties and links operating between members of one faction *vis-à-vis* members of the opposing faction discussed in the preceding four chapters were visible on occasions of (i) disputes over resources and, arising out of such disputes, either immediately or ultimately, (ii) assaults on key persons of the opposing faction, and (iii) court cases. A degree of faction mobilization was also involved in the circulation of slanderous gossip about the leader of the opposing faction. Such gossip was usually passed around before or during an election, on which occasion faction links also tightened because so much was at stake.

Possession of resources was important in the struggle between factions in the local area, for it enabled the police and administration at that level to be bribed. The result of the fight for such resources was held to indicate which of the factions in the local area was the most powerful. A faction always attempted to injure or kill the leader of the opposing faction in the local area so as to create insecurity and demoralization among his followers and also to remove temporarily a link in the chain connecting a political patron at state level with his followers in the villages. Court cases and elections involved the two factions in a public fight. They were disputes for an image, and whoever won on these occasions contributed to reducing the picture of power that the opposing faction presented. An election success meant control of more patronage to the followers of the winning faction. The benefits a man received were from one faction, and this made the division between the two factions very clear, since

187

members of a paarti would fear that these benefits would be lost if their opposing paarti won in the elections.

As the procession of events from 1957 onwards illustrates, occasions for conflict between the two factions were certainly not few in number. In the year 1962, for example, there were four sets of elections. In August there was the court case regarding the beating up of Karam S. and in September Kulwant S.'s conviction in that case. Also in 1962 Kulwant S. started his truck combine. If, to the above, all the innumerable small incidents occurring in villages are added, it would seem that the intervals of time when some of the ties in the faction were not mobilized were very few. These occasions of conflict were marked by the ties and loyalties of the local area lieutenants, particularly *vis-à-vis* each other. A section from the report of a former SP written shortly after the murder of Hardev S. illustrates this:

> The worst aspect of the matter is that every small incident is grossly exaggerated and at once given political colouring. Sides are invariably taken and diametrically opposed views are put up by the opposing party. False motives are frequently attributed to the investigating staff by disgruntled parties, cudgels on whose behalf are at once taken up by the local influential politicians. They [Kulwant S., etc.] enjoy the full confidence and support of S. Bhag Singh, the Congress MLA. Their rival, Mihan S. Gill, commands the support of Gian S. [i.e., Rarewala] and the late Hardev S. of Doraha, whose place is being taken by Balwant S.

This chapter therefore illustrates some actual occasions when factions were mobilized in the villages and local areas. The actions of those involved in particular court cases, and the faction's means of handling situations of strife with the opposing faction, depended on whether there was a possibility of their gaining active support from persons higher in the system. That possibility itself depended on the positions of the factions at state level. The first three types of occasion on which factions mobilized, and which I outlined above, are interrelated and will be discussed concurrently over the period 1957–67.

Factions in the local area were first involved in conflict over the seizure of Ashok Ram's land by Kulwant S.'s family in July 1957. Balwant S. of Lassowal, on Hardev S.'s request, sent truck loads of men in order to seize back the land. On the occasion when the

court heard both the criminal complaint and civil suit filed by
Ashok Ram against Kulwant S. in 1957, many people were afraid to
come forward to act as witnesses against Kulwant S. This is an
instance of a general rule: in court cases, each faction tended to
support its members. However, as the above instance shows, this
pattern could be disturbed on any one occasion by the reality of the
power controlled by each faction *vis-à-vis* the other at that particular
moment. The verdicts in the 1957 case emphasized the structure of a
situation that the land seizure itself had drawn attention to: namely,
that Kulwant S. was a powerful man in the Doraha–Payal area,
that his power was, for a time, being sanctioned by support from
above (from the CM) and that it was therefore unwise to oppose
him.

In Ashok Ram's court case, there were certain persons who did
act as prosecution witnesses against Kulwant S., and what subsequently happened to them was also an indication of the relative
strengths of the local area cores at this time. Harnam S. and a few
of his relatives had appeared as prosecution witnesses in the court
case regarding the land seizure. In December 1957 Jagmohan S.,
Kulwant S.'s brother, in the company of Kamiikar S.'s son, assaulted
a relative of Harnam S. staying in Dhanipur, as a warning to the
others. But Harnam S. again appeared as a prosecution witness
against Kulwant S.'s family in this court case. In the same month,
therefore, Mohinder S. injured two small proprietors also living in
Dhanipur who were Harnam S.'s associates. Harnam S. did not
give way to these threats.

In March 1958 Harnam S. was invited to the betrothal ceremony
of one of his friends in Dhanipur. He 'reached Dhanipur at 8 a.m.,
when recital of the Granth was going on. Bhog ceremony was
observed at 10 a.m. Meals were taken at two o'clock, and two
hours before sunset Harnam S. left for the fields to ease himself.
On the way back he was assaulted'[1] by one of the granthis (readers
of the scriptures) who also happened to be his cousin and, it is
alleged, by Kulwant S. and his brothers Jagmohan S. and Narinder
S., by Kamiikar S. and his son, and by Mohinder S., and stabbed to
death. His body was then taken away on the back of a she-donkey,
cut into pieces with a *kirpan* (the actual words used by Santokh S.
when describing this incident were 'made mincemeat of'), and
thrown into the Sirhind canal. All those who opposed Kulwant S.'s
family in the court case which followed on Harnam S.'s murder

were subsequently attacked. Two friends of Harnam S. were driven out of Dhanipur and sweepers now occupy the house of one of these, while Mohinder S. tills the land of the other.

In the court case concerning the murder of Harnam S., Hardev S. personally initiated a lot of the action in implicating Kulwant S., while at the instance of the Lassowal family the names of Kamiikar S. and his son were included in the list of those responsible for the murder. These accusations were ultimately unsuccessful. Rarewala himself went to see the Union Home Minister and similarly tried to implicate Kulwant S. In the end he failed to do so. Some time, in the course of all this, the CM had indicated to the local administration that they should protect his faction. This vertical link, present in the background, affected the position of the two factions in the local area.

In 1959 Kulwant S. took advantage of what he thought to be the commitment of a leader at state level to their support to obtain more land. Hardev S. had had some gurudwara land in his possession which he had obtained with the help of Rarewala.[2] He had cultivated this for a total period of three years and, according to a court report, he had made use of it for his personal ends. He had also given a sublease of this land to Mihan S. Gill, ex-MLA. At the time of the Rarewala tube well case Kulwant S. intervened to show that the land had been given on less than its rental value. Kairon thereupon suspended the patwari (the keeper of the land records of a group of villages) and the clerk who had seen through the transaction and given the land to Hardev S. The latter had rented out the land at approximately 2,000 rupees a year but had obtained the land on a rental basis of 500 rupees a year. In 1959 Kulwant S. managed to get the land (thirty acres) auctioned, and together with another man from his paarti obtained this land as a part lessee.[3]

In the same year Hardev S., on his side, petitioned that the allocation of brick kilns to Kulwant S.'s family be cancelled and that these be allotted to some members of the Rarewala faction instead.[4]

Concurrent with the fight over resources, the family of Kulwant S. continued to attack those in the Rarewala faction who had opposed them in court cases over the land seizure and the murder of Harnam S. In December 1959 Gian S. was publicly abducted by members of the Kairon faction from a bus at Chawa, in retaliation for the help he had given to the police at the time of Harnam S.'s murder, 'but also as a repayment for other insults'.[5] In the court case that followed it was again Hardev S. who falsely implicated Kulwant S. in the abduction. Then, in 1961, Kulwant S. made an attempt on Karam S.'s life, being joined in the attempt by those who had their own private quarrels with Karam S.[6] Hardev S. implicated Kulwant S. in the case in court in 1962, and the son of Rarewala's watchman (see chapter 13), because of his association with Sham S., and Mihan S. Gill appeared as a prosecution witness against Kulwant S., stating that he had been an eye-witness of the beating up of Karam S. The local area leaders did not receive any backing from the CM on this occasion.

It was thus from 1962 onwards that the CM's support of his faction in the local area became more and more ambiguous. His lieutenants lost their court cases and the opposing faction began making attempts on the life of the dominant personality of the Kairon faction in the local area—Kulwant S. The first attempt on Kulwant S.'s life was made at Khanna in 1963. It was said to have been not only the work of Hardev S. in co-operation with Milkha S. and Harinder S. of Kulwant S.'s own village of Dhanipur, but Sham S. and Mihan S. Gill were also reliably said to have been conspirators.[7] The Kairon paarti retaliated by implicating the son of Hardev S. in the attempt on Kulwant S.'s life. Two further attempts on Kulwant S.'s life were made in 1964, those responsible being a number of assassins who had been hired by the Lassowal family.

It was partly to prevent the erosion of their support in villages that Kulwant S. and his brothers murdered Hardev S. in 1964. In the trial, however, all those members of Kulwant S.'s family who had been accused, although sentenced to be hanged by the sessions court, were acquitted by the high court, on the basis that the evidence given by the witnesses was either interested or had been bought. All the witnesses were Lassowals' truck drivers or had brothers or other relatives in the Lassowals' employ. These were the grounds on which a successful appeal was made. Tejinder S. of Lassowal 'had supplied a contingent of perjured witnesses and along with Mihan S. Gill had dominated the scene right from the start'.[8] The acquittal has to be set in the context of General Mohan S.'s loyalty[9] to the family of Kulwant S. Thus, once again, the intervention of a person higher in the system affected the balance of power between the two factions in the local area. The balance conclusively swung in favour of the Rarewala faction, however, with the assassination of the CM. This was shown at local area level by renewed attempts and threats on the life of Kulwant S.

On 29 September 1965 Kulwant S. applied to the deputy inspector general of police at Patiala for immediate protection for his life, property and honour, alleging that he feared attack from the Lassowal family. In this application he states that Balwant S., Manjeet S. 'and others are now offering huge sums for putting an end to my life. In fact they have engaged six persons from district Bhatinda and seven persons from district Hissar. . . .' He complained that while Balwant S. 'and his relatives have got sixty licences for fire-arms, no such licence is with us. Either some licences be given to us or theirs be cancelled.' In December 1965 Kulwant S. was killed in a gun fight when attacked by a number of Rarewala paarti members in the grounds of his own truck combine. By April 1966 rumours were circulating that 30,000 rupees had been given to a number of persons by the Lassowal family for the life of Jagmohan S. and that almost a *lakh* rupees were being offered if all the brothers could be eliminated. Pressure was also being put by the Lassowal family on the witnesses in the court hearing for the murder of Kulwant S., to give evidence favourable to them. An affidavit filed by a resident of Turan village, near Amloh, Patiala district, illustrates this:

> That the owners of Patiala Goods Carriers have shown their willingness to offer the deponent something, in case the deponent does not give evidence in the murder of the late Kulwant S. In case the deponent does not accede to their wishes they have threatened the deponent to be ready to bear the consequences similar to Kulwant S.

A truck operator resident in Gobindgarh had similar pressure put on him by two drivers of Patiala Goods Carriers. None of the accused in Kulwant S.'s murder has been convicted, all have been acquitted.[10]

In the local area, violence, threats and the winning of court cases were thus associated with the faction whose power could be endorsed, if needed, by its political patron at state level. The very day after Rarewala had been declared the successful candidate in Payal constituency in the 1967 elections, one of his sons beat up the son of an opponent in village Ghaloti and instituted a charge that his victim had insulted him. Similarly, after the 1967 elections, Balwant S. had engaged an ex-army officer, a deserter, to shoot down Santokh S.

Concurrent with the fight for dominance in the courts and during elections, faction leaders in the local area used to indulge in a considerable amount of defamatory gossip against leaders of the opposing faction both at local area and state level.

Members of the Rarewala faction used to spread tales that Kulwant S. and his brothers had murdered their own father. The father of Kulwant S.—Avtar S.—had certainly died in mysterious circumstances. A headman of Dhanipur village had returned a loan of 500 rupees which he owed to the government. Later the government renewed its claim for payment of the loan. It is said that Avtar S. wished to inform the land revenue officer, as a witness, that the loan had been paid, but that Kulwant S. wanted to give the headman some trouble and on his instructions his father did not approach the land revenue officer. It was said by the family that it was shortly after this that Avtar S. committed suicide. The Rarewala faction say that he was murdered by his sons.

Kulwant S. was particularly provocative and insulting in his slander of Rarewala and his family. Members of the Kairon faction reprobated Rarewala's family as being most corrupt. A typical remark passed by one of their paarti men in the 1967 election was: 'They want to rule again. His daughter is standing in Sangrur on the Akali Dal ticket. She sends people to help him and he to help her. Manmohan Kaur [Rarewala's wife] tried for Swatantara ticket. *Koii asul ni hai* [They have no principles].' The Kairon faction would also derogatorily remark that Rarewala was under the domination of his wife and mention that Rarewala was the adopted and not the real son of the Sirdar of Rara.[11]

In those instances when leaders of a faction in a local area managed to snatch resources from the opposing faction and maintain their dominance in the local area by virtue of their having support from above prepared to intervene in their favour, the opposing faction would make attempts to lower the prestige of their political patron at state level by exaggerating the importance of his connexions with lawless elements in rural areas.[12] When, for example, Kulwant S. seized the land in 1957, the gossip was that he had seized it on the strength of Kairon's support. Another similar occasion occurred in 1964, when, after Hardev S.'s murder, Rarewala met the then Union home minister and told him that the central police should investigate the case of Hardev S.'s murder, as it was unlikely that the CM would see 'his own men' convicted.

Massive efforts were indeed made by the Rarewala faction to link
Kairon with Hardev S.'s murder. Mihan S. Gill wrote a letter to the
then Union Home Minister on 18 January 1964 in which he stated
that 'the truck in which the culprits came' to commit the murder 'is
engaged in a company at Halwara aerodrome, which is owned by
S. S. Kairon'. Likewise, a certain Bibi Amar Kaur, whose daughter
was married to one of Hardev S.'s sons, sent a letter on 11 February
1964 also attempting to involve and discredit the CM:[13]

> I have been told that the trucks[14] used by the assailants came from
> Halwara. . . . The contract for the construction of the aerodrome
> is in the name of Surinder Kairon. The trucks were working in the
> construction of the aerodrome. I have incontrovertible evidence
> with me that these trucks originally came from Halwara and after
> murdering Hardev S. they rushed back to Halwara. When the
> police tried to take possession of one of the trucks, S. Hardial S.
> Dhillon, Manager of S. Kairon's construction concern resisted
> the police and threatened them of dire consequences. He said
> 'Do you know the influence of Surinder Kairon? If you show the
> guts of taking possession of the trucks you will have to face untold
> difficulties.'

Elections were another occasion when the ties of members of the
faction in the local area to one another, and their links upward to a
political leader and downward to key supporters in villages, would
be mobilized. In the four constituencies of the Doraha–Payal–
Sirhind area in the 1967 general elections, Ajmer S. together with
Mihan S. Gill and Sham S. (who had come especially from Bihar)
were directing their supporters from the villages. The Lassowal
family appeared to remain in the background and not to campaign
actively, probably for fear of assassination. In the Kairon faction,
Santokh S. and Baljinder S. were campaigning for common candidates: for Beant S., in Payal constituency, Bhag S. in Amloh and
Joginder S. Maan in Sirhind. Despite the fact that the Kairon
faction was without the clear backing of a powerful state political
leader, it won the seats of Amloh and Sirhind.[15]

The electoral situation was the same throughout these four constituencies: for the villagers the election was seen as a paarti matter;
their paarti and its representatives were good and the opposite paarti
and its representatives were bad. They saw the election as involving
them in a fight to deprive key members of the opposing faction of

their resources. One petty proprietor and smuggler talked derogatorily to me about Beant S.:

When he came from West Pakistan he worked as a bus conductor in Calcutta. He has no experience and knows politics only through his association with Dr Baljinder S. On the other hand S. Gian S. [and he detailed the posts Rarewala has occupied] belongs to 'good family'. All in the opposite paarti have served sentences for murder.

Even though Kairon was dead by this time, the label still attached to those associated with him in the local area. The small favours that Kairon used to do for his followers were constantly being recalled by members of the opposing faction, for example, the diversion to Dr Baljinder S.'s village of 4,000 rupees out of 7,000 allocated for a road to another village. Participants of each faction were full of what they would do to their opponents if they won the elections. For example, one man from the Rarewala faction said, 'If Rarewala wills it, we'll see where Dhanipurian's land goes in a few years'; and an opponent from the opposing Kairon faction said, 'Once Beant S. is elected and Kulwant S.'s two daughters are married we'll murder the Lassowals, the Rara Sirdar [i.e., Rarewala] and Sham S.'

Preceding, during and shortly after the elections, enmities were patent, but this was the only time ordinary village participants who had no links flaunted their allegiance: no one, except prominent participants in the factionalism, in the villages and in the local area, liked ordinarily to mention the factionalism in public. If they chanced to be overheard in remarking on their affiliation by a person of the opposing faction that person might then institute a case against them, stating that he apprehended a danger to his life or his property. Such situations always led to the crystallization of a man's allegiance. For example, the maternal nephew of participant 'A'—referred to in chapter 13—was named in such a court case; and he now states himself to be a staunch member of the Rarewala faction, though, in fact, he has never done anything concrete for the faction nor received any favours from it.

Villagers campaigned for certain candidates on the basis of paarti loyalties. State politicians visiting the area to make speeches in favour of candidates did so on a strictly party political basis, for example, Congress ministers would support Congress candidates. The personal enmities that were at the basis of paarti rivalry in the area were thus, at least publicly, given an ideological cover. I give some examples from the speeches of these politicians:

(*i*) S. Gurnam S., the CM of Punjab until November 1967[16] and the then Akali Dal member for Raipur constituency, speaking at a village meeting in Ghuddani Kalan in favour of Beant S., pointed out the corruption in the Congress party and the economic poverty of the electors:

> Congress is giving money for votes . . . Rarewala is dropping pylons as an election stunt. Congress is the party of the rich land-lords but our programme is to have more schools in villages. . . . Out of every fifty *lakhs* the industrialists give the Congress, five to ten *lakhs* are kept for party funds. The CM of Madhya Pradesh made one crore [10 million rupees]. Similarly Patnaik[17] and Kairon also made money. This fight is therefore not between Beant S. and Rarewala, it is between honesty and dishonesty. . . . Congressmen have earned so much money that they have had to put it in the banks overseas. . . . It was Congressmen who were firing into the jails during morcha days[18]. . . . Twenty-seven out of the fifty-seven Congress MLAs left, after the Punjab had been split into Hariana, Himachal Pradesh and Punjabi Suba were Ministers [and he proceeded to mention their 4,000 rupees per month salary and free petrol allowance].

(*ii*) In his speech at another village, as the Congress candidate for Payal, Rarewala focused on the divisions within the Akali Dal and asked the electorate:

> When they are divided among themselves how can they form a strong government? If we have one party, progress will be much faster. I agree Congress isn't good, but people have no choice but to vote for it because there is no other party which can form a government.

Rarewala then, however, went on to praise Congress for establishing the Agricultural University at Ludhiana and Punjabi University at Patiala.[19]

In the February 1967 elections, in the constituencies of Payal, Khanna, Amloh and Sirhind, the same core of people who were canvassing for Congress in Payal and Sirhind (i.e., members of the Rarewala faction) were opposing Congress in Khanna and Amloh (simply because the Congress candidates in those two constituencies were of the Kairon faction), and the same core of people who were canvassing for Akalis in Payal and Sirhind (i.e., members of the Kairon faction) were against Akalis in Khanna and Amloh (because the Akali candidates were members of the Rarewala faction). Individually, Dr Baljinder S., campaigning for Akalis in Payal, was simultaneously campaigning for Congress in the neighbouring constituency of Kum Kalan simply because it was General Mohan S.'s constituency. Similarly, Sham S., supporting a Congress candidate in Payal—i.e., Rarewala—went to oppose a Congress candidate in Kum Kalan because he was of the opposing faction. For all his membership of the Kairon faction and his support for Kairon, Kulwant S., too, did not join the Congress party until 1964, while Beant S. had primary membership of the Congress party until his expulsion on 17 February 1967, i.e., two days before the elections, and had originally tried to get the Congress nomination for Payal constituency. Only when he could not get it did he switch his allegiance to the Akali party. The same set of people were thus supporting two different political parties at one and the same time. Consequently, factional alignments were alignments that bound together people of different political parties.

In court cases and in elections especially, as has been seen, those persons involved usually covered the span of the faction at local level. Persons in the police and administration who were loyal to a particular faction leader at state level or under the influence or pressure of a faction leader in the local area would also be involved. Throughout this chapter the importance of the local area lieutenants retaining and maintaining their upward links has again been demonstrated. The vertical links of local area lieutenants affected the frequency of violence, the outcome of court cases, the power of the faction in the local area, and hence its position *vis-à-vis* its rival. So long as the leader at the apex of the political system had not lost his resources of patronage, the unit that participants in the factionalism called 'paarti' was held together by a common interest in preserving and, if possible, extending its power. For each participant, it was a matter of supporting his paarti and only secondarily of supporting Kairon or Rarewala or whoever was the political patron of their paarti. Although each participant's primary aim and objective was personal, he conceived that the preservation of paarti affected his ability to achieve that aim; hence he became intimately concerned with the paarti as such.[20]

A man's fortunes became sunk in that of his paarti in so far as he believed that he could continue to retain resources and benefits illegally acquired, or acquired with the help of the paarti, only while that paarti was strong. A second central factor in the stability and consistency of faction membership was that each individual participant was able to equate the furtherance of his own ends with membership of a faction. Factions thus commonly tended to lose some supporters on the death or resignation from office of a political leader, since they were dependent on that leader for political patronage in the form of a sanction to the power they exercised over a given area. This was the only sense, however, in which the faction could be said to be linked to a particular leader.

The state political system was characterized by a few alliances that were not formed on the basis of vertical ties. I will stress this further in chapter 16. State-wide faction ties connecting with one another the various local leaders of factions in each area of the province were the most significant type of linkage that existed. Thus, as I briefly mentioned in an earlier chapter, all lieutenants of the Kairon faction in the different local areas of the state knew one another and combined in support of the CM when opposition to him was on a state-wide basis. The local areas of the Punjab were characterized by competition between families and between factions. This competition, which in the Doraha–Payal–Sirhind area resembled strife, was not resolved on the level where it occurred but was always taken to a higher level for resolution and settlement. At times in 1962—for example, when Kairon had achieved a balance of power between the two factions in the Doraha–Payal–Sirhind area—it seemed that the resolving of strife had been centralized.

As has been seen, the characteristic allegiance of the political system was that emerging in collaborative relationships between leaders at the different levels of that system. All participants in the factionalism sought protection for what they possessed and hoped to possess by depriving others of possessing. This was the common denominator of every vertical linkage. It is indeed at this point— that is, on the need of protection—that there is a confluence of all the ethnographic data so far presented. Law was not impartial: it was manipulated by the powerful. In the fieldwork area, a man felt he could protect himself, his family and his property only by placing himself under a protector, i.e., under a powerful man, or by succeeding in becoming powerful enough himself to deter attacks. Kulwant

S. was protector to a host of ordinary participants in the faction, and he in turn received patronage in his protective function from the CM for his usefulness in cutting at the base of power of an important political rival of the CM's. Kairon received the patronage and support of the national leader because he was providing the necessary sort of opposition to elements held to be threatening the solidarity of the nation. At the levels of the state, local area and village, there was a struggle for the links that gave protection. The need to guard oneself, through putting oneself under a protector, and, as one stage towards so augmenting one's influence as eventually to become a protector oneself, was a product of the arbitrariness felt to affect life and property.

16 Assessment

I have previously stated that the units that were integrated into the state political system were factions, at various levels and of varying complexity: they extended throughout the political system and were powerful in all political situations. The political system, therefore, cannot be understood without great emphasis on factions. As well as acting within the formal political structure of the state legislature and in the organizations of each political party, they existed within governmental institutions such as the civil and police administration. I hence found it useful to focus my study on factions, since they were the units through which and in which political activity and political interaction predominantly manifested itself.

At various points throughout the book I have noted the relationships which factional coalitions maintain with other component parts of the governmental organization such as the administrative system and the political parties. It is necessary here to examine these interrelationships further.

The organization of the then ruling Congress party and of administrative and judicial offices in the state was on an hierarchical basis, i.e., each lower office was under the control and supervision of a higher one. During the period of Partap S. Kairon's rule the administration became a 'controlled bureaucracy'.[1] The CM infiltrated its structure, placing those loyal to him and those of exceptional brilliance and merit in important positions. Those administrative officers who acted independently were liable to dismissal or demotion. During Kairon's period of rule Punjab progressed towards having a 'tight'[2] administrative structure in that political direction became increasingly more complete. The scope for administrative participation in policy making was thus small. This is succinctly revealed in the remark of a certain minister on the occasion of his being appointed a head of department. When congratulated by a friend he replied, 'There is only one *mantri* [minister]. Others are *santris* [peons].' The years following Kairon's assassination, how-ever, were marked by a succession of weak CMs, and the administra-tion became steadily more free to make decisions of policy.

The legislative offices, from the State Assembly downwards through the district council and block samiti to pancayats in each village, were not arranged hierarchically; each operated with reference to a smaller unit and controlled smaller resources. The appropriate level of each faction competed to control the relevant legislative offices. The candidate to be elected to the State Assembly from constituencies in the various local areas of the province were effectively chosen by a paarti, and paartis competed in elections for the success of their representatives.

It may be said, therefore, that during Kairon's period in the office of CM effective control of the administrative and legislative systems lay in the hands of the CM's faction within the ruling party. Opponents to that faction within the ruling party struggled to gain control of the state governmental organization at all levels. Political parties, as such, did not compete with one another for such control. They rarely operated as organized groups, for two reasons. First, ideological distinctions between the political parties were a matter of theory alone and they rarely operated in practice. The late CM, as I have shown in chapters 7 and 8, *was* firmly committed to certain policies which were also Congress policies but in this he was almost a lone exception. There was a continuous flow of key figures of the Akali Dal into the Congress when Congress was ruling the state.[3] Since the Congress experienced two electoral defeats in February 1967 and February 1969 this movement has been in a reverse direction, i.e., from the Congress to the Akali Dal.[4] Second, there was a major cleavage within the ruling party (and, to a lesser extent, within the Akali Dal) between urban and rural interests. During Kairon's period of tenure in the office of CM the opposition to the Congress within the legislature therefore came mainly from within the Congress itself: from urban interests and from prominent leaders in rural areas with strong local bases of power. In composition the then ruling party at state level was a coalition of the patrons of locally based factions.

Such factions in the local areas could not remain intact without political patronage from above, and their influence increased and diminished according to the political situation in the state. It was thus impossible to study the factionalism in the local areas and

villages independently of political changes at state level. At state
level the CM used his knowledge and the power of his office to further
his own political interests in specific areas of the province. Those
who had influence in these areas and who at the same time thought
it useful to be his ally he patronized, sanctioning them in their
already existing areas of control. The local level lieutenants of the
faction in no way inherited their positions as leaders. Nor was there
any difference in ranking nor any distinctness in habits and behavioural patterns between them and other villagers. They rarely,
if ever, had their roots in urban areas and were unlikely to have
been brought up in a different tradition or to have come from a
different social environment. Thus there was no barrier to communication between them and ordinary villagers. Communication
was also aided by the web of affinal connexions which any one
family had available to mobilize. However, in the resources at their
disposal, in the formal positions they occupied, in their attachment
(or lack of attachment) to a formal political party, each local level
leader differed from the other. A former president of the Amritsar
District Congress (Urban) Committee, for example, was then a
loyal Congress man and some of Kairon's lieutenants in Karnal
district (a district now part of Hariana) were similarly ideologically
committed to support Kairon. But Kulwant S. had no strong
ideological convictions and only joined the Congress party some
months before Kairon's resignation as CM. Nevertheless all leaders
in the local areas attempted to exercise a local control over government expenditure as channelled through the block samitis; they
sought to get 'their men' into positions of prominence in a village
and on the block samiti itself, to protect 'their men' in court cases,
and to elect 'their' representatives to the State Assembly. They also
mediated between those attached to their faction and the police and
land revenue officers. Equally, they sought to influence those
administrative appointments for their particular local area that they
considered would be valuable.

These, one may say, were the present-day functions of the local
level leaders. They were the modern equivalents of the misl chiefs
referred to earlier and represented a continuation of an historical
type which I delineated in chapter 3 with reference to Ala S., i.e., in
possession of, or in pursuit of the possession of, an area of local
control and seeking confirmation in the power exercised in this
area from the leader on the next level of the political system. The

local level leader sought the support of the state political leader in a local struggle for power and if the latter, as Partap S. Kairon did, needed to build up a strong following in a specific rural area, as part of the drive against all those with bases of power aligned to him, an alignment emerged between the state level and local area leaders. The foundation of the vertical association between leaders of the faction at state level and leaders of the faction in the local area was, for both, the desire to consolidate and maintain power. Even if the type of power they sought was different, complementary interest was the basis of their collaboration. What varied at different periods was the duration of such combinations. On those occasions when political rule at state level remained centralized, the factional collaborations tended to be stable. This leads me into a problem of primarily contemporary relevance, namely, why no form of unitary rule in the province has lasted for long. What are the social and political facts which have prevented the persistence of an effective centralized system of rule in Punjab and which therefore can be understood as contributing to the stability of the traditional system.

In Kairon's period of rule the problem of perpetuating a system of unitary rule was seen by the CM to be, initially, how he was to control existing centres of power and mobilize the resources of the system for his own objectives. The CM tried to do so continuously and independently through personal recruitment. To achieve this he had two courses: personally to gain control of the resources of the state system[5] and thereby secure those services he required; and to encourage certain sections in the society to develop resources which he would then proceed to regulate.[6] Through control of the economy —the distribution of quotas, permits, loans and licences—Kairon tried to strengthen his own supporters and deprive his opponents; thus he aimed at political control over certain sections of society. Through the administration he tried, in the short run, to control the implementation of policy and, in the long run, through his final say in the choice of those on the Punjab Public Services Commission and Subordinate Services Selection Board who would recruit personnel, he attempted to sway the administrative service to his ends. These were the primary resources that were independent of control from any other source. One reason why the CM was unable fully to achieve his political objectives was that he did not succeed in having all political resources completely dependent on him.

Fundamentally, however, it was the structure of the political system that prevented Kairon from achieving his objectives. Political leaders requiring followers and families concerned with raising their prestige and extending their power helped in the perpetuation of a system which kept any form of unitary rule weak. As inside the police and administration, so within political parties and every elective organization, local units, and even smuggling gangs on the border—in many of which organizations Jats dominated—there had always been two opposed factions. It was this widespread condition of divisiveness, uniformly on a non-ideological basis, that had throughout functioned as a principal obstacle in the maintenance of any form of unitary rule.

Another major factor which favoured the persistence of this anarchic distribution of power was that the factional cleavage itself was an important factor in integrating the system. At all levels of the state, power depended on the complementary mutual assistance of persons opposed, in their own interests, to certain others. They were then committed to support and co-operate with one another by their membership of paarti, as also by affinal and kinship ties of economic interdependence. Thus support for factions and faction opposition became vital in the maintenance of a minimal cohesion in rural society.

More fundamentally, the inability to maintain unitary rule was connected with the type of social units which political leaders could mobilize; the manner of generating, and maintaining, support was obviously one that related to the already existent frameworks of social organizations. The ease of winning control of the polity, and the difficulty in maintaining that control, related essentially to the poverty of specialized associations and to the lack of entrenched classes among whom set power and prestige were distributed in standardized modes. Ideological commitments were also weak. All these factors combined forced leaders to continually seek support from among the populace. And only factions based on diverse interests and allegiances were available to provide support.

Factions hampered a leader's centralizing efforts in a number of ways. A leader by favouring one faction always risked alienating his opponents. The implications of this were such that even on vital matters he could never secure the entire support of the rural population. The people he patronized harboured their own ambitions.

Then, too, the rate at which centralization progressed was governed by the services and resources provided by the factions themselves and the viability of the CM's alliance with them. There was no connexion at all, therefore, between strong centralized government and an ending to the anarchic distribution of power in the society. The faction was, in fact, inherent to that type of society: the neglect of such units by a state authority out of weakness, equally with their patronage, enabled them to prosper. In periods when there was an absence of a determined ruling authority the only check on the activities of a faction was the power and influence of the other faction. Equally, in a situation where a strongly centralized government was ruling it relied on a faction whose very *raison d'être* lay in political patronage. Factional disputes within any one village certainly related to specific features of the social structure at that level, but their intensity, and their spread over large areas beyond the village, depended on whether or not they received the patronage of a political leader. Kairon, for example, patronized factions only in those areas of Punjab where there was a powerful political leader to oust. Although the activities of factions in local areas of the province subsequently became controlled under centralized rule, and their leaders could manage to retain their followers only when political patronage was steady, the state government nevertheless maintained its rule only by virtue of the support given to it by some among these units.

The pattern of social and political organization was thus unfavourable to the setting up of unitary rule. Cultural and historical factors also acted against the establishment of such rule. Traditionally, Jats had conceived of 'government' as repression. Historically, small Jat proprietors had carried the greatest burden in terms of revenue taxation. Those small owner-occupiers had contributed most to the military defence of the Punjab and considered that they had received few rewards in return. They therefore had an intense distrust of 'government'. At the same time they felt it was necessary to control the government, since government policy affected things vital to their existence and mode of life. For example, their land ownership was affected, since new laws placed a ceiling on the amount of land that could be owned and hence on a landowner's capacity to accumulate capital, whereas there was no such ceiling placed on the wealth that could be accumulated by owners of industry in urban areas. Again, 'government' determined the Sikh (principally Jat) percentage of military recruitment into the army. Prices for wheat were also regulated by the government.

In the past, Jats had rarely felt that the government was theirs; it had only been something they had had to come to terms with in order to survive. They accordingly had made the necessary alliances. Factions, in the historical context of invasion, foreign rule and perpetual disturbance, had been the pattern of organization evolved by the dominant Jat section of the population. The anti-government attitude of this section of the population, an attitude which they held to be a principle of life, began to change with the passing of the Land Alienation Act,[7] and with this there was participation, in the pre-partition period (along with Hindu and Muslim Jats), in a political party representing rural interests, namely the Unionist party. In 1956, after a period of urban-dominated leadership, the land-holding section of the population (more specifically the many *chooti kisaans*, or small proprietors), came to identify themselves with government because they conceived it to be once again promoting their economic interests *vis-à-vis* the urban section of the population.

In chapter 7 I noted how Kairon, prior to attaining the office of CM, had held the portfolios of Development and Rehabilitation and had had control of the Congress party organization in the state for three years. During this period he initiated many development plans that would improve the standard of living in the rural areas and he had filled the posts in the Congress organization with those loyal to him who were of a rural background. Subsequent to his becoming CM all the political personages who were thereafter to become prominent were of rural origin. He thus raised the political stature of the Jats in the state. He also attempted to improve their economic position: as I mentioned in chapter 7, the implementation of development projects was primarily with reference to rural areas. In addition to aiding people of rural origin in the economic and political spheres, Kairon increased their numbers in the administration. He did so out of an attachment to the Jats but also because the administration was particularly resistant to the implementation of some of his policies. His patronage of the Jats in all these spheres can also be seen as an attempt to eliminate the appeal of the Akali Dal in the rural areas. So long as Master Tara S. retained some following he consistently propagated that the Akali Dal was a party associated with the interests of urban Sikhs.

Kairon's support for those of rural origin and his concern with development in rural areas was not, however, a purely tactical manoeuvre. He had a genuine desire to make the rural Punjab prosperous. To quote one of his closest friends who knew him from his student days in America, 'Whatever he saw in America—the Pasadena orange groves, the grape orchards, the paper mills—he wanted to have in the Punjab.' Nevertheless, while attempting to change the system, Kairon had simultaneously to work with it. Thus to secure his position in the office of CM against rivals in the Congress party with strong bases of power in specific local areas and against the Akali Dal exploiting the emotional strength of such slogans as '*Panth khattre wichh*' ('The Sikh community is in danger'), he had to use the units that were available in the system, i.e., factional coalitions. Those who held down the rural areas for him frequently used violent methods to do so but they continued to receive the CM's patronage because he needed them on his side. A statement often attributed to the CM by his friends was 'I have to deal with the bad elements also. Only a goonda can deal with goondas.'

Factions, then, remained important units whose support had to be sought by a political leader lest it go to an opponent. Kairon, also, like rulers in the past, came up against the jealousy and intense competitiveness of the Jats. He had to cope with their traditional view of life, which saw no complement between an individual's profit and the community's gain. Each Jat concentrated on his own individual profit and gain, an attitude consistent with the lack of a feeling of solidarity among the Jats. Each wanted primarily power over others and a materially good life. As he conceived it, centralization of rule would not help him to achieve these aims.

I consider that before any form of unitary rule can be maintained in the future, some political leader will have to depend not on the forms of organization of the traditional structure but on new social forces; and presumably the structure of the society itself will have to change before such a development can occur. It will perhaps do so when forms of social and political organization cease to be on a vertical, dyadic basis, but are on an associational basis.[8]

I now turn to this problem of the relation of factions to the social structure in Punjab. The support of the faction as a form of social and political organization is clearly economic. Factions in the Punjab would appear to be associated with the pattern of inheritance and disposal of land, the mode of working the land, the prevalence of patron-client relationships, and a lack of permanence in social relationships beyond those established by blood ties between fathers and sons and between brothers. There would seem to be some connexion between the fact that Jat society is loosely structured and the persistence of factions characterized by the vertical links of patronage. Above a Jat and his family there are other Jat families of wealth and power, and he may manage to forge a link with these families through marriage, through the discovery of a previous affinal link, or through joining a faction. The affinal ties significant for political purposes are vertical links, since the affinal ties that are most useful are those to superiors in the polity. A Jat feels that his ability to move upward is not limited. Social mobility often follows on marriage upwards. But upward mobility is also consequent on land seizures. Division of land—consequent on its distribution among his sons—brings downward mobility: no family can conserve the same amount of land in its possession for more than three generations. This perpetuates the use of the faction as a means for social mobility through seizing land. Jats also raise their status (i.e., accumulate more power) through accepting patronage. The patronage system enables each family to manoeuvre to improve its position, and it is flexible enough to allow some to secure help and defence at the required moment. The only meaningful categories of status recognized by the Jats are that some among them are dominant and others are dominated. What characterizes the political system is thus the competition of strong men for bands of followers. Patronage is associated with this: if a Jat is not strong and powerful himself, he seeks the protection or patronage of those who are: and this he usually obtains by joining a faction.

Factions depend on vertical relationships, and where factions are strong, horizontal ties are noticeable by their absence. Thus Jat society is a society with no defined social strata; likewise, caste cannot be said to produce strong groupings, and there are few effective political alignments on the basis of caste. Factionalism is a process dividing society into vertical units, and in the Punjab it occurs in a situation where ties on the basis of village residence, clan, caste and class are weak.

Factionalism is also associated with the mode of working the land. First, the mode of production isolates each Jat family from others[9] and competition over land divides their interests. There is very little familial interdependence except that which is freely chosen. In the rural areas each Jat family is self-sufficient in terms of food production, in irrigation water for crops, and, increasingly, in agricultural implements. There were, however, a number of notable instances of economic co-operation between farmers. One of these was the development of a Cane Growers' Association at Phagwara in 1956–7 (with the encouragement of Partap S. Kairon) to pressurize mill owners to buy their sugar cane from Punjab's farmers and not from Uttar Pradesh.

Second, the patron-client relationships of landowner and tenant, landowner and landless labourer, landowner and peasant proprietor, also militates against the establishment of horizontal ties. But it may be noted that the ultimate consequence of certain of Kairon's economic plans, had they been effectively implemented over a longer period, would have been the breakdown of the economic system that sustained such vertical ties. For example, if the law regarding land 'ceilings' had been fully implemented this would have meant eventually smaller landholdings which farmers would have worked themselves without landless labour and without tenants. The economic system whereby land is worked with the help of landless labourers and tenants is slowly breaking down, however, owing to other factors. Particularly in certain districts of the Punjab, there is a shortage of agricultural labour due to the sons of landless labourers receiving education and moving off the land into skilled posts in the cities. Also, a number of those landless labourers who have migrated overseas and accumulated savings have returned to buy their own land and are now no longer economically dependent on the Jats. Intensive farming in some areas has also caused an acute labour shortage. As these developments affect the entire province, together with increasing mechanization of agriculture, the economic dependence of landless labourers and tenants on those who are the owners of land will disappear and with it the ability of landowners to collect political followings on the basis of ties of economic dependence.

Third, not only vertical relationships of the patronage system but also too affinal ties have the effect of organizing the Jats into multitudes of small isolated units, each of which has no other reason for establishing connexions with another save to serve the purposes of their common political association with the same political leader. Aside from this, there is nothing in the structure that will provide a means for a more continuous form of linkage between different, locally based units of the rural population. It is possible to foresee changes in this pattern as the rural economy of the Punjab becomes more diversified. For example, in the future Doaba (the area between the Beas and Sutlej rivers) could become an area dominantly given up to market gardening, with farmers growing wheat only for their own consumption. It is such developments that will lead to an economic interdependence between the various local areas of the Punjab and perhaps result in a more integrated province.[10] The fundamental feature explaining the continuance of the system is that each family, through an affine, through membership of a faction, has access to the protective relationships that guarantee the maintenance and accumulation of property; no category of persons is deprived in actuality of such protection. As has been adequately illustrated, the maintenance and accumulation of resources depends on access to upward connexions and links and is guaranteed by law only in name. The need for protective relationships therefore remains. The political and social links of a participant in the factionalism with a political leader is therefore rarely exploitative, but functions, at least for a period, as a link of mutual benefit. Politics is a source of enrichment not only for the person holding office but it is also a source of gain to those who co-operate with him as supporters. This situation may be expected to continue until politicians no longer retain their present power to allocate and reallocate resources and to interfere with the functioning of the administration. Political and economic resources are allocated via persons, and not according to rule; hence links with these persons become important. The faction performs important economic functions and, because it does so, allows its members to prevent the depreciation of their family resources and hence maintain their family honour. Not only the families of certain individuals have benefited from this system but, indeed, whole areas owe their economic development to the interest taken in them by political leaders.

Effective safeguards to property ownership, by impartial and meticulous law enforcement, will undoubtedly affect the durability of the support structures of the political system encouraging more stability, but it is questionable whether the factional system itself will change. It is also problematical whether industrial growth can stimulate a change in the pattern of vertical economic and political division in rural society. The development of heavy industry would certainly expand the forms of economic association—classes and trade unions—and with this development the pattern of traditional political associations would certainly undergo change. However, there is little heavy industry in the state and a lack of accumulation of bulk capital. The emphasis has been on the development of small-scale industries, and this trend in industrial growth shows every sign of continuing.[11]

Moreover, many of these small-scale enterprises, such as mills, machine tool shops and transport companies are organized on a co-operative basis where those who are the investors and owners are also the workers. Class loyalties and divisions do not tend to develop in such a situation. A large number of these units are, in addition, family based, and this means that the range and extent of co-operative economic endeavour remains limited. Further, if one takes the example of the two truck combines that have been referred to in this book, it can be seen that factional divisions and alignments had penetrated the transport industry. The change-inducing potential of the type of industrial development proceeding in the Punjab on the traditional political organization is therefore likely to be marginal and factions will remain the typical structures of support for leadership that they are at present.

W. Moore (*Social Change*, pp. 52–3) has argued that where there is a high degree of intensity of personal interaction on a societal basis the spread of change is greater. I would disagree. Radical social change does not take place through the medium of relationships more especially when the individuals that are party to these relationships are, as in the Punjab, among the Jat Sikhs, interdependent of their own choice and for purposes and interests of their own. Moreover, as is noted by M. Argyle ('The social psychology of social change'), the individual who is most likely to put across new ideas for social re-organization is one not too dependent on the affiliative satisfactions provided by his community. This the Jats are; and these connexions are regarded as binding and obligatory as well as satisfying. It also should be noted that for a Jat to be given support from his own community on the basis of his ideas would be extremely rare. He would have to also be a god, respect being given to a man for his personal character, not for his ideas.

The fact that there is no accumulation of *bloc* capital in any particular section of the Jat population is not a factor favouring system maintenance as might be expected. The argument that Jats can never get bitter about their differences because these are not so great and because any equality in wealth that does exist is not institutionalized, does not apply since even minor differences in wealth between families are matters of honour. However, the nature of power, whereby gain of any sort is legitimate only if dispensed and can be maintained only by attendance to the requests of those who ask for favours, *is* an important factor in system maintenance. Resulting from it there is none of the social distance and separation that exists in a stratified society and each family has the wherewithal to maintain its izzat.

As noted frequently throughout the text, the affiliations of Jats are multiple: their connexions and friendships are in all parts of the social structure. These many different kinds of people that are known to a man are known as people, i.e., a person is not reduced to his role as a policeman or an administrative officer. He is always Amar S. or Kartar S. and, as such, is not representative of anything but his own individual self. The patronage system in the Punjab therefore allows for human contact on the scale of the society as such and its values and institutional arrangements protect such contacts.[12] The multiple friendships are associated with the pragmatism of its people, with the primacy they attach to relationships as opposed to principles in the sense that they are concerned that the immediate interests of their own family and of families to whom they are connected in some way be looked after. If such a situation were to arise where faithfulness to one's friends and loyalty to ideas were in conflict, the former would have the power to displace the latter as the focus for concern. Jats can thus never be 'maniacs of a beautiful idea',[13] nor can a Rousseau flourish among them. They would take one look at his manner of conducting his life and before they reached his ideas dismiss him as a deplorably immoral creature. Persons are important and the attachment to principle with all the rigidity that it implies is not a factor in their social and political collaborations. This concern for persons and their interests at any given moment means that through their relationships men are constantly making adjustments to each other in the sense of attending to each other's grievances. One consequence of the existence of multiple ties and their use is that there is no accumulation of hatreds. And thus the factor of gathering and accumulating resentment,[14] so important in European movements for social change, cannot be a significant factor in change in the Punjab.

17 Personal postscript: real people and images

In the last chapter, I explored the practical difficulties affecting the likelihood of structural change within the Sikh Jat community. I did so purely as an academic exercise. Also, however, I had been accustomed to hearing the familiar characterization of patronage systems as 'unjust' and 'corrupt' and I was interested to see whether this was really so. Among the Jats, I found that such a system need not, by its nature, exclude the notion of or practice of equality in human relationships. Thus the question posed on p. 203 as to what would disrupt the present system of socio-political relationships in the rural areas implies no evaluation on my part that change is desirable in the Punjab. Rather the reverse. For, let us say, if A and Z (A and Z being representative of two different categories of people) can be brought together by a network of linkages ramifying through the entire structure of a society, then with the communication that implies and the polarization it evades, there is no reason why those linkages should be destroyed. Inevitably I could not but compare the Punjab cultural context with my own European one. It seemed that in societies characterized by patronage and egalitarianism, as indeed (though to a lesser degree) by patronage and inegalitarianism, a man was never so detached from others that either his concern about them or his hatred for them became an abstraction, i.e., a product of his ideas and values rather than of his interactions. By contrast, the society to which I belonged had achieved precisely that.[1] It is one of the unhappier expressions of our structural complexity that it has fostered enormous distance and lack of communication between individuals. A man is overburdened by the duties and activities attached to his role, 'taken over' by it and characterized accordingly. Only in this sort of system (I believe it is called 'highly differentiated') could the writings of certain philosophers and social and political theorists have had the influence they did. Had they not lived in 'an academic world', socially separate and distant by virtue of their role and their 'specialized knowledge', it is doubtful if they would have been accorded their semi-prophetic status. It was the significance of this development that prompted Benda to write in 1927: 'Our age is indeed the age of the intellectual organization of political hatreds.'[2]

An enormous interest has been shown in altering the social structures of 'underdeveloped' countries. In one of the articles appearing in *Agricultural Development and Economic Growth*, the following quotation appears:[3]

> In thus enabling the individual to feel caught up in the concerns of vast units of humanity outside his kin, the social structures of technologically advanced societies inculcate a width of inter-personal allegiances which is incomprehensible in economically backward societies.

This is an extremely dubious assertion. Responses to or on behalf of specific groups of men in the societies spoken of are responses not to interpersonal allegiances but to the views contained in particular ideologies as to who ought to be shown concern.[4] Marxist political and philosophical thinking, for example, took the collective entity of the people—Comte's *'humanité'* or greater being—to be the unit for which an individual should show concern on a world-wide, non-national basis. This concern should receive its appropriate expression in changing society. And thus Sholokhov in his novel *And Quiet Flows the Don*, gives the final, decisive judgment on Melekhov (the principal character) that he does: 'His own Cossack traditions sucked in with his mother's milk rose above the greater human truth.' In these lines immediate loyalties to family and to community are depreciated; one must suffer the loss of these when they come in conflict with wider human ties. Concern for persons close to one is either displaced or replaced by loyalty to ideals—the ideal in this instance being the good of man in general. Such an abstracted vision of man has no relation to any concrete human person and as Camus, in *The Rebel*, pointedly states, one's concern becomes with humanity in general so as to avoid showing concern with anybody in particular. With the 'good of man' as his ideal thus it has been possible for European man to produce Raskolnikovs many times over and the mentality of a Marat—'Who cannot see that I want to cut off a few heads to save a great number.'—in the hearts and intellects of many. There is thus no irrelevance to the question asked by Scheler (*The Nature of Sympathy*, p. 190), namely, which is more worthy of our consideration and concern—family, nation or humanity? There is much relevance in the answer:

> Assuredly, mankind as a whole is intrinsically more worthy of love than any one nation or country! But it can then no longer be assumed that he who exercises this act of love is specifically human in doing so. For it is already implied of man that in his specific capacity as a bearer of values he can never apprehend the whole of the generic unit to which he belongs with the same adequacy as those partial collective units of which he is necessarily a member.

The 'highly differentiated' 'structurally complex', social structures praised and set up as models in so much sociological literature (Eisenstadt, *Essays on the Sociological Aspects of Political and Economic Development*; 'The continuity of modernization and the development of administration'; Hagen, *On the Theory of Social Change*; Hoselitz, *Sociological Aspects of Economic Growth*; Mc-Clelland, *The Achieving Society*) have merely developed and perfected the organizational procedures in which hatred as well as concern can operate with great ease. Wasn't it the reputed assertion among so many 'kleinburger' Germans that they only obeyed orders and did their duty because they couldn't devolve their *bureaucratic* responsibility further, and thus were coerced by their system into cruelty? The differentiation and specialization so characteristic of the more 'advanced' societies produces as its complement an individual identified with his role rather than with his own human identity. The nature of this structural complexity is not accurately portrayed in the works of the advocates of 'modernization' but is tellingly spoken of by Steiner (in *Bluebeard's Castle*, p. 31):

> Art, intellectual pursuits, the development of the natural sciences, many branches of scholarship flourished in close spatial, temporal proximity to massacre and the death camps. It is the structure and meaning of that proximity which must be looked at.

Part four
Appendices

I Uttar Pradesh Chief Minister's reply to S. Hukam S., Deputy Speaker, Lok Sabha

Lucknow

29 August 1959

My dear Sardar Sahib

Kindly refer to your DO letter of the 20th instant complaining about the expression 'Rai Singh and other Sikh' in our Uttar Pradesh Public Land (Eviction and Recovery of Rent and Damages) Bill, 1959. It is true that this expression had crept into the Bill as originally drafted but it was realized at once that the phraseology was unfortunate. It was, therefore, changed to 'Rai Sikhs, Jat Sikhs, Virk Sikhs, and Kamboh Sikhs, who were classified as criminal tribes in the erstwhile Punjab'. The present wording is a bare statement of fact, and does not cast any reflection on the Sikh community as a whole. The Minister of Revenue also made it clear in his speech that no aspersion was sought to be cast on any other section of Sikhs.

You have raised the question as to what will happen to these people if they are ousted from the land now in their occupation. I am hardly in a position to answer this question fully. Some of these people are in lawful possession of land. There is no intention of taking these lands away from them. We have stretched law a little and allowed those who had no strong legal claim but were in possession on the strength of some kind of an oral commitment made by someone in authority at some time in the past to remain. But the great majority of these men did not come to us under any arrangement with the Government of India as refugees looked after by the Rehabilitation Dept. have done. They infiltrated into the State uninvited and in many cases have absolutely no right to the land which they are occupying. We cannot be held responsible for them, particularly when we have on our lands a large population within the State itself which is absolutely landless. It would be too much for us to grant priority to these trespassers. We had written to the Punjab Govt. to provide for them but to no purpose. The Govt. of

India also expressed its inability to do anything in the matter, as a recent correspondence has shown. The Rajasthan Govt., may be able to absorb a few some time next year. That is about all. We must clearly disown any responsibilities for providing these men with land. This will be unfair to the State.

I trust the situation is quite clear to you now.

Yours sincerely,
Sd.
Sampurnanand

Sardar Hukam Singh
Dy. Speaker, Lok Sabha,
New Delhi

II Regional formula

Following prolonged negotiation between Mr Nehru and other government and Congress leaders on the one hand and representatives of the Akali Dal on the other, an agreement was reached early in March [1956] on the reorganization of the Punjab, PEPSU and Himachal Pradesh, and approved on 11 March by the General Council of the Akali Dal. The main provisions of the agreement, which represented a compromise between the Hindu demand for the union of all three states in a Greater Punjab and the Akali Sikhs' demand for a separate Punjabi-speaking state, were as follows:

1 The Punjab and PEPSU should be merged in a single bilingual state with a common governor, ministry, legislature, public service commission and high court. The predominantly Hindu state of Himachal Pradesh would provisionally become a Union territory.

2 For the transaction of government business with regard to certain specified matters the state would be divided into two regions, one Hindi-speaking and the other Punjabi-speaking.

3 For each region there would be a regional committee of the Punjab State Assembly consisting of members of the Assembly, including the ministers belonging to the region, but excluding the Chief Minister.

4 Legislation regarding the specified matters would be referred to the regional committees, who could also make legislative proposals to the state government. Advice tendered by the regional committees would normally be accepted by the government and the state legislature, but in the event of difference of opinion the matter would be referred to the governor, whose decision would be final and binding.

5 The regional committees would deal *inter alia* with development and economic planning (within the framework of general development plans formulated by the state legislature), local

221

government, public health, primary and secondary education, agriculture, cottage and small-scale industries, livestock, fisheries, co-operative societies and charitable and religious institutions.

6   The demarcation of the Hindi and Punjabi regions would be carried out in consultation with the state government and other interests concerned.

7   Both Punjabi and Hindi would be recognized as official languages of the state. At district level and below, the official language of each region would be the regional language. The state government would set up two separate departments for promoting the Punjabi and Hindi languages. The proposals contained in the State Reorganization Bill were unanimously approved by the PEPSU legislative assembly on 22 March.

III   Jawaharlal Nehru's speeches*

(i) **Extracts from a speech in Parliament, New Delhi, 7 July 1952:**

... We must give the topmost priority to the development of a sense of unity in India. ... Any decision that might come in the way of that unity should be delayed till we have laid a strong foundation for it. ... It is infinitely better even if it takes a little more time to form linguistic provinces only when the goodwill and consent of all concerned are forthcoming. ...

(ii) **Part of a speech on emotional integration delivered at Bangalore on 6 October 1955:**

The main thing we have to keep in mind is the emotional integration of India. ... Political integration has already taken place to some extent, but what I am after is something much deeper than that— an emotional integration of the Indian people so that we might be welded into one and made into one strong national unit, maintaining at the same time all our wonderful diversity. I do not want this diversity to be regimented and taken away but we must be wary of losing ourselves in 'petty quarrels'.

(iii) **Part of a speech made during the debate on the report of the States Reorganization Commission:**

There may be things which are more important and we must not lose ourselves in passionate excitement over the boundary of a State. ... This question of language has somehow come to be associated with the question of states re-organization. I repeat that I attach the greatest importance to language but I refuse to associate it necessarily with a state.

* Ministry of Information and Broadcasting, Government of India. *Jawaharlal Nehru's Speeches.*

223

IV Note by Dr Gursham S., Dean, College of Agriculture, Ludhiana, on Kairon's role in setting up the university

Shri Partap Singh Kairon took over as Development Minister and Minister in Charge of Agriculture in the year 1952. His very first act on taking over as Minister of Agriculture was to take some active steps for the starting of an Agricultural College and Research Institute on this side of Punjab at some well centrally located place. This certainly needed some decision with determination, as in a democratic set-up every MLA feels that his is by far the best constituency for starting any educational institution. Shri Kairon gave a practical shape to this proposition, once and for all, by deciding that the location of this college be at Ludhiana, which was not only a centrally located place but also, more or less, represented a uniform region. It was with his persistent efforts and active interest that an area of about 500 acres was allotted to begin with at the present site. Necessary funds were also provided for starting a building and the present college building was taken up in the year 1956 and the college moved into it in 1958. Although by about this time Shri Kairon had taken over as Chief Minister, he continued to take a personal interest in the welfare and development of this institution, which in a way owed its very existence to him. Whereas in the beginning instruction was being imparted up to BSc level only, it was felt that in view of the vast expanding requirements for well trained agricultural graduates, starting of postgraduate classes leading to at least Master's degree in agriculture was a dire necessity. Shri Kairon, in his capacity as Chief Minister, not only gladly responded to such a request but here again made all the necessary funds available so that the postgraduate classes could be started with the minimum possible time. Such classes were taken up on regular basis in the year 1959.

The great part played by Shri Kairon in the establishment of Punjab Agricultural University will remain a landmark for the establishment of any such institution in this country.

It may not be out of place to mention that this state, like any other state, had inherited the British system of running of Agriculture Departments, where the Director of Agriculture, a technically trained man, was the chief executive. Under him were three different main activities, namely, teaching, research and extension, including services and supplies. The formation of the agricultural universities envisaged the transfer of a greater portion of these activities to these universities. Such a gesture was certainly not appreciated by those in power at the Directorate of Agriculture level. It was through the sheer initiative and bold steps taken by the then Chief Minister, Mr Kairon, that the Act of Punjab Agricultural University was framed, exactly in accordance with the recommendations made by the government of India, in the year 1961. Even after the enactment of this Act interested parties continued to do their best to see that the university should not get exactly what was listed there in the Act. But here again, Mr Kairon made it a point to see that there was no diversion from what was already indicated in the said Act. According-ing to schedule, the Agricultural University came into existence within about a year of the passing of this Act, where again Mr Kairon played a prominent part. It would not have been surprising that even with the passage of this Act the formation of such a university may have dragged on and on, but for Mr Kairon, who had it initiated in time.

Mr Kairon took personal interest in selecting Shri P. N. Thapar, ics, an able administrator and an experienced organizer, to be the first vice-chancellor. It was, in fact, on a personal request from Mr Kairon that Shri P. N. Thapar agreed to give up a very high post in the government of India, and to take over as the chief executive of this university.

This university started with a total outlay of Rs. 80 lacs. Shri P. N. Thapar, the vice-chancellor, felt that, to give a shape to the university of the kind that each one of us wanted to have, this amount was hardly sufficient to meet the bare needs. The Chinese aggression in September 1952 turned out to be a blessing in disguise, at least to the Punjab Agricultural University, in as much as that with the starting of this aggression a heavy cut was imposed on all the plan schemes throughout the state but, with the cessation of hostilities, the cuts were restored. The vice-chancellor of the Punjab Agricultural University lost no time to impress upon Shri Kairon that this could be a good occasion to give some additional funds to this university from the overall third plan of the state. Shri Kairon responded to this request very frankly in as much as that an additional sum of Rs. 1.75 crores was allocated over and above the initial amount of Rs. 80 lacs already earmarked for this university.

V Figures indicating the rate of progress in the Punjab in the period 1950–65

	1950–1	1960–1	1963–4	1964–5
Consolidation of land in *lakh* acres	1.44	147.28	209.72	218.40
Electrification of towns and villages	91	3,016	4,932	5,225
Metalled road mileage	3,239	6,313	7,250	7,600
Hospitals and dispensaries	765	1,051	1,073	1,077
Industries and registered factories	1,486	4,709	4,776	5,145

Figures supplied by the Punjab Public Relations Department.

During the Kairon era, co-operation was established with various overseas firms, for which the CM himself was either directly or indirectly responsible—a sanitary ware factory at Bahadurgarh, near Patiala, in collaboration with a British firm; Nestlé International at Moga in District Ferozepur, the arrangement for which had been made in 1954 while he was Development Minister and for which construction started in 1956; an Indo-Swiss training centre in precision tools at Chandigarh in 1964; the arrangement for the Pfizer–Dumex antibiotic plant in 1960.

VI   Extracts from notes on charges brought against S. Partap S. Kairon

1. Certain charges were brought against Sardar Partap Singh Kairon, Chief Minister of the Punjab. These charges were communicated to Sardar Partap Singh, who has sent his replies and explanations. We have given the most careful thought to this matter, as it related to a person in the high and responsible position of a Chief Minister of a state and to his administration. We have repeatedly laid stress in Congress resolutions and our directions on the maintenance of high standards and conventions in public life and administration, and it is from this point of view that we have to consider any charges that might be made. It is also our duty to protect persons in high and responsible positions from harassment and unfair charges.

2. It is necessary to bear in mind the background of the Punjab and of the Congress party there during the past year, as well as the relationship of the groups and parties involved. Even since the last general election there has been continuous agitation in the Punjab and there has at the same time been an inner conflict in the Congress party. Certain elements in the state started what is known as the Hindi agitation against the regional formula. The Arya Samaj, as well as some communal Hindu organizations, supported this agitation and large numbers of persons committed breaches of the law and were arrested. The Akalis also carried on a counter-agitation, though this was more restrained at this time, as the Punjab government itself was opposing the Hindi agitation. The Punjab thus became a battleground of communal forces and the whole atmosphere of the state was vitiated. The government had to deal with a very difficult situation.

3. During this period of continuing crises, a number of Congress members of the legislature withheld their full support from the government and some even encouraged the forces which were attacking government. Some very regrettable incidents took place in the course of this agitation. Sardar Partap Singh faced this serious

228

situation with courage and determination. Though the Chief Minister was not personally responsible for the regrettable incidents referred to above, they resulted in adding to the communal bitterness in the state and were utilized for the purpose of attacking the Chief Minister. Sardar Partap Singh emerged from this long trial of strength with credit and with enhanced reputation so far as the administration was concerned

4. The charges under investigation have been put forward by some members of the Congress party of the Punjab legislature, and the leader of this group is Shri Prabodh Chandra. It is the well-known fact that after a brief period of initial support he has been opposed to Sardar Partap Singh and has sought to get him removed from the Chief Ministership. A group gathered round him and something in the nature of a vendetta was carried on against the Chief Minister. The Congress party in the Assembly became a scene of unseemly conflicts between rival groups. Repeated efforts were made to put an end to this rivalry and conflict, but they did not succeed. An atmosphere was thus created which encouraged the group opposed to the Chief Minister to put forward all kinds of charges.

5. Sardar Partap Singh's reputation during his long career of public service has been that of a man of personal integrity and of complete freedom from communal bias. He is a man of the people, simple in his life and devoting his great energy to the work for which he was responsible. His very virtues to some extent became his defects. His constant tours, more especially in the rural areas, led to a lesser degree of time and interest being given to the normal work of administration, and his anxiety to deal with problems on the spot and with speed led sometimes to his by-passing normal administrative procedures.

6. This has been the broad background of the Punjab during the past year, and no government there has had an easy time. The people are virile and hard-working and full of vitality; the peasantry are tough, capable and resourceful; the city people are also full of initiative. Some of the best engineers and mechanics come from Punjab. The very vitality of the people spills over sometimes into conflict and there is a tendency to create factions, which is reflected in the political life of the Punjab. The police, which is efficient, have played an important part in the state. Because of the tough elements in the population, the police had developed some rough-and-ready methods which were equally tough. On some occasions some action

of the police during the past year or two appeared to us to be improper, and the attention of the Chief Minister was drawn to it. The Chief Minister dealt with the situation in his own informal way, which was not always in keeping with normal administrative methods. This procedure is not to be commended and, in the long run, it is bound to produce difficult situations, even though it leads to immediate results.

7. There are in all twenty-five charges preferred against the Chief Minister. They can be divided into three categories:

    (i) charges insinuating corruption;

    (ii) charges alleging misuse of powers in the interest of his family or friends;

    (iii) charges alleging irregularities in the administration.

8. Some of the charges in the third category have not been considered fully, as they are the subject matter of pending proceedings in court or are under investigation otherwise.

9. In regard to charges in category (i), that is, relating to some kind of corruption, none of them have been substantiated, and some have been completely disproved. We regret that serious charges of this kind should be casually brought without any justification.

10. In the second category are charges relating to some action taken in the interest of the family or others connected with him. In the main, these relate to the by-passing of normal administrative machinery by ordering the withdrawal of a case and the non-suspension of a public servant arrested by the Customs authorities for smuggling. We are of the opinion that some of these charges are established in the sense that improprieties were committed. Sardar Partap Singh has told us that he was ignorant of what had been done either by some relative of his or some other person. It may well be that owing to the heavy burden he carried and his working at high pressure he could not keep in touch with these matters or could not pay much attention to them. Normally we cannot consider him responsible for the failings of some members of his family, but a person in his high position cannot rid himself of such responsibility. . . .

16. We have referred briefly above to the various charges against Sardar Partap Singh Kairon and indicated our views in regard to them. We have, in fact, considered these charges very fully separately. As a result of our investigation, we have come to the conclusion that

there is no basis at all for any corruption; that in some of the charges relating to his family members or others associated with him, certain improprieties were committed; while Sardar Partap Singh might not have personally been aware of these, a person in his position must be deemed to be constructively responsible; and that there were certain procedural irregularities in administrative matters. 17. We have discussed all these matters fully with Sardar Partap Singh. In regard to some of the matters relating to his family or the administration, he has told us that he had no personal knowledge, and so the replies he has given are really the replies supplied to him by the persons more intimately concerned. He spoke to us frankly and fully in regard to all these matters and has offered to resign from his high office, should this be considered necessary. It is not for us, however, in view of all the circumstances and the view we have expressed above, to accept or reject this offer of resignation. It is for the Congress party in the legislature to indicate in the normal way whether they have confidence in him as Chief Minister or not. An early meeting of the party should therefore be held for this purpose.

(SHRIMAN NARAYAN)
General Secretary All India Congress
Committee and Secretary
Central Parliamentary Board
(1952–8).

19 May 1958

VII Details of votes polled to Rarewala and Beant S. in Payal Assembly constituency

		SGS Rarewala (Congress)	Beant S. (Akali)
1	Khera	153	243
2	Pohir	306	294
3	Nanakpur Jagera	222	182
4	Lehra	252	224
5	Jhamat	286	215
6	Buthari	476	275
7	Khatra Churharmi	191	169
8	Khatra Bhikki	280	160
9	Hens I	379	282
10	Hens II	295	129
11	Kular	273	227
12	Siar I	441	156
13	Siar II	416	126
14	Saharon Majra	380	326
15	Dhaul Kalan	363	418
16	Lehal I	350	171
17	Lehal II	273	169
18	Kuli Kalan	378	246
19	Chomo	366	218
20	Ber Kalan	322	284
21	Maloud I	597	243
22	Maloud II	371	330
23	Ramgarh Sardarn I	277	292
24	Ramgarh Sardarn II	447	309
25	Sohian	372	326
26	Sekha	172	199
27	Siahan Daud I	92	185
28	Siahan Daud II	295	51
29	Dudhal	369	266
30	Rabbon Unchi	430	209
31	Lassara Lakhowas	403	242
32	Nizampur	195	230
33	Sirthala	339	238
34	Bhurthla Randhawa	227	514
35	Rauni I	232	355

36	Rauni II	352	363
37	Hoal	371	372
38	Jarg I	231	285
39	Jargari	576	335
40	Jarg II	338	189
41	Jandali	238	201
42	Sihora I	395	263
43	Sihora II	423	270
44	Dhamot I	341	145
45	Dhamot II	423	131
46	Dhamot III	278	119
47	Ghudhani Khurd	320	337
48	Ghudhani Kalan I	352	439
49	Ghudhani Kalan II	224	588
50	Ghaloti I	463	285
51	Ghaloti II	343	348
52	Ghangas	282	350
53	Kathari	346	298
54	Lapran	234	267
55	Bilaspur	202	539
56	Gidhari	293	321
57	Daborji	—	—
58	Ajnaud	315	208
59	Bowani	464	264
60	Rajgarh	307	420
61	Doraha Pind	340	147
62	Doraha I	362	258
63	Doraha II	355	320
64	Doraha III	420	310
65	Jaipura	387	469
66	Kaddon	471	427
67	Barmalipur	299	248
68	Shah Pur	349	460
69	Maksudra I	360	109
70	Maksudra II	454	137
71	Payal I	470	391
72	Payal II	415	315
73	Majri	224	253

It can be seen from this table that twenty-three of the seventy-three polling stations were won by Beant S. of the Kairon faction.

VIII   References to cases tried in court

Channan S. murder case	Appeal against sentence passed by the Additional Sessions Judge, Patiala (February 1965) High Court of Punjab.
Hazara S. murder case	(October 1958) Sessions Court, Patiala.
R. P. Kapur – Partap S. Kairon	(1961) All India Reporter, Supreme Court.
R. P. Kapur – the state of Punjab	(1960) All India Reporter, Supreme Court.
Karnal murder case	Garewal's memorial of the events leading up to his trial and also containing extracts from the judgment of the court case (1960), presented to the President of India in a letter appealing for reinstatement in the IAS.
Kartar Kaur murder case	(December 1965) Sessions Court, Patiala.
Piara S. murder case	Criminal Appeal no. 344 of 1964; High Court of Punjab.
Sirdar Nishan S. and others – the state through Shri Ram Piara	(1964) Court of the Sessions Judge, Meerut.
State of Punjab (appellant) – D. S. Garewal	(1960) Circuit Bench of the Punjab High Court, Delhi.
The State – Gurmel S. Jagpal S. Dangal S. Harchand S.	(August 1964) Sessions Case no. 52, Sessions Court, Patiala.

Notes

1 Introduction

1 East Punjab has one of the best networks of road transport within India, with more than a thousand vehicles of the state-owned Punjab Roadways covering a mileage of 110,000 miles per day. The mileage covered by private operators has to be added to this.

2 Very few modern anthropological accounts focus on this. It is mentioned by G. H. Almond and V. S. Coleman in *The Politics of Developing Areas* (p. 154), who briefly note that northern India as such has 'strong linguistic, cultural and military ties to Central Asia and the Middle East'.

3 West Punjab retained the important canals and 70 per cent of the fertile canal-irrigated tracts of the undivided province, with their revenue. East Punjab was left with 34 per cent of the total area and 20 per cent of the irrigated area.

4 It was indeed as recognition of the common cultural heritage of its people irrespective of religious community that a Pakistan Embassy official once remarked to a Sikh political leader during negotiations to allow more Sikhs to visit Nankana Sahib (the birthplace of Nanak, the founder of the Sikh religion): 'He was born with us. Only you have taken him over.'

5 This point is noted, although it is not developed upon, by L. W. Hazelhurst (in *Entrepreneurship and the Merchant Castes in a Punjab City*) who, quoting from P. Tandon, *Punjabi Century 1857–1957*, states that the caste structure is weak among Hindus.

6 As a modern novelist has so concisely put it (L. Durrell, *The Spirit of Place*, p. 156): 'the important determinant of any culture is after all— the spirit of place' and '. . . a Spain, an Italy, a Greece, will always give you the same type of culture—will express itself through the human being just as it does through its wild flowers'.

7 Generally the limit was not in excess of sixty ordinary acres but it was raised to eighty ordinary acres in the case of the drier and less intensively irrigated zones of southern Punjab.

8 Yields in some irrigated areas must now be more than twice as high as at the time when this evaluation was introduced, that is, if the food grain production can be used as an indication. In Ludhiana district, in the Central Punjab, where I did my fieldwork, in 1950–1 only 162,700 tons of food grains were produced, while the figure for 1964–5 was 459,700 tons (figures from Punjab Public Relations Department,

Ludhiana marches ahead). Ludhiana was, along with the other two districts of Central Punjab, Amritsar and Jullundur, the most intensively irrigated zone.

9 Punjab Public Relations Department, *Facts about Punjab*, p. 1.
10 One-third was the proportion calculated by the 1961 census.
11 Figures mentioned in a debate in the Upper House of Parliament in September, 1969.
12 These are: Amritsar, Jullundur, Ludhiana, Ferozepur, Bhatinda, Sangrur, Patiala, Gurdaspur, Hoshiarpur, Kapurthala and Ambala.

2 Perspective on community studies

1 H. E. Barstow, *Handbooks for the Indian Army: the Sikhs*, p. 196.
2 J. Cutileiro (in *A Portuguese Rural Society*), with specific reference to south-eastern Portugal.
3 A. Weingrod, with reference to Sardinia ('Patrons, patronage and political parties', pp. 387–400).
4 J. Pitt Rivers (*The People of the Sierra*) states that proximity is a social bond in Spain: 'The nation is an agglomeration of . . . communities founded each upon a territorial basis.' (p. 209.) Cutileiro notes that in Portugal, neighbourhood is not determined by proximity but by equality of status. He gives the example that a latifundist's land may be close to the land of a small proprietor but he will not regard that man as his neighbour. However, latifundists, where their lands adjoin, regard themselves as neighbours.
5 E. Friedl ('The role of kinship', pp. 30–8) notes the extensive use of kin in northern Greece and that members of the 'élite' would be one's own relatives.
6 This can be contrasted with Portugal where class rather than kinship is the key determinant of relationships. A statement recorded by Cutileiro evidences this: 'The Manager of one of the freguesia's [administrative area] wealthiest latifundists told me that he was a distant cousin of his employer's. "But I would not dare tell him so," he added.'
7 F. G. Bailey, *Politics and Social Change*. The book is the only other significant attempt by a social anthropologist to describe the system of interactions of a state political system in India.
8 Ibid., pp. 221–2.
9 C. Morrison, 'Dispute in Dhara', thesis, p. 31.
10 Ibid., p. 2.
11 H. J. Izmirlian, *Caste, Kin and Politics in a Village*, p. 5.
12 J. H. Steward, 'Area research'.
13 M. N. Srinivas, *Caste in Modern India*, p. 134.
14 'Empiricism has engendered so many different ideas. . . . If we look for common factors in these diverse approaches we find a central idea: the function of cognitive mechanisms is to submit to reality, copying its features as much as possible.'
15 J. G. Kennedy, 'Peasant society and the image of limited good'.

3 Significant events in Jat history

1 *Singh* means literally a lion and metaphorically connotes physical bravery. Rajputs commonly attach it to their names and so do Hindu Jats.

2 *Kaur* means princess.

3 See, for example, the legend of Mirza and Sahiban, *The Legends of the Punjab*, vol. 3.

4 Many of the utterances attributed to Guru Nanak facilitated the unity of Jats who were both Hindu and Muslim as well as Sikh; for example, the statement '*na ko Hindu hai na ko Musalaman hai* (there is neither Hindu nor Musalaman)'. Likewise his teachings, which laid little stress on formal outward religious observance. (See W. H. McLeod, *Guru Nanak and the Sikh Religion*, pp. 208–19.)

5 The Jat upsurge in the Punjab occurred at the same period (i.e., the sixteenth century) as the revolt of the Mahrattas under Shivaji and the rebellion of the Jats in the Agra-Mathura area. The only difference, as I. Habib notes (*The Agrarian System of Moghul India*, pp. 137–41), was that its cementing bond was religious community and not caste. All three revolts he indicates as being the consequence of the oppression of the peasants by the Moghul rulers and the disaffection of the zamindars (landlords) with imperial rule.

6 W. H. McLeod, in *The Evolution of the Sikh Community*, notes the influence of the dominant Jat component among the Sikhs on the ideology and religious institutions of Sikhism.

7 H. R. Gupta, *A History of the Sikhs*, vol. 3, pp. 33–4: 'The overflowing energy of the Sikhs was not spent so much in expanding their territories as in their civil warfare.' Except in the early stages 'this period was not one of conflict between the Sikhs and Musalmans, as the latter had been subdued; but of Sikh against Sikh, Sirdar against Sirdar, and misl against misl'.

8 In presenting this account, I am aware of the unsatisfactory state of eighteenth-century historical studies of the Punjab and of the unreliability of the English sources. Of this period, W. H. McLeod notes (*Guru Nanak and the Sikh Religion*, p. 2): 'The period of almost one hundred years which intervenes between the death of Guru Govind Singh and the emergence of Ranjit Singh is an obscure one. The broad outline of Sikh military and political activity is known and has been recorded many times but much remains to be done in terms of an analysis of the military and political activity.'

9 The word *misl* is from an Arabic word which means 'likeness'. J. D. Cunningham (*A History of the Sikhs*, p. 69, n. 1) notes also that in India the term *misl* has generally denoted anything that was placed in ranks.

10 The more prominent and larger of the misls were the Bhangis, Kanheyas, Ramgarhias, Ahluwalias and Sukerchakias.

11 'Each was intensely jealous of the other and even a soldier considered himself the equal to a chief of high rank' (H. R. Gupta, *A History of the Sikhs*, vol. 2, p. 16). 'In the country of the Punjab from the Indus to

the banks of the Jumna,' a Mohammedan observer noted, 'there are thousands of chiefs in the Sikh community and none obeys the other. If a person owns two or three horses he boasts of being a chief and gets ready to fight against thousands. When a village is besieged by the Sikhs to realise tribute which the zamindars cannot afford they intrigue with other Sikhs and the Sikhs begin to fight among themselves.' (Quoted ibid., vol. 2, pp. 19–20.)

12 Ibid., vol. 1, p. 315.
13 At that time the territory of Sirhind extended from the Jumna river in the east to Bahawalpur state in the west and from the Sutlej river in the north to the environs of Delhi in the south.
14 Jassa S. Ramgarhia was not a Jat but a carpenter (Tarkhan).
15 Jassa S. Ahluwalia was similarly not a Jat but a Kalal. The Kalals were originally hereditary distillers. Jassa S. adopted the title of Ahluwalia from the name of his ancestral village and it is generally used now by all Sikh Kalals.

4 Patterns of allegiance I

1 H. R. Gupta, *A History of the Sikhs*, vol. 1, p. 17, n. 2.
2 Ibid., vol. 1, p. 103, n. 2.
3 Ibid., vol. 1, p. 305, n. 1.
4 The census now provides no figures on a caste basis and hence the present number of Sikh Jats cannot be given. In 1931, when the Sikh population numbered 4,071,624, the number of Jats was 2,133,152. (*Census*, 1931, vol. 17, *Punjab*, part I, 'Report by Khan Ahmed Hasan Khan'.)
5 It is said (K. R. Quanungo, *History of the Jats*, pp. 2–4) that by virtue of their physique 'they belong to the same ethnic group as the Rajput ... the stature is mostly tall, complexion fair, head long, nose narrow and prominent'. This view holds that the Jats are degraded Rajputs and that by practising widow remarriage, allowing their women to work, and also by tilling the land with their own hands they lost caste and were considered by the Rajputs as socially inferior. Another view holds that the Jats came from Asia Minor and Armenia in the successive invasions during the period 600 BC to AD 600.
6 There are many exceptions to this rule but by and large it is followed.
7 The rule of exogamy is not always adhered to; Garewals, who are a large clan, intermarry with one another. A. H. Bingley, in *Sikhs*, mentions that some clans do not intermarry with each other, since they claim common descent.
8 There were twenty-one major clans in Ludhiana district, of which the fieldwork area was a part. The following figures indicate the size of the more prominent and largest clans in 1911: Garewal, 15,112; Gill, 9,367; Sidhu, 8,249; Sandhus, 3,243; Maan, 3,522; Dhillon, 3,286; Chahal, 4,538.
9 This differs from the pattern found among the Hindu Jats of Meerut Division in north-west Uttar Pradesh (see M. C. Pradhan, *The Political*

System of the Jats of Northern India), where each clan is associated with a definite geographical area. Clans were formerly much more important than at present. When the Jats migrated to the Punjab, for example, those who settled to the west of the fieldwork area, where the imperial authority was weak, settled in clans. Thus Garewals to this day have a group of seventy-five villages in the south of Ludhiana and Gills have a group of villages in the Jagraon tehsil of Ludhiana district and in the adjoining parts of Ferozepur district. This clustering, however, was not typical and a variety of clans in any one area and in any one village was the rule. Although the leadership of a misl remained in the hands of a particular family from a particular clan, it cannot be reliably ascertained that their followers were of the same clan.

10 A village, for census purposes, is defined as an area for which a separate record of rights exists, which has a population of under 5,000, and which is separately listed for revenue purposes.

11 Also it is not meaningful, on a Punjab-wide basis, to distinguish strata on the basis of the amount of land owned, since the average land acreages owned by these three categories vary between different areas.

12 According to an article in *Advance* (June–September 1967), the magazine of the Public Relations Department, Punjab, 65 per cent of peasant proprietors had under fifteen acres.

13 The number per 1,000 workers engaged in their traditional occupation, according to the 1931 census, was 843 for the Jats; this was the highest incidence.

14 These persons had already generally risen to positions that were higher than that which a Mazhbi normally attained. In three cases I know of the persons concerned were MLAs.

15 Mazhbis were the caste that stuck to their traditional occupation the least, according to the 1931 census. Only 176 out of 1,000 were engaged in shoe-making.

16 There were, of course, exceptions. For example, some Jat MLAs who were friends with Mazhbi MLAs, would dine with the latter at their houses.

17 L. Dumont, *Homo Hierarchicus*, chapter 3.

18 D. G. Mandelbaum, *Society in India*, p. 217.

19 Most of the social anthropological literature on India relates to caste and hence to its two most characteristic features: inequality and hierarchy based on ritual position. G. D. Berreman ('The study of caste ranking', pp. 115–29) suggests that 'the system of interaction is to a large extent the hierarchy'. A. C. Mayer notes various empirical evidences of the principle of hierarchy ('Some hierarchical aspects of caste') in eating, smoking and drinking relationships, and in occupations.

20 For further discussion of these concepts see pp. 56–9.

21 H. J. Izmirlian, *Caste, Kin and Politics in a Village*, p. 29.

22 A. C. Mayer, *Caste and Kinship in Central India*, p. 3.

5 Patterns of allegiance II—Sikh Jat families

1 From p. 5 of the third of three papers ('Social organization in a pathan district') given at School of Oriental and African Studies and entitled 'Women and honour' by Audrey Boorne.

2 Formerly this shortage of women was spoken of as being the combined result of the polygyny of men from richer families and the practice of female infanticide among small landholders.

3 L. H. Griffin (*The Law of Inheritance to Chiefships* . . .) notes that *karewa* was, at the time of writing, a very common occurrence. Stating (p. 43) that 'supersession of the widow was the rule and her succession the exception', he gives as a reason that the succession of a woman to an estate left it a prey to the powerful. It would seem more appropriate to say 'left her a prey to the powerful', and hence the family honour.

4 Under customary law, daughters were excluded from inheriting any share of the ancestral property (*jadii zamiin*). A daughter was entitled to be maintained while she was unmarried, and to be married at the expense of her father or whosoever held the ancestral land. On completion of her marriage she was transferred to her husband's household and became dependent on him and his land for support. Sons shared equally in ancestral property. This arrangement for equal inheritance was termed *bhaiband* or *pagvand*. In the past there had sometimes been an equal division of land among the mothers and not among their sons. Thus if a man had four children, one of whom only was from one wife while three others were from a second wife, according to *chutavand* the single son of the first wife would receive half the estate and his three half-brothers would each receive one-sixth (i.e. a house property system). A few families also practised the custom of *Haq sardari*, or primogeniture. But the first custom of dividing the land was the most usual.

5 Control of credit relationships in one village leading to the acquisition of wealth on the part of the landlord allowed the latter to dispose of it to powerful affines involved in the factionalism of the Doraha–Payal–Sirhind area, who required help in litigation.

6 The situation to which this proverb refers is, of course, the invasions, when the rural population was frequently plundered of its possessions, while there was also no point in keeping stored away what they had managed to save from destruction at those times, as it was likely to be seized by a neighbouring chief or in tax. Even today one can note that there is no attempt to preserve possessions from generation to generation.

7 *Izzat* was attached to landholding, and to sell one's land was not honourable. It was attached to certain occupations, for example the military service and the administrative service; it also covered a multitude of rules concerning the behaviour expected of men in relation to women, and vice versa, which I do not elaborate here.

8 The area continues to be without peace. I returned to Doraha in 1970, and during my two-and-a-half-year absence there had been four murders.

6 The structure of coalitions—factions at all levels

1 P. R. Brass, *Factional Politics in an Indian State*, p. 244.
2 Ibid., p. 238.
3 P. Friedrich ('The legitimacy of a cacique' in M. J. Swartz, *Local-Level Politics*, pp. 243–69), concentrating on the activities of the political middlemen in southwestern Mexico over a period of forty years and not restricting his observations to a village, indicates that his data may suggest 'important qualifications to the currently developing theories of factionalism' (p. 258).
4 B. Benedict, 'Factionalism in Mauritian villages', *British Journal of Sociology*, 8, 1957, pp. 328-42.
5 D. F. Pocock, 'The bases of faction in Gujerat', *British Journal of Sociology*, 8, 1957, p. 296.
6 See A. Sindler, *Huey Long's Louisiana*.
7 D. F. Pocock, 'The bases of faction in Gujerat', *British Journal of Sociology*, 8, 1957, p. 296.
8 B. Benedict, 'Factionalism in Mauritian villages', *British Journal of Sociology*, 8, 1957, pp. 337, 338, 340.
9 Morris, 'Communal rivalry among Indians in Uganda', *British Journal of Sociology*, 8, 1957, p. 306.
10 R. W. Nicholas, 'Factions: a comparative analysis', in M. Banton, *Political Systems and the Distribution of Power*, Association of Social Anthropologists, Monograph 2, 1965, p. 30.
11 A. C. Mayer, 'Factions in Fiji Indian rural settlements', *British Journal of Sociology*, 8, 1957, pp. 323, 325, 327 respectively.
12 Nicholas's own field data were on a Govindapur village in the deltaic area of West Bengal: article in M. Banton, *Political Systems and the Distribution of Power*, p. 45. The above statement, however, has to be modified with respect to factions whose persistence is due to their being representative of stable social classes with opposed interests and distinct political attitudes. The factions discussed by Sindler in the state of Louisiana, which recruit their supporters on the basis of class interests and political ideology, are an example.
13 F. G. Bailey, *Stratagems and Spoils*, p. 52.
14 R. W. Firth, 'Introduction' to 'Factions in Indian and overseas Indian societies', *British Journal of Sociology*, 8, 1957, p. 292.
15 Ibid., pp. 292 and 294.
16 See A. C. Mayer, 'The significance of quasi-groups in the study of complex societies', p. 116.
17 F. G. Bailey, *Politics and Social Change*, pp. 143–54, and A. C. Mayer, 'The significance of quasi-groups in the study of complex societies', p. 114.
18 A. C. Mayer, 'The significance of quasi-groups in the study of complex societies'.
19 A. Sindler (*Huey Long's Louisiana*) similarly concludes for Louisiana state politics that the bi-factional system is stronger than personal loyalties to a leader. In Louisiana the factions represent class interests

and definite ideological programmes. The durability of the factional system in the Punjab is due to other factors, which are made explicit in the latter half of this chapter and in chapter 16.

20 Thus Shastri '. . . opposed Nehru's reluctance to dismiss Kairon as CM of the Punjab' as quoted in M. Brecher, *Succession in India*, p. 243, n. 28.

21 A similar system appears to be operative in the state of Uttar Pradesh, as is indicated by B. D. Graham in his article 'The succession of factional systems in the Uttar Pradesh Congress party, 1937–66' in M. J. Swartz, *Local-level Politics* (pp. 323–60). Referring to a faction leader in Uttar Pradesh on pp. 330 and 342, he speaks of the support provided him by faction leaders from different parts of the province with their personal followings, and mentions how the same faction leader had allied himself with minor factions in the various local areas of the state.

7 Vertical links of a state leader with a national leader

1 Under the rule of Maharajah Ranjit S., when Sikhs achieved supremacy in the Punjab in an area stretching from the Khyber Pass to the Sutlej river, and northwards into the Ladakh area of Tibet, the term 'Khalsa' had a strictly secular meaning. It referred to the kingdom of the Maharajah, and to the Sikhs who inhabited that stretch of territory. Customarily, however, the 'Khalsa', as well as meaning the existing government of the Sikhs, has also had a more mystical meaning, implying that superior government under whose protection the community lives.

2 Egerton, for example, records that when the British took the Punjab 'the Sikh population were soldiers almost to a man'. (D. C. Ibbetson, *Outlines of Punjab Ethnography*, p. 139.)

3 This persecution is regarded by the Sikhs as being religious persecution, but it clearly was not. Their fifth guru was tortured to death for refusing to pay tax levied on him for aiding the Emperor Jahangir's son (Prince Khusrau) in a rebellion; the seventh guru became a political partisan of the eldest son of the Emperor Shah Jehan (Dara Shikoh), while Tegh Bahadur, the ninth guru, was put to death because, according to J. D. Cunningham (*A History of the Sikhs*, p. 67) 'his power was interfering with the prosperity of the country'.

4 There have been innumerable recognitions of this fact; for example, the inscription on Banda's seal in 1710: '*Degh tegh fateh nusrat i bedrang; yaft az Nanak Guru Gobind Singh* [through hospitality and the sword unending victory granted by Nanak and Guru Gobind Singh].' Similarly, an inscription on the sword of the ex-rulers of Nahba is '*Badhe degh te yaa tegh tee* [a man becomes great by ready patronage for the needy or by taking to arms].' It is significant that a langar used to be attached to the household of each Sikh chief.

5 It is held that the Sikhs have preserved and will continue to preserve their separateness through these symbols and that they constitute a

substantial part of the meaning of being Sikh. It is felt that the reason why Sikhs can now claim to be identified with no other empirical community is that they wear these symbols. 'Community', as a visible entity on the ground, is held to exist only so long as it can be denoted by the group of people wearing turbans, steel bracelets, etc., and having uncut hair. Once a Sikh discards these symbols, it is held, he discards his cultural tradition. Hindus and Sikhs alike then assume that he is non-Sikh, or, if they knew he once wore a turban, etc., they will classify him as a Hindu believing in Sikhism.

6 I make no reference to the abundant literature on the partition period in view of the fact that this section of chapter 7 is only designed to provide background material for understanding the nature of the link between the Prime Minister and Kairon.

7 In the undivided Punjab, Muslims constituted 57 per cent of the total population in 1941.

8 Baldev S. had capital in other states of the Union, while his constituency was in Punjab (Rupar)—'He wanted both his capital and his constituency to be in the same country.' (From a conversation with an advocate prominent in the Akali Dal and associated in 1946–7 with the All-India Sikh Students' Federation.)

9 It is said that Lord Wavell offered a Sikh state to Master Tara S. and that the offer was repeated by Churchill when S. Baldev S. visited England. This opinion was current among those active in the All-India Sikh Students' Federation at the time.

10 In Lyallpur canal colony, for example, the Sikhs had owned 80 per cent of the land and in Shahpur almost as much.

11 Source: an advocate in the Akali Dal at that time prominent in the All-India Sikh Students' Federation.

12 'In the past there had been a splendid police force to deal with disturbances . . . but they had ceased to be fully reliable from the moment that our impending departure from India had been announced. Until then, the Indian policeman had seldom hesitated to act against his co-religionists. He knew that if he did his duty he would be supported by higher authority. . . . But soon the British would no longer have the power either to reward or to punish; and it was only natural that the policeman should not be willing to compromise himself with his new masters.' (*The Memoirs of General the Lord Ismay*, pp. 414–15.)

13 P. Moon (*Divide and Quit*, p. 279) notes the resolve of the Akali leaders 'to ensure the survival of the Sikhs as a compact community' by expelling Muslims from East Punjab so as to accommodate those fleeing from West Punjab.

14 Information from an interview with Mohan S. Nagoke.

15 Note on the Sikh Plan, Government of Pakistan, 1948.

16 The states of Patiala, Jind, Nabha, Kapurthala, Faridkot and Kalsia, together these states constituted PEPSU.

17 It was said to be an act of discrimination against the Sikhs and it was rightly pointed out that the whole trend and pattern of Congress resolutions up to 1947 had been in favour of the setting up of linguistic

provinces. For example, (i) 'if a province has to educate itself and do its daily work through the medium of its own language, it must necessarily be a linguistic area' (Nehru Committee report, 1928, p. 62); and (ii) 'the main purpose of the creation of linguistic states is that the culture, language and script of the minorities shall be preserved' (Congress resolution, 1937). In 1953, however, the States Reorganization Commission came to the conclusion that because Punjabi and Hindi were so akin to each other and were understood by all sections of the state's population there was no real problem on a language basis at all.

18 This was approximately the area from Ambala city to the border with Pakistan. The area beyond Ambala down to Delhi, now the state of Hariana, had always been Hindi-speaking and was detached from the present province of Punjab in 1966. It was to the urban Hindus from the Punjabi-speaking region that the States Reorganization Commission of 1953 was referring when it said that Punjabi Suba was opposed by large sections of the population who spoke that language.

19 Speech in Parliament of Rajagopalacharia as quoted from the memorandum submitted to the States Reorganization Committee by the Shiromani Akali Dal, p. 6.

20 This allegation was made by Sant Fateh Singh, a prominent leader of the Akali Dal, as quoted in A. S. Bhudiraja, *Facts about Punjabi Suba* Shiromani Akali Dal, 1965, p. 3.

21 For further information on the Sikh community's sense of discrimination and on the demand for a Punjabi-speaking province, see B. R. Nayar, *Minority Politics in the Punjab*, chapters 1–3.

22 See 'Apostasies of Sikh officers', *Spokesman*, 4 February 1953.

23 'But discrimination is made against the Sikhs, who are treated as Hindus for the purposes of all other laws. This is the only law for the purposes of which the Sikhs are treated as different from the Hindus. It is quite clear that this is a part of the clever move of reabsorbing the Sikhs into Hinduism. As a result of this discrimination more than 200,000 Sikhs of the Scheduled Castes have been recently absorbed into Hinduism in UP alone. The Sikh population in UP, according to the census of 1941, was about 233,000 and according to the census of 1951 the population has dwindled to 192,000. Ordinarily it should have increased as the result of natural growth and the immigration of thousands of Sikh refugees from West Punjab.' (Speech of Master Tara S. as quoted in *Tribune*, 20 August 1953.)

24 See Appendix I.

25 The private view of an Akali Dal leader was that the issue had been exacerbated by the dispute of a certain settler in the Terai area with a particular UP Congress MLA over a piece of land. The UP government successfully used it as a pretext to dislodge some of the Sikhs. The Akali Dal transferred the incident onto the level of discrimination against the Sikh community as a whole. Undoubtedly individual cases of discrimination did occur.

26 This distrust expressed itself once again in November 1966, when on

the concession of the demand for a Punjabi-speaking state, key economic projects and economic resources were included within the boundaries of other states, notably Hariana and Himachal Pradesh while the state capital of Punjab, Chandigarh, became Union territory.

27 '... previous to this Kairon had been made President of the State Congress only to ... deceive and hoodwink the Sikh masses into the belief that the said organisation was nationalistic.' (*Spokesman*, editorial, 5 March 1952.)

28 In May 1966. The same point was also stressed by a former Home Minister in one of the Kairon cabinets.

29 Information from a former Home Minister associated with Kairon.

30 Information gathered from a source close to a former CM.

31 Information from a former Deputy Speaker in the Vidhan Sabha.

32 For the full text of the regional formula, see Appendix II.

33 Candidates at that time fought on a joint Congress-cum-Akali ticket except in two constituencies: Lahore West and Patti, where each put up their own separate candidates.

34 The scope of this study—which aims solely at providing the data thought to be necessary for understanding his relations with a particular faction in a particular local area—prevents me from detailing Kairon's role in all spheres. It is pertinent to note, for example, that figures show Punjab as progressing at a rapid rate from 1952 onwards, when Kairon became Development Minister, a progress which was very marked during his period of tenure in the office of CM (1956–64); see Appendix V. But I concentrate on how his support in the rural areas of the province was built up.

35 This had been earlier noted by the States Reorganization Committee of 1953, which found that large sections of the population in Punjab who spoke Punjabi (i.e., the Hindus of the Punjabi-speaking region) were opposed to the formation of a Punjabi-speaking state. The report mentioned that there was really no language problem in Punjab, as Punjabi and Hindi were well understood by all sections of the people in the state.

36 30 May 1957, as quoted in *Tribune*, 2 June 1957.

37 This period in the history of the relationship between the Akali Dal and the Congress party is a subject in itself, and as a fuller account would involve an interruption of the narrative I here merely indicate the sources for my statement. These were chiefly conversations held with members of the Working Committee of the Akali Dal, members of the SGPC and a number of High Court lawyers prominent in the Akali party in the period August 1966 to January 1967. Above all, I am indebted to Jai Inder S., the former president of Amritsar District Congress Committee (Urban) for much of the supporting data for this statement. The latter was one of Kairon's lieutenants in Amritsar district and more than anyone else was responsible for the breaking of the 1960 *morcha*. Certain documents that I obtained from the late Master Tara S. and certain discussions that I had with some of his lieutenants also led me to the same conclusion.

38 See Appendix III.
39 Most of the benefits went to the Jats, not solely because Kairon was partial to them but because the bias of the policies of the central government was to develop rural areas. In the rural areas of Punjab, Jats controlled the institutions through which such aid was channelled. A review of the work done by the Punjab Vidhan Sabha during the years 1957–62 reveals that most of the development projects related to rural areas.
40 1960–1 Budget; plan head: Agricultural production.
41 It was remarked to me confidentially by an officer in the Department of Public Relations in May 1967 that not a single village had been electrified since Kairon's resignation. This same officer also mentioned that the number of small industrial units on Kairon's resignation was 15,000; and that it was still 15,000.
42 See Appendix IV.
43 Statement at a press conference in Chandigarh on 25 May 1960.
44 As quoted in Department of Public Relations, *Stronger Punjab through Unity, not Turmoil*, p. 13.
45 Equally, however, the position of the Punjab, between Pakistan and China, was a major factor influencing the central government's decision to concede the demand for a Punjabi-speaking state.
46 Statement at a press conference in Chandigarh on 25 May 1960.
47 Of the officers recruited during the Chinese emergency of 1962, 80 per cent were Sikh. (Source: various officers of the armed forces. The figure may be exaggerated.)
48 He arranged for one *lakh* acres of land to be granted for Punjabi soldiers in the states of Rajasthan and Madhya Pradesh. (As quoted in the address delivered by the Governor of Punjab on 18 February 1963.)
49 In this connexion Kairon liberalized the policy on state loans. He is also said to have got more than the normal amount of raw material at the disposal of the central government allotted to the Punjab. Of the industrial training institutes which were part of an all-India centrally-sponsored scheme of which the government of India shared the expenditure to an extent of 60 per cent, Kairon on his own initiative, out of the state funds, had a number of others installed in the Punjab. He gave a maintenance allowance to 60 per cent of the trainees at a rate of forty rupees per month, whereas the government was committed to provide only one-third of the trainees with twenty-five rupees per month. (Information from the Director, Industrial Training Department, January 1966.)
50 The Prime Minister, as quoted in Department of Public Relations, *Towards Wider Horizons, Nobler Goals*, pp. 35 and 36.
51 'It seems that you think there is no other influential and strong man than Mr Kairon and that he commands a clear majority in the Assembly as well as in the PPCC [Punjab Provincial Congress Committee]. This may be true to some extent. But has anybody ever tried to think as to how he secured this majority? He misused his vast powers as CM for establishing and consolidating his group. He would

not have been so strong even after using all such means, had your expression of opinion about him not created an impression in the minds of congressmen that he was not going to be dislodged as the supreme leader of the nation was at his back . . .' (Part of a letter from an ex-CM of Punjab to the Prime Minister.)
52 For a fuller statement of this report see Appendix VI.
53 As quoted in R. S. Bhattia, *Quami Ekta.*
54 The Vidhan Sabha report (p. 11) sums up these men as being 'a small but very determined group of opponents ever anxious to find fault with him and ever ready to strike grievous blows to destroy his reputation and shatter his career'.
55 Summary of the opposition to Partap S. Kairon, Vidhan Sabha report, p. 10.
56 Partap S.'s friend from his student days in America, the late Dr Anup S., member of the Upper House of Parliament, implicated certain persons in the Home Ministry.

8 The relationships of the Chief Minister at state level

1 Vallabhai Patel had dominated the organization of the Indian National Congress. He had been Deputy Prime Minister in the period 1948–51.
2 Cf. Patel's statement as quoted in *Tribune*, 7 October 1950: 'When democracy itself has a rather unsteady existence, opposition also becomes a drag and a drawback—we have to build so many things that we have hardly any time for mutual fault-finding. . . . I cannot see any prospect of a rival organisation [to Congress] for the next ten to fifteen years. This is to the good of the country.'
3 Certain newspaper commentaries at the time of the report of the All-India Congress Committee's enquiry in 1958 into charges of mal-administration on the part of the CM clearly stated that Kairon was playing on Nehru's fear of the effects of communalism in order to establish complete and total dominance in the state: 'It would not be surprising if the Congress Parliamentary Board's condoning of "procedural irregularities" in the administration was also secured by representing that the suspensions and supersessions of officials were a necessary precaution against violation of the sanctity of the newly acquired freedom from communal bias of the Punjab Congress under the aegis of Sardar Partap S. Kairon.' (Extract from 'Verdict on Punjab', *Tribune*, 23 May 1958.)
4 The sister of the former Chief Justice A. N. Bhandari was implicated in a court case. This is said to have been done with a view to bringing pressure on the then Chief Justice in whose court certain election matters, in which the CM was personally interested, were pending. It is said it was given to Bhandari to understand that he had to support the CM. This, in fact, he was regarded as doing when he cancelled the bail application of a high administrative officer, R. P. Kapur. And Kapur also was a relative of Bhandari's (Bhandari's sister was Kapur's mother-in-law). (Source: (i) 'An open letter to the President of India

and an appeal by the Members of Parliament' signed A. Ghani Dhar, MP, 12 September 1963, and (ii) Chairman of the Praja Socialist Party, Punjab. Both, it is fair to mention, were resolute opponents of Partap S. Kairon. (iii) Criminal Revision No. 1402, of 1962. Allahabad High Court.)

5 Thus one Ram Piara, the then MLA for Karnal, who alleged he was beaten up by Kairon's supporters in Karnal itself in 1963 for being a vociferous opponent of the CM in the Vidhan Sabha, insisted that his case be transferred to a court outside the Punjab for investigation as he claimed the Punjab High Court could be influenced by the CM, who was inimical to him. (See S. Nishan S. and others v. the State through Ram Piara. Criminal Revision No 167 of 1964. Court of the Sessions Judge Meerut.)

6 Kairon is said to have himself attempted to influence S. D. Singh: the latter's younger brother was public prosecutor at Ambala when Garewal was being tried in Delhi. S. D. Singh was not subordinate to the Punjab government but it has been alleged that Kairon summoned his younger brother, who was, and told him that his services would be terminated were his elder brother to decide the case in favour of Garewal. (Information from a friend of S. D. Singh's younger brother.)

7 Information from the Registrar, High Court of Punjab, January 1966.

8 Defending himself against criticisms that he interfered in the administration too frequently and explaining his action at a later period, he said: 'Severe action was taken against erring officials because I knew that delay was the root cause of corruption. It is absolutely necessary in a democracy that the people get that to which they are entitled promptly and expeditiously without undergoing the humiliating process of laying themselves prostrate before an impervious bureaucratic machinery.' (From a written statement by Partap S. Kairon entitled 'I and my Accusers', given to me by the then President of the Punjab Provincial Congress Committee.)

9 The most notable examples of this were (i) Ranjit S., who was made SP of district Amritsar, superseding innumerable others; and (ii) P. N. Sahni, who in the joint Punjab had been an ordinary inspector in the Transport Department, and who, while Kairon was CM, became general manager in charge of government transport and was brought into the IAS service in recognition of his special ability. (Information from a former private secretary of Kairon.)

10 Officers were always under the control of the CM, and this situation was merely intensified in Kairon's period of rule.

11 A notorious example was that of Ram Singh, who was deputy inspector general of police at Ambala at the time of the Garewal case. On this occasion he made full use of his position to ingratiate himself with the CM. Even though Ram Singh had sent a message of congratulation to Garewal on the liquidation of the criminals and confirmed that they had been killed in an encounter, in the witness box he spoke against Garewal and said that actually they had been murdered by him. The

following strictures were passed on him by the judge: 'The high police officers, Chaudhri Ram Singh included . . . appear to have believed that they would be pleasing the cm and thereby serving their own ends if they went out of their way and arranged false and fabricated evidence which might somehow secure the conviction of the accused, particularly D. S. Garewal.' (Judgment, Karnal murder case, p. 854.)

12 As quoted in the Calcutta newspaper *The Statesman*, 24 February 1965.
13 In June 1957 R. P. Kapur, the Commissioner, Ambala Division, had sold a piece of land to one M. L. Sethi, a lawyer, who was a friend of the cm. Later Sethi alleged that Kapur had fraudulently concealed from him that proceedings were pending for the purchase of his land by the government, and he took a complaint to Kairon on 10 December 1958. Seven months afterwards no further action had been taken on the complaint lodged by Sethi. It had been filed at a time when Garewal was being tried and the cm was trying to pressurize Kapur to give evidence for the prosecution in this case. The complaint which Sethi had lodged was therefore kept pending to give Kapur time to think over his position. Only when Kapur did not prove amenable was the inspector-general of police directed to commence the investigation against Kapur. Had he acted as a prosecution witness in the Karnal murder case, the case concerning his financial misrepresentation to Sethi would have been quietly dropped. (All India Reporter, Supreme Court, 1960 and 1961.)
14 P. 157, Partap S. Kairon, 'I and my Accusers' (see note 8).
15 Ibid., pp. 26-7.
16 Kairon made the Punjab civil service of equivalent status to the ias and gave new selection grades to various officers in the ias. He preferred to depend on them because they were appointed by the state.
17 I give some examples: (i) S. Mohan S., who came from a village in Kairon's constituency and who had been a consistent member of the Congress party from 1936 and who always saw to it that the majority of the votes of his village went to Kairon; (ii) Jathedar Mohan S.— Kairon wanted to accommodate him, as he had brought two votes in favour of Kairon in the 'no confidence' motion against the latter in June 1958, after he had lost his seat in the elections of 1962; (iii) Gorakh Nath, a veteran Congressman and loyal supporter of Kairon in district Gurdaspur, who also had lost his Assembly seat; (iv) Anup S., an extremely loyal friend of Kairon's since the latter's student days in America, who was made Chairman of the Public Services Commission; (v) Atma S., who had been a co-worker of Kairon's in the National movement.
18 For example, Kairon was responsible for the location in Punjab of one of India's three Hindustan machine tools factories. Under this scheme land and power had to be provided by the state government. Kairon took the initiative and informed Nehru that power, water supplies and land would be arranged within three days.
19 Political considerations were clearly present in the disposal of loans and in the giving of quotas (steel, copper, glass, etc.). Loans were not

given to political opponents as it would have merely made the opposition stronger, economically. It is alleged by a former member of the Jan Sangh (the Hindu communal organization) that the denial of industrial development to whole areas was used as a means of penalizing them. Rohtak city is pointed out as an example of this: it is said that there was no industrial progress in the region because it always returned a candidate from the Jan Sangh. Supporters were given small industrial units on a rental basis, with the rent adjusted to the cost of construction of the concern: the units were the property of those operating them.

20 His motto was, 'You work for Punjab, I'll work for you.' Patronage, however, did not imply the return of a very secure support unless bolstered by the requisite sanctions. Immediately prior to the 1962 elections it is reported that Kairon called a meeting of Ludhiana's industrialists in which, commenting on a lack of enthusiasm in their support, he said, 'It is I who have built up the industry and if necessary I will demolish it with a bulldozer. Do remember that.'

9 The Kairon–Rarewala rivalry

1 This indeed became the basis in 1953 for a split in the Akali Dal. Certain leaders representative of the small proprietors inside PEPSU held that Master Tara S. was co-operating with feudal elements.

2 In fact the law and order situation remained unchanged. Rarewala was a minimum of eleven months in office, during which period forty-seven outlaws were eliminated. Rao was Adviser in PEPSU for six or seven months, and thirty-two outlaws were eliminated. (*Spokesman*, 29 July 1953.)

3 'Development was not a mere economic programme it was a philosophy evolved to create a new social order. Realizing that agriculture was the bedrock of prosperity, agrarian reforms received the most urgent attention at my hands. I knew that these reforms would annoy vested feudal interests—the rajas, the big landlords. But land must belong to the tiller and intermediaries must be eliminated. Being a man of the soil myself, I realized that unless the tenant enjoyed a security of tenure, agriculture could not be revolutionized because the element of personal participation would be absent; modern farming would not be possible unless the age-old evil of fragmentation of holdings was eliminated. It is a measure of legitimate pride that . . . 623,794 tenants have been raised to the status of landowners in an area of 1,762,829 acres. As a result of the imposition of a ceiling on landholdings . . . by the middle of 1963 an area of 412,513 standard acres had been declared surplus, an achievement which has won the appreciation of the Planning Commission. But this levelling process upset quite a few . . . big landlords.' (Partap S. Kairon's own statement.)

4 Rarewala's position was not a unique one. Many Sikh leaders in the Congress party were with the Congress solely because it was the party then in power. Their hearts were with the Akali Dal's political demands, and their antipathies against Congress leaders persisted. In the

February 1969 mid-term elections, Rarewala fought as an Akali Dal candidate.
5 Rattan S.'s wife and General Mohan S.'s wife were sisters.

10 The general nature of factional rivalries in rural areas

1 Figures given by Ludhiana Tehsil Office.
2 The average landholding of a farmer in the West Punjab was much higher than that of a farmer in the East Punjab. East Punjab was also smaller in area than West Punjab. Hence, with the influx of refugees after partition, the amount of land allotted to each refugee farmer could only be a proportion of what he had held in the West Punjab. Owners of ten acres had to part with 25 per cent of their area; owners of between ten and thirty acres experienced a 30 per cent cut, while owners of 500 acres and more lost 95 per cent of their land.
3 For example, such basic commodities as cement, paraffin, oil and sugar.
4 It was also not until November 1966 that power-driven pumps and agricultural sprayers were delicensed.
5 The word *dacoit* was, of course, used very freely in ordinary conversation in Punjab, especially in a derogatory manner, to cast aspersions on opponents. When the word was used in this sense it clearly implied roughness and lawlessness.

11 Factional participants in the local area

1 This comment was made with reference to a village in Taiwan and discussed in a paper 'Political factionalism and its impact on Chinese village school organization in Taiwan' in M. J. Swartz, *Local-Level Politics*, pp. 377–99.
2 The grim evidence is fully recorded in the Shiromani Gurudwara Parbhandhak Committee publication, *Muslim League Attack on Sikhs and Hindus*, Amritsar, 1950. The incitement to murder continued after Pakistan had achieved independence, as can be witnessed by the last line of an incendiary poem printed in the 5 September issue of the *Daily Zamindar*, Lahore, namely '*Koii Sikh rehna na pae Maghribi Punjab men*' ('Let no Sikh be allowed to remain in West Punjab').
3 I discuss these and other internal divisions in the Rarewala faction later in this chapter.
4 The sho or station house officer is in charge of the police station that covers a subdivision of a district.
5 The following were the assets of Balwant S.: the owner of sixty lorries, he was managing director of the Patiala Bus Service, Sirhind; of the Indian Motor Transport Company, Karnal; of the Fatehgarh Bus Service, Sirhind; he was also director and partner in a large mechanized farm between Sirhind and Gobindgarh, as well as a managing director with Gurbachan S. of Patiala Goods Booking Agency, Delhi and Bombay. Gurbachan S. and Malkeet S. were managing directors of

Malerkotla Bus Service and Dasmesh Transport Company, Ludhiana.
6 See chapter 14.
7 See chapters 12 and 15.
8 By the summer of 1968 the family had acquired a further 400 acres of land in Uttar Pradesh.
9 Santokh S. regarded him as useless and used to dismiss him by saying bluntly, 'He drinks too much.'
10 Gurnam S. again became CM in February 1969.
11 He won this seat against Gian S. Rarewala in February 1969.
12 The same inspector general who is mentioned on p. 166.
13 I do not think one should underplay the personal ambition of Kulwant S. Those who were not interested in local area and state politics used their outside links only to preserve their power in the village. Kulwant S., however, was using his links to rise to power over an area.
14 The family was 'izzat-centred'. After an attempt on the life of Kulwant S. in the main bazaar of the city of Ludhiana in 1964, Jagmohan S., his brother, had remarked (according to a close friend of the family): 'I always warned him to take more care. It will be a disgrace to our family if he is killed. Sometime I think I should finish him off myself. Why should I let our enemies do it?'
15 Bhag S. had been, as was noted earlier, a lieutenant in the INA, with which General Mohan S. himself had been associated. Kulwant S. and the general had been friendly since 1957. It was alleged by a member of the Rarewala faction that the general had an interest in helping Kulwant S.'s family retain the land that they seized in 1957, as he received, at each harvest, a half share of the produce. This allegation, however, may be only one of the many typical expressions of factional enmity.
16 His actual statement was 'The electorate is not such a fool' (interview in April 1967). This statement does not imply that the electorate played a significant role in determining a local area leader's choices. Kairon was dead. Accordingly, his faction had also lost some of their prestige and its leaders in the local area had to foster their support carefully. During Kairon's period of rule, lack of electoral support did not pose a threat to the CM so long as the leaders in the local area remained attached to him and were able to commit a following from the village.
17 I mean here a rather unpolished man who would not, for example, be acceptable in the homes of the urban middle class.
18 I have shown that Ajmer S., Sham S., Balwant S., etc., had risen to their intermediary positions in the same way. What they had done had paid off: Sham S. had trucks in Bihar; Ajmer S., keeping out of litigations, had two of his sons at university; and one of Gurbachan S.'s sons had done an engineering degree course in England.

12 Vertical links between leaders of the faction in the local area and those at state level

1 Whereas the data presented on ties between local leaders within both the Kairon and Rarewala factions is equivalent in amount, the quantity of data I can present on the vertical linkages within the Rarewala faction is sparse. This is due to the fact that I was related by marriage to the leading family of the Kairon faction.

2 S. M. Rai, *The Partition of the Punjab*, p. 94: 'The government issued a circular to the district magistrates to prepare lists of persons who participated in killing, arson and loot. The officers were also instructed to recover the looted property from the local people, so that it could be distributed among the refugees. But this order was not carried out, for a number of reasons. Officials were themselves involved in it and an honest implementation of the order would perhaps have led to the collapse of the whole administration. Speaking on the subject Mr Prabodh Chandra said: "I do not know how far the killing of Muslims by the Hindus and Sikhs was considered a step in the right direction; but the fact this should happen . . . [yet] under the garb of this circular the poor people will be made the scapegoats and all the officers and men of influence including goondas who were the recipient of the booty will be shielded." '

3 At this stage it is pertinent to note the opinion of P. Moon (*Divide and Quit*, p. 261): 'In some of the Princely States of East Punjab, notably Patiala Kapurthala and Faridkot, the slaughter of Muslims had been particularly high.'

4 Evidence for Hardev S.'s motives comes from Santokh S. and from Ajmer S. and Dr Gurdarshan S. The latter were both members of Rarewala's faction.

5 'People called Avtar S.'s sons the Kairon of the ilaaqa [local area].' (Statement made in Kartar Kaur murder case.)

6 See the court case on Hazara S.'s murder, October 1958.

7 See chapters 13 and 15.

8 Ibid.

9 Written statement of Santokh S.'s lawyer. See also p. 192.

10 The general's own testimony.

11 The officer was posted to the Punjab Armed Police and was given a promotion. Police officers, if especially rough on the public, always tended to get posted to the Punjab Armed Police.

12 Elaborating on this to me, Rarewala said: 'These atrocious people [i.e., Kulwant S. and his brothers] even came and stood outside my house in Chandigarh with their guns.'

13 The 1960 SGPC elections and their results have already been referred to in chapter 7.

14 From a personal interview.

15 The sources of this information are from a number of lawyers conversant with the case; the facts they gave me were confirmed in a talk with the sub-editor of *Tribune* (Ambala).

16 To provide Klaire's action with a context, an indication may be given
here of the kind of power a CM had over an administrative officer and
the kind of pressure under which an administrative officer was placed
when he fell foul of the CM. In this connexion I quote the example of
D. S. Garewal, to whom I have already had occasion to refer in
chapter 8. In a letter to the President of India, Garewal remarks that
he was demoted from his position as SP Karnal to that of an assistant
sub-inspector of police because he had incurred the CM's displeasure
(he had in fact disobeyed the CM's orders). A high CID official (the same
CID official who was enquiry officer in the Rarewala tube well case)
was sent to Garewal's previous place of posting to make enquiries into
certain malpractices alleged to have been committed by him. 'This
was done on the strength of an anonymous letter which was not only
inspired but despatched' by this CID official himself 'to get an excuse
to start an enquiry. This was an opportunity to enable this officer to
fabricate evidence against me to arm the CM to secure my dismissal. . . .
Due to the fabrication of false cases and worries, my health completely broke down. All medical facilities were denied to me in the
Punjab and no doctor was willing to attend on me [for fear of the CM
and not because Kairon himself requested them to behave in this
manner].' (These facts are taken from Garewal's memorial about
his trial as contained in his request to the president for reinstate-
ment.)
17 For the basis of their enmity, which was, in effect, the background to
Kulwant S.'s request for protection, see chapter 13.
18 This story was very reluctantly told to me by General Mohan S.
Because of Milkha S.'s known connexion with Rarewala and Balwant
S. the terms 'Sirdar of Chandigarh' and 'Sirdar of Sirhind' referred,
according to the general, to Rarewala and Balwant S. respectively.
19 The sum of 75,000 rupees was collected at the rate of 200 rupees per
truck owner. It was said by a lawyer attached to the Ludhiana district
court, however, that this money was obtained from Balwant S. by
threats to involve him in court cases. Another opinion is that the
money was given with a view to obliging the CM.
20 Department of Public Relations, *Towards Wider Horizons, Nobler
Goals*.
21 After the 1962 elections, for example, a number of villages that were
pro-Rarewala were detached at the CM's instance from the then
constituency of Doraha. The names of the villages were Rampur,
Kuba, Begowal, Haraich, Khera, Mehdudan, Lal Kiilan, Niilon and
Lopan Bollala.
22 Testimony of General Mohan S., Santokh S. and lawyers in the
district courts, Ludhiana.
23 Information from Santokh S. and a former SHO, now in the CID.
24 High court writ petition.
25 It was categorically asserted by one of Kairon's chief lieutenants in
Amritsar district that Hardev S.'s murder was a political murder.
26 It can be noted here that Kulwant S.'s lawyer, a man of singularly sober

and unexpansive temperament, certainly not prone to exaggeration, remarked that they were 'very thick with Surinder'.

27 The small number of mills then in existence—there were only seven in Punjab as a whole—meant that the total quantity of sugar produced by the farmers of any given area could not be absorbed. In Payal constituency only Kulwant S.'s family and the family of Gian S. Rarewala had their sugar taken on this particular occasion.

28 A typical act of Satnam S.'s, for example, was to keep the car of the superintending engineer for a month at a time. He would not be ordered to return it, and state officials would therefore assume (and probably the act was designed to make them assume this in the first place) that he was so close to Kairon that he might possibly be able to obtain favourable promotions and transfers for them.

29 His actual remark concerning Kairon was said in a tone of despair, '*Thak gaia*', i.e., 'He's worn out', and, by implication, 'Of what use can an exhausted man be to me?'

30 This was not a remote possibility as the United Front government was very unstable and there were innumerable crossings of the floor. The government actually did fall in November 1967.

31 These are the words of Lieutenant Bhag S.

32 This link was not such as would allow Santokh S. to take any extreme step such as murdering any important member of the opposing faction. Joginder S. Maan was an extremely close friend of the Maharajah of Patiala. That Santokh S. chose to move into such a system of ties can only reflect how desperate he was for links in the situation following the death of Kairon. Maan was otherwise also associated with persons who were pro-Rarewala. For Santokh S. this was a political tie-up that was purely situational, following on the death of Kairon, when, owing to lack of a single strong patron, he needed several weaker ones. Santokh S.'s alliances at this time may, in their nature and purpose, be compared with those of Ala S. in chapter 3.

33 The various local level leaders knew one another; for example, Satnam S. was on very friendly terms with Kairon's men in Karnal district.

34 Information given by a CID officer attached to neither of the factions.

35 See chapter 15.

36 Kulwant S.'s eldest son.

37 High court report: 'Application for the Cancellation of Bail' of members of the opposing faction.

13 The factional attachments of village participants

1 Under bathai a landowner rents out a proportion of his land to a peasant family, who work that land for him and who give him a share of the produce at harvest time as rent.

2 Information regarding the basis of their enmity is taken from Criminal Appeal No 344.

3 This incident was widely reported by several sources.

4 Criminal Appeal No 344 of 1964, high court of Punjab.

5 Information from a police informant attached to the district courts, Patiala, and from a lawyer in Ludhiana.
6 These were Santokh S.'s words. It presumably meant that he did something for them that benefited them in some way. A friend, in the Punjab, is one to whom one can turn for help and who is duty bound to give that help.
7 See chapter 11.
8 Santokh S.'s words.
9 Santokh S.'s words.
10 See chapter 12.
11 The father of Karam S.'s wife's sister-in-law, for example. Karam S. also said (Hazara S. murder case, October 1958) that a brother-in-law of his who was an uncle of Milkha S. had appeared as a prosecution witness. Two associates of Harnam S. from the village of Dhanipur and from the same village in West Punjab were also prosecution witnesses in the murder case.
12 They later murdered the widow because they heard she was going to sell the land to another man from Kulwant S.'s village of Dhanipur.
13 Those attaching themselves to the Kairon faction from the villages of Barmalipur and Jargari (mentioned earlier) had definitely had the idea in their minds that they would 'pull the big men down'.

14 Relationships between village participants and local area leaders

1 To give only one example, Gurbachan S.'s sister was married into the family of the vice-chairman of Doraha block samiti.
2 The function of the gram sewak is to educate the villagers in the use of sanitation, manure pits and other aspects of development.
3 For example, the letter of one Rattan S., dated 21.4.53 and addressed to the Adviser in PEPSU states: 'I am a headman of village Haraich and was also a member of the small town committee, Doraha. During the general elections S. Gian S. Rarewala exerted direct and indirect pressure on me to cast my vote in his favour, but I did not yield to this pressure and cast my vote in favour of the Congress candidate. ... Rarewala got my removal from the membership of the small town committee through the DC Fatehgarh Sahib, who is a close relative of his. ... I was never informed of any charges under which I was removed from membership. Secondly, a file to remove me from lambardarship of my village was started. ...'
4 *Bhog*, in common usage, means any Sikh religious service at which reading of the Sikh scriptures is concluded by the singing of the Ardas and the distribution of pershad.
5 This was Lieutenant Bhag S.'s comment regarding Kulwant S. and his brothers.
6 According to Criminal Appeal No 344, this happened in the court case which Gian S. of Jhabbowal instituted against Santokh S. for the alleged beating up of Gian S.'s servant (see chapter 13).
7 This happened, for example, in Ashok Ram's case.

15 Factions in competition

1 Details from Hazara S. murder case, October 1958.
2 Similarly, Kulwant S.'s land was kept with the help of General Mohan S.
3 High Court of Punjab, Criminal Appeal No 344 of 1964.
4 Details from Hazara S. murder case, October 1958.
5 These are Santokh S.'s words. Quoting the latter: 'At the place where we were keeping him captive, we served him his food on his hands [i.e., not as an equal]. Gian S. had once insulted me, saying "You are not a *nadir* [emperor] that you can claim these three thousand rupees [this was the amount outstanding for the bus: see p. 169]." For this we beat him. He had sixty lathi marks on his legs and feet.'
6 For example, one man of Payal, a refugee, had joined in the attempt to beat up Karam S. because the latter had been a witness against his uncle in a court case regarding the distillation of illicit liquor.
7 Letter to the Home Minister, 1964.
8 P. 122 of the appeal made on 8 February 1965 against the sentence passed by the additional sessions judge, Patiala, on 29 January, in the trial for Channan S.'s murder.
9 It is said that the general was on friendly terms with the judge of the high court who heard the appeal in the trial for Hardev S.'s murder.
10 Those accused were the son of Karam S., two relatives of Balwant S. of Lassowal, and Milkha S.
11 'His real name is Kartar S., son of Hari S., resident of village Bhari, District Ludhiana. His real relation with Rattan S. Rarewala whose son he is now called was that Rattan S.'s wife was the sister of Hari S., real father of Gian S. . . . While he was at City High School, Patiala, his name was changed to Gian S., son of Rattan S., with the help of Rattan S.'s daughter, who was married to the late His Highness Bhupindra S., father of the present Maharajah of Patiala. Rattan S. in fact had no son and this drama was played after his death. But the Punjab Government, in whose territory Rattan S. had landed property at village Safulwala in District Ferozepur, did not recognize this Kartar S., now Gian S., to be the real heir to Rattan S.'s property.' (Part of a letter addressed to the Adviser of PEPSU by some citizens of Doraha.)
12 Rarewala spoke of Kairon as a goonda (lawless person) and in an interview in December 1966 said he was an 'upstart'.
13 Both these letters were in the possession of a particular SP and were shown to me by him.
14 Shortly before the murder of Hardev S. two trucks belonging to Kulwant S.'s family had been sent with Surinder S. Kairon to engage in construction work at Halwara airport, as it was feared that the trucks would be seized by the local police at the instance of Balwant S. of Lassowal. This was mentioned to me by Santokh S. but the fact is also detailed in 'Kartar Kaur murder case' (December 1965). If the trucks were with the CM's son no one would dare touch them for fear of the CM.

15 For the results of the elections see Appendix VII.
16 And now again the CM from February 1969.
17 The former CM of Orissa.
18 The reference here is to the shooting of a number of Akali Dal prisoners in Bhatinda and Ferozepur jails during the 1960 Akali demonstration to demand a Punjab-speaking province.
19 Rarewala's opinions on the Congress as stated in n. 4 of the closing chapter should therefore be noted.
20 And it was because of this that he was loyal to the paarti as such, supporting its candidate at election time, acting as a witness in favour of paarti members or as a prosecution witness against members of the opposing paarti in successive court cases.

16 Assessment

1 Quoting M. G. Smith, *Government in Zazzau*, p. 25: 'The controlled bureaucracy is simply an administrative structure subordinate to the holders of power, and is not itself a system of power, but its instrument.'
2 Ibid., p. 28.
3 See B. R. Nayar, *Minority Politics in the Punjab*, chapter 4.
4 The history of Gian S. Rarewala exemplifies my point. In 1956 he was one of a number of prominent Akalis to join the Congress party. In January 1969 he resigned as leader of the Congress opposition in the State Assembly and fought as an Akali Dal candidate in Payal constituency. In a speech given at an election meeting in a village in his constituency he is reported as having said, 'History is going to hurl doom on the Congress. . . . The people of Punjab . . . will be blazing a new path for their countrymen if they make Punjab a real graveyard of the Congress misrule and ambition.' ('Rarewala roars: now or never!', report in the *Punjab Mail*, 12 January 1969.)
5 A respected Communist, for example, once remarked that Kairon's motto had been to become like Birla and Tata (two of India's prominent capitalists, who are reputed to influence the making of decisions in Delhi) in order to avoid being controlled by the kinds of interests that Birla and Tata represented.
6 This has been amply illustrated by his attitudes towards the industrialists already noted in chapter 8.
7 In the period 1857–1947 landlords became a privileged class and British rule depended on them. This indeed is one reason, according to N. G. Barrier (*The Punjab Alienation of Land Bill 1900*), why the Land Alienation Bill was enacted. For an interesting discussion of this period see also B. Moore, *Social Origins of Dictatorship and Democracy*, chapter 6.
8 E. Durkheim, *The Division of Labour*, pp. 55, 124, 130, 131, 180, 181, implies this by his suggestion that organic solidarity arises only when the parts of society both differ from and depend on one another. In

Punjabi rural society, as has been seen, the social and political units are similar to one another rather than characteristically different.

9 In this respect one can compare the situation of both small and large landowners in the Punjab with that of the French peasantry whom K. Marx describes in *The Eighteenth Brumaire of Louis Bonaparte* at p. 109 as a 'sackful of potatoes'.

10 M. Gluckman makes this point when discussing the development of state forms of government in Africa in *Politics, Law and Ritual*, at p. 163: 'Even in those states where central administration is relatively strong and there is some degree of social stratification these are insufficient to counter the divisive effects of sectional interests in the absence of a complex economic interdependence of regions.'

11 W. Goode, on p. 593 of his article 'Family and mobility' in R. Bendix and S. M. Lipset (eds), *Class Status and Power*, 1967, suggests that there may be some association between the equal division of property and the development of small-scale industries.

12 Brewster's assessment (in 'Traditional social structures as barriers to social change') that the social structure and value system of 'underdeveloped' countries limit co-operation and collective action to small numbers of people, can clearly be dismissed with respect to the Punjab.

13 M. Gorky, *Untimely Thoughts: Essays on Revolution, Culture and the Bolsheviks.*

14 This has been eloquently commented upon by G. Steiner (*In Bluebeard's Castle*, p. 38): 'The holocaust is a reflex, the more complete for being long inhibited.'

17 Personal postscript: real people and images

1 Witnessing a German officer whip to death in the street an old unknown person, C. Kaplan (*Scroll of Agony*) asks, 'How is it possible to attack a stranger to me . . . without any reason?' And part of the answer is that the person is but an image, the objectification of some hated idea. F. Stern (*The Politics of Cultural Despair*, p. 142) focuses on this point when commenting on the anti-semitism of the German idealist Langbehn. He says, 'There was no personal experience that could have aroused his hatred', but for him the Jews and modernity were one and his anti-Semitism sprang from his own disgust of modernity and Jews then became the visible materialization of non-value, i.e., evil.

2 J. Benda, *The Betrayal of the Intellectuals*, pp. 135 and 21.

3 In this connexion Koestler (*Beyond Reductionism*, p. 230) can be quoted: 'The damages wrought by individual violence for selfish motives are insignificant compared to the holocausts resulting from self-transcending devotion to collectively shared belief systems.'

4 J. M. Brewster, 'Traditional social structures as barriers to social change'.

Bibliography

ALMOND, G. A. and COLEMAN, J. S., *The Politics of Developing Areas*, Princeton University Press, 1960.

ARENSBURG, C. M. and KIMBALL, S. T., *Culture and Community*, Harcourt Brace & World, 1965.

ARGYLE, M., 'The social psychology of social change' in T. Burns and S. B. Saul (eds), *Social Theory and Economic Change*, Tavistock Publications, 1967.

ASBURY, H., *Gangs of New York*, Knopf, 1928.

AYROUT, H. H., *The Egyptian Peasant*, The Beacon Press, 1963.

BADEN POWELL, B. H., *The Indian Village Community*, Longmans, 1896.

BAILEY, F. G., *Politics and Social Change: Orissa in 1959*, University of California Press, 1963.

BAILEY, F. G., 'Two villages in Orissa' in M. Gluckman (ed.), *Closed Systems and Open Minds*, Oliver & Boyd, 1965.

BAILEY, F. G., *Stratagems and Spoils*, Blackwell, 1969.

BANFIELD, E. C., *The Moral Basis of a Backward Society*, Free Press, 1958.

BARTH, F., *Political Leadership among Swat Pathans*, Athlone Press, 1959.

BARZINI, L., *The Italians*, Hamish Hamilton, 1964.

BEALS, A. R. and SIEGAL, B. J., 'Conflict and factionalist dispute', *JRAI*, 90, 1960, pp. 107–17.

BENDA, J., *Treason of the Intellectuals*, trans. R. Aldington, Norton, 1969.

BENDIX, R., *Nation Building and Citizenship*, John Wiley, 1964.

BERREMAN, G. D., 'The study of caste ranking', *South Western Journal of Anthropology*, 21, 1965, pp. 115–29.

BLOCH, M., *Feudal Society*, Routledge & Kegan Paul, 1962.

BLOK, A., 'The Mafia and peasant rebellion as contrasting factors in Sicilian latifundism', *European Journal of Sociology*, 10, 1969, pp. 95–116.

BOISSEVAIN, J., 'Maltese village politics and their relation to national politics', *Journal of Commonwealth and Political Studies*, 1, 1961–3, pp. 211–27.

BOISSEVAIN, J., 'Patronage in Sicily', *Man*, 1, 1966, pp. 18–33.

BRASS, P. R., *Factional Politics in an Indian State*, University of California Press, 1965.

BRECHER, M., *Succession in India*, Oxford University Press, 1966.

BREWSTER, J. M., 'Traditional social structures as barriers to social change', in H. M. Southworth and B. F. Johnston (eds), *Agricultural Development and Economic Growth*, Cornell University Press, 1967, pp. 66–106.

CAMPBELL, J. F. K., *Honour, Family and Patronage*, Oxford University Press, 1964.

CAMUS, A., *The Rebel*, trans. A. Bower, Hamish Hamilton, 1953.

COHEN, A., 'Political anthropology: the analysis of the symbolism of power relations', *Man*, 4, 1969, pp. 215-35.

CUTILEIRO, J., *A Portuguese Rural Society*, The Clarendon Press, 1971.

DEUTSCH, M., 'Group behaviour', *International Encyclopaedia of the Social Sciences*, 6, 1966, pp. 265-76.

DOLCI, D., *To Feed the Hungry, an Inquiry in Palermo*, MacGibbon & Kee, 1959.

DOLCI, D., *The Outlaws of Partinico*, MacGibbon & Kee, 1960.

DOLCI, D., *Waste: an Eyewitness Report on some Aspects of Waste in Western Sicily*, MacGibbon & Kee, 1963.

DUMONT, L., *Homo Hierarchicus*, Weidenfeld & Nicolson, 1970.

DUMONT, L. and POCOCK, D. F., 'Village studies', contributions to *Indian Sociology*, 1, 1957, pp. 23-41.

DURKHEIM, E., *The Division of Labour*, Free Press, 1964.

DURRELL, L., *The Spirit of Place*, Faber, 1969.

EISENSTADT, S. N., *Essays on the Sociological Aspects of Political and Economic Development*, Mouton, The Hague, 1961.

EISENSTADT, S. N., *The Political Systems of Empires*, Free Press, 1963.

EISENSTADT, S. N., 'The continuity of modernization and the development of administration', CAG Occasional Papers, International Development Research Centre, University of Indiana, 1965.

EPSTEIN, A. L., 'The network and urban social organization', *Rhodes Livingstone Institute Journal*, 29, 1961, pp. 29-62.

FENTON, W. H., 'Factionalism in American Indian society', *Actes du IVme Congres international des Sciences anthropologiques et ethnologiques Vienne, 1-8 Septembre 1952*, vol. 2, pp. 330-40, Verlag Adof Holzhausens NFG, Vienna, 1955.

FIRTH, R. W. (ed.), 'Factions in Indian and overseas Indian societies', *British Journal of Sociology*, 8, 1957, pp. 291-342.

FLORIS, G., 'A note on dacoits in India', *Comparative Studies in Society and History*, 4, 1962, pp. 467-72.

FRANKENBERG, R., *Communities in Britain*, Penguin, 1966.

FRIEDL, E., 'The role of kinship in the transmission of national culture to rural villages in mainland Greece', *American Anthropologist*, 1, 1959, pp. 30-8.

GELLNER, E., *Thought and Change*, Weidenfeld & Nicolson, 1964.

GINSBURG, N., *The Pattern of Asia*, Constable, 1958.

GLUCKMAN, M., 'Anthropological problems arising from the industrial revolution' in A. W. Southall (ed.), *Social Change in Modern Africa*, Oxford University Press, 1961.

GLUCKMAN, M., *The Ideas in Barotse Jurisprudence*, Yale University Press, 1965.

GLUCKMAN, M., *Politics, Law and Ritual*, Blackwell, 1965.

GORKY, M., *Untimely Thoughts: Essays on Revolution, Culture and the Bolsheviks*, Eriksson, 1971.

HABIB, I., *The Agrarian System of Moghul India*, Asia Publishing House, 1963.

HAGEN, E. E., *On the Theory of Social Change*, Dorsey Press, 1962.

HAYEK, F. A., 'The primacy of the abstract' in A. Koestler and J. R. Smythies (eds), *Beyond Reductionism—New Perspectives in the Life Sciences*, 'The Alpbach Symposium', Hutchinson, 1968, pp. 309–33.

HOSELITZ, B., *Sociological Aspects of Economic Growth*, Free Press, 1960.

IONESCU, G. and GELLNER, E., *Populism. Its Meanings and National Characteristics*, Weidenfeld & Nicolson, 1969.

KAPLAN, C., *Scroll of Agony: the Warsaw Diary of Chaim A. Kaplan*, Hamish Hamilton, 1967.

KEFAUVER, E., *Crime in America*, Gollancz, 1952.

KENNEDY, J. G., 'Peasant society and the image of limited good: critique', *American Anthropologist*, 68, 1966, pp. 1212–25.

KOESTLER, A. and SMYTHIES, J. R. (eds), *Beyond Reductionism—New Perspectives in the Life Sciences*, 'The Alpbach Symposium', Hutchinson, 1968.

KRADER, L., *Formation of the State*, Prentice-Hall, 1968.

LEWIS, N., *The Honoured Society*, Collins, 1964.

LEWIS, O., *Village Life in Northern India*, University of Illinois, 1958.

LOPREATO, J., *Peasants No More*, Chandler, 1967.

MCCLELLAND, D. C., *The Achieving Society*, Van Nostrand, 1961.

MANDELBAUM, D. G., *Society in India, Continuity and Change*, vol. 1, University of California Press, 1970.

MARRIOTT, MCK., 'Village India', American Anthropological Association Memoir No. 83, 1955.

MARX, K., *The Eighteenth Brumaire of Louis Bonaparte*, International Publishers, 1957.

MATHUR, H. C., 'Pancayati Raj and political parties', *Indian Journal of Public Administration*, 8, 1962.

MAXWELL, G., *God Protect Me from my Friends*, Longmans, 1957.

MAYER, A. C., 'Some hierarchical aspects of caste', *South-western Journal of Anthropology*, 2, 1956.

MAYER, A. C., *Caste and Kinship in Central India: a Village and its Region*, Routledge & Kegan Paul, 1960.

MAYER, A. C., 'The significance of quasi-groups in the study of complex societies' in M. Banton (ed.), *The Social Anthropology of Complex Societies*, Association of Social Anthropologists, 4, 1966, pp. 97–122.

MINISTRY OF INFORMATION AND BROADCASTING, GOVERNMENT OF INDIA, *Jawaharlal Nehru's Speeches*, vols 2 and 3, Government of India, Publications Division, 1954 and 1958.

MINISTRY OF INFORMATION AND BROADCASTING, GOVERNMENT OF INDIA, *India Reference Manual*, Government of India, Publications Division, 1966.

MOORE, B., jun., *Social Origins of Dictatorship and Democracy*, Penguin, 1967.

MOORE, W., *Social Change*, Prentice-Hall, 1963.

MUZAFER, S. and C. W., 'Group formation', *International Encyclopaedia of the Social Sciences*, 6, 1966, pp. 276–83.

NEWMAN, R. E., *Pathan Tribal Patterns*, Foreign Studies Institute, Ridgewood, N.J., 1965.

NICHOLAS, R. W., 'Village factions and political parties in rural West Bengal', *Journal of Commonwealth and Political Studies*, 2, 1963, pp. 17–32.

NICHOLAS, R. W., 'Factions: a comparative analysis' in M. Banton (ed.), *Political Systems and the Distribution of Power*, Association of Social Anthropologists, 2, 1965, pp. 21–61.

ORENSTEIN, H., 'The structure of Hindu caste values: a preliminary study of hierarchy and ritual defilement', *Ethnology*, 4, 1965, pp. 1–15.

PAZ, O., *The Labyrinth of Solitude*, Penguin, 1961.

PERISTIANY, J. A. (ed.), *Honour and Shame*, Weidenfeld & Nicolson, 1965.

PIAGET, J. and INHELDER, B., 'The gaps in empiricism' in A. Koestler and J. R. Smythies (eds), *Beyond Reductionism—New Perspectives in the Life Sciences*, 'The Alpbach Symposium', Hutchinson, 1968, pp. 118–60.

PITT RIVERS, J., *The People of the Sierra*, University of Chicago Press, 1954.

PLANNING COMMISSION, GOVERNMENT OF INDIA, *Third Five-Year Plan*, Government of India, 1961.

POCOCK, D. F., 'Inclusion and exclusion: a process in the caste system of Gujerat', *Southwestern Journal of Anthropology*, 13, 1957, pp. 19–31.

PRADHAN, M. C., *The Political System of the Jats of Northern India*, Oxford University Press, 1967.

PUZO, M., *The Godfather*, Heinemann, 1969.

QUANUNGO, K. R., *History of the Jats*, Calcutta, 1925.

REDFIELD, R., *The Little Community*, University of Chicago Press, 1956.

REDFIELD, R., *Peasant Society and Culture*, University of Chicago Press, 1956.

RUSSETT, B. M., 'The relation of land tenure to politics' in R. A. Dahl and D. E. Neubaurer (eds), *Readings in Modern Political Analysis*, Prentice-Hall, 1968.

SCHELER, M., *The Nature of Sympathy*, Routledge & Kegan Paul, 1954.

SCHELER, M., *Philosophical Perspectives*, The Beacon Press, 1958.

SHANIN, T., *Peasants and Peasant Societies*, Penguin, 1971.

SHOLOKHOV, M. A., *And Quiet Flows the Don*, trans. S. Garry, Putnam, 1934.

SILVERMAN, S. F., 'Patronage and community-nation relationships in central Italy', *Ethnology*, 4, 1965, pp. 172–89.

SINDLER, A., *Huey Long's Louisiana: State Politics 1920–52*, Johns Hopkins University Press, 1959.

SMITH, M. G., *Government in Zazzau*, Oxford University Press, 1960.

SOUTHWORTH, H. M. and JOHNSON, B. F., *Agricultural Development and Economic Growth*, Cornell University Press, 1967.

SPRINIVAS, M. N., *Caste in Modern India*, Asia Publishing House, 1962.

SPROTT, W. J. H., *Human Groups*, Penguin, 1958.

STEINER, G., *In Bluebeard's Castle: Some Notes Towards the Redefinition of Culture*, Faber, 1971.

STERN, F., *The Politics of Cultural Despair*, University of California Press, 1963.

STEVENSON, H. N. C., 'Status evaluation in the Hindu caste system', *Journal of the Royal Anthropological Institute*, 84, 1954, pp. 45–65.

STEWARD, J. H., 'Area research. Theory and Practice', Social Science Research Council, *Bulletin*, 63, 1950.

STEWARD, J. H., *Theory of Culture Change*, University of Illinois, 1955.

STIRLING, P., *A Turkish Village*, Weidenfeld & Nicolson, 1965.

SWARTZ, M. J., *Local-Level Politics*, Aldine Publishing Company, 1968.

WEINGROD, A., 'Patrons, patronage and political parties', *Comparative Studies in Society and History*, 10, 1967–8, pp. 377–400.

WERTHEIM, W. F., 'Patronage, vertical organization and populism', *VIIIth Congress of Anthropological and Ethnological Sciences II*, Science Council of Japan, Tokyo, 1968, pp. 16–18.

WHYTE, W. F., *Street Corner Society*, University of Chicago Press, 1955.

WOLF, E. R., 'Aspects of group relations in a complex society', *American Anthropologist*, 58, 1956, pp. 1065–78.

WOLF, E. R., 'Kinship, friendship and patron-client relations in complex societies' in M. Banton (ed.), *The Social Anthropology of Complex Societies*, Tavistock Publications, 1966, pp. 1–22.

WOLF, E. R., *Peasants*, Prentice-Hall, 1966.

Punjab

Akali Dal and the SGPC, Superintendent of Government Printing, Simla, 1921–2 .

ALL INDIA CONGRESS COMMITTEE, *Resolutions on State Reorganization, 1920–55*, New Delhi, 1956.

BARRIER, N. G., *The Punjab Alienation of Land Bill 1900*, Comparative Studies on Southern Asia, Monograph and Occasional Papers Series, no. 2, Duke University, 1966.

BARRIER, N. G., *The Sikhs and their Literature*, Manohar Book Service, Darya Ganj, 1970.

BARSTOW, H. E., *Handbooks for the Indian Army: the Sikhs*, New Delhi, 1941.

BHATTIA, RAJINDER S., (ed.), *Quami Ekkta*, S. Partap S. Kairon Commemoration Volume, Delhi, 1966.

BINGLEY, A. H., *Sikhs*, Superintendent of Government Printing, Calcutta, 1918.

CALVERT, H., 'The wealth and welfare of the Punjab', *Civil and Military Gazette*, Lahore, 1936.

Census of India, 1931, vol. 17, *Punjab*, part I, 'Report by Khan Ahmed Hassan Khan', Civil and Military Gazette Press, Lahore, 1933.

Census of India, 1961, Punjab, District Census Handbook no. II, 'Ludhiana District', Government of India, 1965.

Census of India, 1961, 'Kunran, a village in Sangruur District of Punjab', Village Survey Monographs of Punjab, Government of India, 1965.

CUNNINGHAM, J. D., *A History of the Sikhs*, S. Chand, New Delhi, 1966.

DARLING, M., *The Punjab Peasant in Prosperity and Debt*, Oxford University Press, 1925.

DARLING, M., *Wisdom and Waste in the Punjab Village*, Oxford University Press, 1934.

DEPARTMENT OF PUBLIC RELATIONS, *Papers Relating to the Hindi Agitation in Punjab*, Chandigarh, 1957.

DEPARTMENT OF PUBLIC RELATIONS, *Stronger Punjab through Unity, not Turmoil*, Chandigarh, 1960.

DEPARTMENT OF PUBLIC RELATIONS, *Selections, State Publicity Talks (1959–69)*, Chandigarh, 1961.

DEPARTMENT OF PUBLIC RELATIONS, 'Address delivered by the Governor of Punjab to the Joint Session of the Vidhan Sabha and the Legislative Council on 18 February 1963', Chandigarh, 1963.

DEPARTMENT OF PUBLIC RELATIONS, 'Extracts from a speech of S. Partap S. Kairon, CM in the Punjab Vidhan Sabha, delivered on 18 September 1963', Chandigarh, 1963.

DEPARTMENT OF PUBLIC RELATIONS, *Towards Wider Horizons, Nobler Goals*, Chandigarh, 1963.

DEPARTMENT OF PUBLIC RELATIONS, *Fact Sheets on Punjab*, Chandigarh, 1964.

DEPARTMENT OF PUBLIC RELATIONS, *Facts about Punjab*, Chandigarh, 1966.

DEPARTMENT OF PUBLIC RELATIONS, *Ludhiana Marches Ahead*, Chandigarh, 1966.

DHAR, A. G., *Misery of the Punjab*, New Delhi, 1963.

EGLAR, Z., *A Punjabi Village in Pakistan*, Columbia University Press, 1960.

GRIFFIN, L. H., *The Law of Inheritance to Chiefships as Observed by the Sikhs previous to the Annexation of the Panjab*, Lahore, 1869.

GRIFFIN, L. H., *The Rajas of Panjab*, Lahore, 1870.

GRIFFIN, L. H., *The Panjab Chiefs*, Government of the Punjab Press, Lahore, 1890.

GRIFFIN, L. H., *Ranjit Singh*, Oxford University Press, 1905.

GRIFFIN, L. H. and MASSEY, C. F., *Chiefs and Families of Note in the Punjab*, Government Printing Press, Lahore, 1940.

GUPTA, H. R., *A History of the Sikhs*, vols I–III, Sarkar, Calcutta, 1939–44.

HAZELHURST, L. W., *Entrepreneurship and the Merchant Castes in a Punjabi City*, Comparative Studies in Southern Asia, Duke University, 1966.

IBBETSON, D. C., *Outlines of Punjab Ethnography*, Calcutta, 1883.

ISMAY, H. L. I., *The Memoirs of General the Lord Ismay*, Heinemann, 1960, chapter 33, 'Last days of the Raj'.

IZMIRLIAN, H. J., 'Caste, Kin and Politics in a Village', University Microfilms, High Wycombe, 1964.

MCLEOD, W. H., *Guru Nanak and the Sikh Religion*, Oxford University Press, 1968.

MCLEOD, W. H., *The Evolution of the Sikh Community*, Cambridge University Press, forthcoming.

MOON, P., *Divide and Quit*, Chatto & Windus, 1961.

MORRISON, C., 'Dispute in Dhara: a study of village politics in Eastern Punjab', unpublished Ph.D. thesis, University of Chicago, 1965.

MOSLEY, L., *The Last Days of the British Raj*, Weidenfeld & Nicolson, 1961.

NARAYAN, S., 'Notes on the charges brought against S. Partap S. Kairon', New Delhi, 19 May 1958.

NAYAR, B. R., *Minority Politics in the Punjab*, Princeton University Press, 1966.

PAKISTAN, GOVERNMENT OF, *Note on the Sikh Plan*, Lahore, 1948.

PHILLIPS, C. H. and WAINWRIGHT, M. D. (eds), *The Partition of India. Policies and Perspectives 1935–47*, Allen & Unwin, 1970.

PUNJABI UNIVERSITY, LANGUAGE DEPARTMENT, *The Legends of the Punjab*, Patiala, 1962.

PUNJAB VIDHAN SABHA, *The Beginning of the Opposition against S. Partap S. Kairon and its Culmination in his Resignation from the Chief Ministership*, Chandigarh, 1958.

PUNJAB VIDHAN SABHA, *Who's Who, 1962–7*, Chandigarh, 1965.

RAI, S. M., *The Partition of the Punjab*, Asia Publishing House, 1965.

RANDHAWA, M. S., *Out of the Ashes*, Department of Public Relations, Chandigarh, 1954.

RANDHAWA, M. S., 'Punjab Agricultural University, pivot of green revolution in Punjab', *Punjab Mail*, 24 August 1969.

RANDHAWA, M. S., 'Implication of wealth tax on agriculture', *Tribune*, Ambala, 26 March 1970.

RUSTOMJI, K. J., *A Treatise on Customary Law in the Punjab*, University Book Agency, Allahabad, 1949.

SARHADI, A. S., *Punjabi Suba*, U. C. Kapur & Sons, Delhi, 1970.

SHARMA, B. D., *Anatomy of Accusations: Spotlight on the Background of Allegations Against S. Partap S. Kairon*, Chandigarh, 1964.

SHIROMANI AKALI DAL, *Memorandum on Punjabi-speaking States Submitted to the States Re-organization Commission in 1956*, Amritsar, 1956.

SHIROMANI AKALI DAL, *Facts about Punjabi Suba Agitation: a collection of memoranda presented before the Das Commission*, Amritsar, 1960.

SHIROMANI AKALI DAL, *Facts about Punjabi Suba*, Amritsar, 1965.

SHIROMANI GURUDWARA PARBHANDAK COMMITTEE, *Muslim League Attack on Sikhs and Hindus in the Punjab*, Amritsar, 1950.

SHIROMANI GURUDWARA PARBHANDAK COMMITTEE, *Discrimination against the Sikh Backward Castes*, Amritsar, 1953.

SHIROMANI GURUDWARA PARBHANDAK COMMITTEE, *Memorandum submitted to the consultative committee of Parliament on the issue of Punjabi Suba*, Amritsar, 1965.

SINGH, DALIP, *The Tragedy of the Terai*, Terai Kisan Relief and Defence Committee, Rudrepur, 1959.

SINGH, DALIP, *Punjab Government and the Gurudwara Elections*, New Delhi, 1960.

SINGH, DURLABH, *The Valiant Fighter*, Hero Publications, Lahore, 1942.

SINGH, G. and GYANI, L. S., *The Idea of the Sikh State*, Jiwan Singh for Lahore Bookshop, Lahore, 1946.

SINGH, I. P., 'A Sikh Village', *Journal of American Folklore*, 71, pp. 479–54.

SINGH, K., *A History of the Sikhs*, vol. 1, Princeton University Press, 1963.

SINGH, M. (ed.), *Kairon*, Mubarak Singh for Abhinandan Granth Committee, Ludhiana, 1965.

SINGH, P., *The Sikh Gurus and the Temple of Bread*, SGPC, Amritsar, 1964.

SINGH, S. S., *The Sikhs demand their Homeland*, Sikh University Press, Lahore, 1946 .

SMITH, M. W., 'Social structure in the Punjab', *Economic Weekly*, 47, 1953.

TANDON, P., *Punjabi Century 1857–1947*, Chatto & Windus, 1961.

THORBURN, S. S., *Musalmans and Moneylenders in the Punjab*, Blackwood, 1886.

TREVASKIS, H. K., *The Land of the Five Rivers*, Oxford University Press, 1928.

TUPPER, C. L., *Punjab Customary Law*, Calcutta, 1881.

Reports

The Commission of Inquiry, constituted under Home Ministry notification No S.O. 3109, New Delhi, 1964.

The Punjab Boundary Commission, Manager of Publications, Delhi, 1966.

Sikh Memorandum to the Punjab Boundary Commission, Lahore, 1947.

Index

action set, 66, 67, 72
administration: high status of, 4, 55, 108, 159; Kairon's control over, 107–12, 114, 123, 162, 200, 203; operation as affected by factions, 135–40, 146–8, 151–4, 156, 159, 160, 162–6, 178, 181–5, 188, 192, 201, 204, 212; structure, 9–11, 200
Afghans, Afghan invasions, 4, 27–31, 33
agriculture: crops, 3, 7, 43, 98, 210; harvests, 7, 43–4, 121
agricultural interests, 42, 54, 83, 99; holdings, 7, 98
Agricultural University, Ludhiana, 54, 55, 98, 196
agricultural yields, 7, 121
Ahmed Shah Abdali, 27–31, 35, 58
Akali Dal: and Congress, 139, 196, 197, 201, 206, 207; and partition, 86, 87, 88; and Punjabi Suba, 78, 79, 82, 83, 88–91, 93–101; and Rarewala, 115–19, 142, 193
Akhand Path, 94
Ala S., 30, 31, 202
All India Sikh Students Federation, 84, 87
Amritsar: city, 8, 10, 86; district, 42, 59, 87, 90, 94, 117, 133; District Congress, 123, 202
Ardas, 80, 81
army, 16, 17, 35–7, 41, 42, 59, 92, 101, 114, 118
Aroras, see businessmen
Arya Samaj, 91, 94, 95, 96
Aurungzeb, 27

authority, attitudes to, 6, 19, 28–30, 45, 46, 57, 206
Ayub Khan, 97

Bailey, F.G., 22, 23, 66
Baldev S., 84, 86, 96
Beant S., MLA, 132–3, 139, 161, 182, 195
behaviour, 4, 5, 17–20, 32, 37, 38, 41, 44, 48–52, 57–9, 103–4, 122–3, 183, 189
Bhag S., Lt., MLA, 132, 138–41, 175, 182
Bhargava, Gopi Chand, 86
bhog ceremony, 184, 189
Block Development Officer (BDO), 12, 111–12
Brass, Paul, 63
British and the Sikhs, 6, 35, 42, 83, 84, 88, 92, 111, 118
business, Congress patronage of, 113
businessmen: Aroras, Khatris, 40–43, 90, 98, 206; Hindus, 8, 41, 91–92, 94, 113

canal colonies, 35
canals, 3; Sirhind canal, 15, 189
castes, caste system, 4, 11, 26, 40–47
central government and Sikh community, 78, 79, 90–2, 94–5, 97, 105
Chandigarh, 11, 15, 20, 159, 165
class, 16–21, 37–39
communal group, 78, 97
communalism, 79, 94, 97, 98, 101

Routledge Social Science Series

Routledge & Kegan Paul   London and Boston

68–74 Carter Lane   London EC4V 5EL
9 Park Street   Boston   Mass 02108

Contents

*Authors wishing to submit manuscripts for any series in
this catalogue should send them to the Social Science Editor,
Routledge & Kegan Paul Ltd, 68–74 Carter Lane,
London EC4V 5EL*

*●Books so marked are available in paperback
All books are in Metric Demy 8vo format (216 × 138mm approx.)*

International Library of Sociology

General Editor John Rex

GENERAL SOCIOLOGY

Barnsley, J. H. The Social Reality of Ethics. *464 pp.*
Belshaw, Cyril. The Conditions of Social Performance. *An Exploratory Theory. 144 pp.*
Brown, Robert. Explanation in Social Science. *208 pp.*
● Rules and Laws in Sociology. *192 pp.*
Bruford, W. H. Chekhov and His Russia. *A Sociological Study. 244 pp.*
Cain, Maureen E. Society and the Policeman's Role. *326 pp.*
Gibson, Quentin. The Logic of Social Enquiry. *240 pp.*
Glucksmann, M. Structuralist Analysis in Contemporary Social Thought. *212 pp.*
Gurvitch, Georges. Sociology of Law. *Preface by Roscoe Pound. 264 pp.*
Hodge, H. A. Wilhelm Dilthey. *An Introduction. 184 pp.*
Homans, George C. Sentiments and Activities. *336 pp.*
Johnson, Harry M. Sociology: *a Systematic Introduction. Foreword by Robert K. Merton. 710 pp.*
Mannheim, Karl. Essays on Sociology and Social Psychology. *Edited by Paul Keckskemeti. With Editorial Note by Adolph Lowe. 344 pp.*
Systematic Sociology: *An Introduction to the Study of Society. Edited by J. S. Erös and Professor W. A. C. Stewart. 220 pp.*
Martindale, Don. The Nature and Types of Sociological Theory. *292 pp.*
●**Maus, Heinz.** A Short History of Sociology. *234 pp.*
Mey, Harald. Field-Theory. *A Study of its Application in the Social Sciences. 352 pp.*
Myrdal, Gunnar. Value in Social Theory: *A Collection of Essays on Methodology. Edited by Paul Streeten. 332 pp.*
Ogburn, William F., and **Nimkoff, Meyer F.** A Handbook of Sociology. *Preface by Karl Mannheim. 656 pp. 46 figures. 35 tables.*
Parsons, Talcott, and **Smelser, Neil J.** Economy and Society: *A Study in the Integration of Economic and Social Theory. 362 pp.*
●**Rex, John.** Key Problems of Sociological Theory. *220 pp.*
Discovering Sociology. *278 pp.*
Sociology and the Demystification of the Modern World. *282 pp.*
●**Rex, John** (Ed.) Approaches to Sociology. *Contributions by Peter Abell, Frank Bechhofer, Basil Bernstein, Ronald Fletcher, David Frisby, Miriam Glucksmann, Peter Lassman, Herminio Martins, John Rex, Roland Robertson, John Westergaard and Jock Young. 302 pp.*
Rigby, A. Alternative Realities. *352 pp.*
Roche, M. Phenomenology, Language and the Social Sciences. *374 pp.*
Sahay, A. Sociological Analysis. *220 pp.*
Urry, John. Reference Groups and the Theory of Revolution. *244 pp.*
Weinberg, E. Development of Sociology in the Soviet Union. *173 pp.*

FOREIGN CLASSICS OF SOCIOLOGY

●**Durkheim, Emile.** Suicide. *A Study in Sociology. Edited and with an Introduction by George Simpson. 404 pp.*
Professional Ethics and Civic Morals. *Translated by Cornelia Brookfield. 288 pp.*
●**Gerth, H. H.,** and **Mills, C. Wright.** From Max Weber: *Essays in Sociology. 502 pp.*
●**Tönnies, Ferdinand.** Community and Association. (*Gemeinschaft und Gesellschaft.) Translated and Supplemented by Charles P. Loomis. Foreword by Pitirim A. Sorokin. 334 pp.*

SOCIAL STRUCTURE

Andreski, Stanislav. Military Organization and Society. *Foreword by Professor A. R. Radcliffe-Brown. 226 pp. 1 folder.*
Coontz, Sydney H. Population Theories and the Economic Interpretation. *202 pp.*
Coser, Lewis. The Functions of Social Conflict. *204 pp.*
Dickie-Clark, H. F. Marginal Situation: *A Sociological Study of a Coloured Group. 240 pp. 11 tables.*
Glaser, Barney, and **Strauss, Anselm L.** Status Passage. *A Formal Theory. 208 pp.*
Glass, D. V. (Ed.) Social Mobility in Britain. *Contributions by J. Berent, T. Bottomore, R. C. Chambers, J. Floud, D. V. Glass, J. R. Hall, H. T. Himmelweit, R. K. Kelsall, F. M. Martin, C. A. Moser, R. Mukherjee, and W. Ziegel. 420 pp.*
Jones, Garth N. Planned Organizational Change: *An Exploratory Study Using an Empirical Approach. 268 pp.*
Kelsall, R. K. Higher Civil Servants in Britain: *From 1870 to the Present Day. 268 pp. 31 tables.*
König, René. The Community. *232 pp. Illustrated.*
●**Lawton, Denis.** Social Class, Language and Education. *192 pp.*
McLeish, John. The Theory of Social Change: *Four Views Considered. 128 pp.*
Marsh, David C. The Changing Social Structure of England and Wales, 1871-1961. *288 pp.*
Mouzelis, Nicos. Organization and Bureaucracy. *An Analysis of Modern Theories. 240 pp.*
Mulkay, M. J. Functionalism, Exchange and Theoretical Strategy. *272 pp.*
Ossowski, Stanislaw. Class Structure in the Social Consciousness. *210 pp.*
Podgórecki, Adam. Law and Society. *About 300 pp.*

SOCIOLOGY AND POLITICS

Acton, T. A. Gypsy Politics and Social Change. *316 pp.*
Hechter, Michael. Internal Colonialism. *The Celtic Fringe in British National Development, 1536–1966. About 350 pp.*
Hertz, Frederick. Nationality in History and Politics: *A Psychology and Sociology of National Sentiment and Nationalism. 432 pp.*

Kornhauser, William. The Politics of Mass Society. *272 pp. 20 tables.*
Laidler, Harry W. History of Socialism. *Social-Economic Movements: An Historical and Comparative Survey of Socialism, Communism, Co-operation, Utopianism; and other Systems of Reform and Reconstruction. 992 pp.*
Lasswell, H. D. Analysis of Political Behaviour. *324 pp.*
Mannheim, Karl. Freedom, Power and Democratic Planning. *Edited by Hans Gerth and Ernest K. Bramstedt. 424 pp.*
Mansur, Fatma. Process of Independence. *Foreword by A. H. Hanson. 208 pp.*
Martin, David A. Pacifism: *an Historical and Sociological Study. 262 pp.*
Myrdal, Gunnar. The Political Element in the Development of Economic Theory. *Translated from the German by Paul Streeten. 282 pp.*
Wootton, Graham. Workers, Unions and the State. *188 pp.*

FOREIGN AFFAIRS: THEIR SOCIAL, POLITICAL AND ECONOMIC FOUNDATIONS

Mayer, J. P. Political Thought in France from the Revolution to the Fifth Republic. *164 pp.*

CRIMINOLOGY

Ancel, Marc. Social Defence: *A Modern Approach to Criminal Problems. Foreword by Leon Radzinowicz. 240 pp.*
Cain, Maureen E. Society and the Policeman's Role. *326 pp.*
Cloward, Richard A., and Ohlin, Lloyd E. Delinquency and Opportunity: *A Theory of Delinquent Gangs. 248 pp.*
Downes, David M. The Delinquent Solution. *A Study in Subcultural Theory. 296 pp.*
Dunlop, A. B., and McCabe, S. Young Men in Detention Centres. *192 pp.*
Friedlander, Kate. The Psycho-Analytical Approach to Juvenile Delinquency: *Theory, Case Studies, Treatment. 320 pp.*
Glueck, Sheldon, and Eleanor. Family Environment and Delinquency. *With the statistical assistance of Rose W. Kneznek. 340 pp.*
Lopez-Rey, Manuel. Crime. *An Analytical Appraisal. 288 pp.*
Mannheim, Hermann. Comparative Criminology: *a Text Book. Two volumes. 442 pp. and 380 pp.*
Morris, Terence. The Criminal Area: *A Study in Social Ecology. Foreword by Hermann Mannheim. 232 pp. 25 tables. 4 maps.*
Rock, Paul. Making People Pay. *338 pp.*
● **Taylor, Ian, Walton, Paul, and Young, Jock.** The New Criminology. *For a Social Theory of Deviance. 325 pp.*

SOCIAL PSYCHOLOGY

Bagley, Christopher. The Social Psychology of the Epileptic Child. *320 pp.*
Barbu, Zevedei. Problems of Historical Psychology. *248 pp.*
Blackburn, Julian. Psychology and the Social Pattern. *184 pp.*

5

●**Brittan, Arthur.** Meanings and Situations. *224 pp.*

Carroll, J. Break-Out from the Crystal Palace. *200 pp.*

●**Fleming, C. M.** Adolescence: Its Social Psychology. *With an Introduction to recent findings from the fields of Anthropology, Physiology, Medicine, Psychometrics and Sociometry. 288 pp.*

● The Social Psychology of Education: *An Introduction and Guide to Its Study. 136 pp.*

Homans, George C. The Human Group. *Foreword by Bernard DeVoto. Introduction by Robert K. Merton. 526 pp.*

● Social Behaviour: *its Elementary Forms. 416 pp.*

●**Klein, Josephine.** The Study of Groups. *226 pp. 31 figures. 5 tables.*

Linton, Ralph. The Cultural Background of Personality. *132 pp.*

●**Mayo, Elton.** The Social Problems of an Industrial Civilization. *With an appendix on the Political Problem. 180 pp.*

Ottaway, A. K. C. Learning Through Group Experience. *176 pp.*

Ridder, J. C. de. The Personality of the Urban African in South Africa. *A Thematic Apperception Test Study. 196 pp. 12 plates.*

●**Rose, Arnold M.** (Ed.) Human Behaviour and Social Processes: *an Interactionist Approach. Contributions by Arnold M. Rose, Ralph H. Turner, Anselm Strauss, Everett C. Hughes, E. Franklin Frazier, Howard S. Becker, et al. 696 pp.*

Smelser, Neil J. Theory of Collective Behaviour. *448 pp.*

Stephenson, Geoffrey M. The Development of Conscience. *128 pp.*

Young, Kimball. Handbook of Social Psychology. *658 pp. 16 figures. 10 tables.*

SOCIOLOGY OF THE FAMILY

Banks, J. A. Prosperity and Parenthood: *A Study of Family Planning among The Victorian Middle Classes. 262 pp.*

Bell, Colin R. Middle Class Families: *Social and Geographical Mobility. 224 pp.*

Burton, Lindy. Vulnerable Children. *272 pp.*

Gavron, Hannah. The Captive Wife: *Conflicts of Household Mothers. 190 pp.*

George, Victor, and **Wilding, Paul.** Motherless Families. *220 pp.*

Klein, Josephine. Samples from English Cultures.
 1. Three Preliminary Studies and Aspects of Adult Life in England. *447 pp.*
 2. Child-Rearing Practices and Index. *247 pp.*

Klein, Viola. Britain's Married Women Workers. *180 pp.*

 The Feminine Character. *History of an Ideology. 244 pp.*

McWhinnie, Alexina M. Adopted Children. *How They Grow Up. 304 pp.*

● **Myrdal, Alva,** and **Klein, Viola.** Women's Two Roles: *Home and Work. 238 pp. 27 tables.*

Parsons, Talcott, and **Bales, Robert F.** Family: Socialization and Interaction Process. *In collaboration with James Olds, Morris Zelditch and Philip E. Slater. 456 pp. 50 figures and tables.*

SOCIAL SERVICES

Bastide, Roger. The Sociology of Mental Disorder. *Translated from the French by Jean McNeil. 260 pp.*

Carlebach, Julius. Caring For Children in Trouble. *266 pp.*

Forder, R. A. (Ed.) Penelope Hall's Social Services of England and Wales. *352 pp.*

George, Victor. Foster Care. *Theory and Practice. 234 pp.*
Social Security: *Beveridge and After. 258 pp.*

George, V., and **Wilding, P.** Motherless Families. *248 pp.*

● **Goetschius, George W.** Working with Community Groups. *256 pp.*

Goetschius, George W., and **Tash, Joan.** Working with Unattached Youth. *416 pp.*

Hall, M. P., and **Howes, I. V.** The Church in Social Work. *A Study of Moral Welfare Work undertaken by the Church of England. 320 pp.*

Heywood, Jean S. Children in Care: *the Development of the Service for the Deprived Child. 264 pp.*

Hoenig, J., and **Hamilton, Marian W.** The De-Segregation of the Mentally Ill. *284 pp.*

Jones, Kathleen. Mental Health and Social Policy, 1845-1959. *264 pp.*

King, Roy D., Raynes, Norma V., and **Tizard, Jack.** Patterns of Residential Care. *356 pp.*

Leigh, John. Young People and Leisure. *256 pp.*

Morris, Mary. Voluntary Work and the Welfare State. *300 pp.*

Morris, Pauline. Put Away: *A Sociological Study of Institutions for the Mentally Retarded. 364 pp.*

Nokes, P. L. The Professional Task in Welfare Practice. *152 pp.*

Timms, Noel. Psychiatric Social Work in Great Britain (1939-1962). *280 pp.*

● Social Casework: *Principles and Practice. 256 pp.*

Young, A. F. Social Services in British Industry. *272 pp.* .

Young, A. F., and **Ashton, E. T.** British Social Work in the Nineteenth Century. *288 pp.*

SOCIOLOGY OF EDUCATION

Banks, Olive. Parity and Prestige in English Secondary Education: a Study in Educational Sociology. *272 pp.*

Bentwich, Joseph. Education in Israel. *224 pp. 8 pp. plates.*

● **Blyth, W. A. L.** English Primary Education. *A Sociological Description.*
1. Schools. *232 pp.*
2. Background. *168 pp.*

Collier, K. G. The Social Purposes of Education: *Personal and Social Values in Education. 268 pp.*

Dale, R. R., and **Griffith, S.** Down Stream: *Failure in the Grammar School.* *108 pp.*

Dore, R. P. Education in Tokugawa Japan. *356 pp. 9 pp. plates.*

Evans, K. M. Sociometry and Education. *158 pp.*

●**Ford, Julienne.** Social Class and the Comprehensive School. *192 pp.*

Foster, P. J. Education and Social Change in Ghana. *336 pp. 3 maps.*

Fraser, W. R. Education and Society in Modern France. *150 pp.*

Grace, Gerald R. Role Conflict and the Teacher. *About 200 pp.*

Hans, Nicholas. New Trends in Education in the Eighteenth Century. *278 pp. 19 tables.*

● Comparative Education: *A Study of Educational Factors and Traditions.* *360 pp.*

Hargreaves, David. Interpersonal Relations and Education. *432 pp.*

● Social Relations in a Secondary School. *240 pp.*

Holmes, Brian. Problems in Education. *A Comparative Approach. 336 pp.*

King, Ronald. Values and Involvement in a Grammar School. *164 pp.*

School Organization and Pupil Involvement. *A Study of Secondary Schools.*

●**Mannheim, Karl,** and **Stewart, W. A. C.** An Introduction to the Sociology of Education. *206 pp.*

Morris, Raymond N. The Sixth Form and College Entrance. *231 pp.*

●**Musgrove, F.** Youth and the Social Order. *176 pp.*

●**Ottaway, A. K. C.** Education and Society: An Introduction to the Sociology of Education. *With an Introduction by W. O. Lester Smith. 212 pp.*

Peers, Robert. Adult Education: *A Comparative Study. 398 pp.*

Pritchard, D. G. Education and the Handicapped: *1760 to 1960. 258 pp.*

Richardson, Helen. Adolescent Girls in Approved Schools. *308 pp.*

Stratta, Erica. The Education of Borstal Boys. *A Study of their Educational Experiences prior to, and during, Borstal Training. 256 pp.*

Taylor, P. H., Reid, W. A., and **Holley, B. J.** The English Sixth Form. *A Case Study in Curriculum Research. 200 pp.*

SOCIOLOGY OF CULTURE

Eppel, E. M., and **M.** Adolescents and Morality: *A Study of some Moral Values and Dilemmas of Working Adolescents in the Context of a changing Climate of Opinion. Foreword by W. J. H. Sprott. 268 pp. 39 tables.*

●**Fromm, Erich.** The Fear of Freedom. *286 pp.*

● The Sane Society. *400 pp.*

Mannheim, Karl. Essays on the Sociology of Culture. *Edited by Ernst Mannheim in co-operation with Paul Kecskemeti. Editorial Note by Adolph Lowe. 280 pp.*

Weber, Alfred. Farewell to European History: *or The Conquest of Nihilism. Translated from the German by R. F. C. Hull. 224 pp.*

SOCIOLOGY OF RELIGION

Argyle, Michael and **Beit-Hallahmi, Benjamin.** The Social Psychology of Religion. *About 256 pp.*
Nelson, G. K. Spiritualism and Society. *313 pp.*
Stark, Werner. The Sociology of Religion. *A Study of Christendom.*
Volume I. *Established Religion. 248 pp.*
Volume II. *Sectarian Religion. 368 pp.*
Volume III. *The Universal Church. 464 pp.*
Volume IV. *Types of Religious Man. 352 pp.*
Volume V. *Types of Religious Culture. 464 pp.*
Turner, B. S. Weber and Islam. *216 pp.*
Watt, W. Montgomery. Islam and the Integration of Society. *320 pp.*

SOCIOLOGY OF ART AND LITERATURE

Jarvie, Ian C. Towards a Sociology of the Cinema. *A Comparative Essay on the Structure and Functioning of a Major Entertainment Industry. 405 pp.*
Rust, Frances S. Dance in Society. *An Analysis of the Relationships between the Social Dance and Society in England from the Middle Ages to the Present Day. 256 pp. 8 pp. of plates.*
Schücking, L. L. The Sociology of Literary Taste. *112 pp.*
Wolff, Janet. Hermeneutic Philosophy and the Sociology of Art. *About 200 pp.*

SOCIOLOGY OF KNOWLEDGE

Diesing, P. Patterns of Discovery in the Social Sciences. *262 pp.*
●**Douglas, J. D.** (Ed.) Understanding Everyday Life. *370 pp.*
●**Hamilton, P.** Knowledge and Social Structure. *174 pp.*
Jarvie, I. C. Concepts and Society. *232 pp.*
Mannheim, Karl. Essays on the Sociology of Knowledge. *Edited by Paul Kecskemeti. Editorial Note by Adolph Lowe. 353 pp.*
Remmling, Gunter W. (Ed.) Towards the Sociology of Knowledge. *Origin and Development of a Sociological Thought Style. 463 pp.*
Stark, Werner. The Sociology of Knowledge: *An Essay in Aid of a Deeper Understanding of the History of Ideas. 384 pp.*

URBAN SOCIOLOGY

Ashworth, William. The Genesis of Modern British Town Planning: *A Study in Economic and Social History of the Nineteenth and Twentieth Centuries. 288 pp.*
Cullingworth, J. B. Housing Needs and Planning Policy: *A Restatement of the Problems of Housing Need and 'Overspill' in England and Wales. 232 pp. 44 tables. 8 maps.*

Dickinson, Robert E. City and Region: *A Geographical Interpretation* *608 pp. 125 figures.*
The West European City: *A Geographical Interpretation. 600 pp. 129 maps. 29 plates.*
● The City Region in Western Europe. *320 pp. Maps.*
Humphreys, Alexander J. New Dubliners: *Urbanization and the Irish Family. Foreword by George C. Homans. 304 pp.*
Jackson, Brian. Working Class Community: *Some General Notions raised by a Series of Studies in Northern England. 192 pp.*
Jennings, Hilda. Societies in the Making: *a Study of Development and Redevelopment within a County Borough. Foreword by D. A. Clark. 286 pp.*
●**Mann, P. H.** An Approach to Urban Sociology. *240 pp.*
Morris, R. N., and **Mogey, J.** The Sociology of Housing. *Studies at Berinsfield. 232 pp. 4 pp. plates.*
Rosser, C., and **Harris, C.** The Family and Social Change. *A Study of Family and Kinship in a South Wales Town. 352 pp. 8 maps.*

RURAL SOCIOLOGY

Chambers, R. J. H. Settlement Schemes in Tropical Africa: *A Selective Study. 268 pp.*
Haswell, M. R. The Economics of Development in Village India. *120 pp.*
Littlejohn, James. Westrigg: *the Sociology of a Cheviot Parish. 172 pp. 5 figures.*
Mayer, Adrian C. Peasants in the Pacific. *A Study of Fiji Indian Rural Society. 248 pp. 20 plates.*
Williams, W. M. The Sociology of an English Village: *Gosforth. 272 pp. 12 figures. 13 tables.*

SOCIOLOGY OF INDUSTRY AND DISTRIBUTION

Anderson, Nels. Work and Leisure. *280 pp.*
●**Blau, Peter M.,** and **Scott, W. Richard.** Formal Organizations: *a Comparative approach. Introduction and Additional Bibliography by J. H. Smith. 326 pp.*
Eldridge, J. E. T. Industrial Disputes. *Essays in the Sociology of Industrial Relations. 288 pp.*
Hetzler, Stanley. Applied Measures for Promoting Technological Growth. *352 pp.*
Technological Growth and Social Change. *Achieving Modernization. 269 pp.*
Hollowell, Peter G. The Lorry Driver. *272 pp.*
Jefferys, Margot, *with the assistance of Winifred Moss.* Mobility in the Labour Market: *Employment Changes in Battersea and Dagenham. Preface by Barbara Wootton. 186 pp. 51 tables.*

Millerson, Geoffrey. The Qualifying Associations: *a Study in Professionalization. 320 pp.*

Smelser, Neil J. Social Change in the Industrial Revolution: *An Application of Theory to the Lancashire Cotton Industry, 1770-1840. 468 pp. 12 figures. 14 tables.*

Williams, Gertrude. Recruitment to Skilled Trades. *240 pp.*

Young, A. F. Industrial Injuries Insurance: *an Examination of British Policy. 192 pp.*

DOCUMENTARY

Schlesinger, Rudolf (Ed.) Changing Attitudes in Soviet Russia.
2. The Nationalities Problem and Soviet Administration. *Selected Readings on the Development of Soviet Nationalities Policies. Introduced by the editor. Translated by W. W. Gottlieb. 324 pp.*

ANTHROPOLOGY

Ammar, Hamed. Growing up in an Egyptian Village: *Silwa, Province of Aswan. 336 pp.*

Brandel-Syrier, Mia. Reeftown Elite. *A Study of Social Mobility in a Modern African Community on the Reef. 376 pp.*

Crook, David, and **Isabel.** Revolution in a Chinese Village: *Ten Mile Inn. 230 pp. 8 plates. 1 map.*

Dickie-Clark, H. F. The Marginal Situation. *A Sociological Study of a Coloured Group. 236 pp.*

Dube, S. C. Indian Village. *Foreword by Morris Edward Opler. 276 pp. 4 plates.*

India's Changing Villages: *Human Factors in Community Development. 260 pp. 8 plates. 1 map.*

Firth, Raymond. Malay Fishermen. *Their Peasant Economy. 420 pp. 17 pp. plates.*

Firth, R., Hubert, J., and **Forge, A.** Families and their Relatives. *Kinship in a Middle-Class Sector of London: An Anthropological Study. 456 pp.*

Gulliver, P. H. Social Control in an African Society: a Study of the Arusha, Agricultural Masai of Northern Tanganyika. *320 pp. 8 plates. 10 figures.*

Family Herds. *288 pp.*

Ishwaran, K. Shivapur. *A South Indian Village. 216 pp.*

Tradition and Economy in Village India: *An Interactionist Approach. Foreword by Conrad Arensburg. 176 pp.*

Jarvie, Ian C. The Revolution in Anthropology. *268 pp.*

Jarvie, Ian C., and **Agassi, Joseph.** Hong Kong. *A Society in Transition. 396 pp. Illustrated with plates and maps.*

Little, Kenneth L. Mende of Sierra Leone. *308 pp. and folder.*

Negroes in Britain. *With a New Introduction and Contemporary Study by Leonard Bloom. 320 pp.*

Lowie, Robert H. Social Organization. *494 pp.*
Mayer, Adrian C. Caste and Kinship in Central India: *A Village and its Region. 328 pp. 16 plates. 15 figures. 16 tables.*
  Peasants in the Pacific. *A Study of Fiji Indian Rural Society. 248 pp.*
Smith, Raymond T. The Negro Family in British Guiana: *Family Structure and Social Status in the Villages. With a Foreword by Meyer Fortes. 314 pp. 8 plates. 1 figure. 4 maps.*

SOCIOLOGY AND PHILOSOPHY

Barnsley, John H. The Social Reality of Ethics. *A Comparative Analysis of Moral Codes. 448 pp.*
Diesing, Paul. Patterns of Discovery in the Social Sciences. *362 pp.*
●**Douglas, Jack D.** (Ed.) Understanding Everyday Life. *Toward the Reconstruction of Sociological Knowledge. Contributions by Alan F. Blum. Aaron W. Cicourel, Norman K. Denzin, Jack D. Douglas, John Heeren, Peter McHugh, Peter K. Manning, Melvin Power, Matthew Speier, Roy Turner, D. Lawrence Wieder, Thomas P. Wilson and Don H. Zimmerman. 370 pp.*
Jarvie, Ian C. Concepts and Society. *216 pp.*
Pelz, Werner. The Scope of Understanding in Sociology. *Towards a more radical reorientation in the social humanistic sciences. 283 pp.*
Roche, Maurice. Phenomenology, Language and the Social Sciences. *371 pp.*
Sahay, Arun. Sociological Analysis. *212 pp.*
Sklair, Leslie. The Sociology of Progress. *320 pp.*

International Library of Anthropology

General Editor Adam Kuper

Brown, Paula. The Chimbu. *A Study of Change in the New Guinea Highlands. 151 pp.*
Lloyd, P. C. Power and Independence. *Urban Africans' Perception of Social Inequality. 264 pp.*
Pettigrew, Joyce. Robber Noblemen. *A Study of the Political System of the Sikh Jats. 284 pp.*
Van Den Berghe, Pierre L. Power and Privilege at an African University. *278 pp.*

International Library of Social Policy

General Editor Kathleen Jones

Bayley, M. Mental Handicap and Community Care. *426 pp.*
Butler, J. R. Family Doctors and Public Policy. *208 pp.*
Holman, Robert. Trading in Children. *A Study of Private Fostering. 355 pp.*

Jones, Kathleen. History of the Mental Health Service. *428 pp.*
Thomas, J. E. The English Prison Officer since 1850: *A Study in Conflict. 258 pp.*
Woodward, J. To Do the Sick No Harm. *A Study of the British Voluntary Hospital System to 1875. About 220 pp.*

International Library of Welfare and Philosophy

General Editors Noel Timms and David Watson

● **Plant, Raymond.** Community and Ideology. *104 pp.*

Primary Socialization, Language and Education

General Editor Basil Bernstein

Bernstein, Basil. Class, Codes and Control. *2 volumes.*
 1. *Theoretical Studies Towards a Sociology of Language. 254 pp.*
 2. *Applied Studies Towards a Sociology of Language. About 400 pp.*
Brandis, W., and **Bernstein, B.** Selection and Control. *176 pp.*
Brandis, Walter, and **Henderson, Dorothy.** Social Class, Language and Communication. *288 pp.*
Cook-Gumperz, Jenny. Social Control and Socialization. *A Study of Class Differences in the Language of Maternal Control. 290 pp.*
● **Gahagan, D. M.,** and **G. A.** Talk Reform. *Exploration in Language for Infant School Children. 160 pp.*
Robinson, W. P., and **Rackstraw, Susan D. A.** A Question of Answers. *2 volumes. 192 pp. and 180 pp.*
Turner, Geoffrey J., and **Mohan, Bernard A.** A Linguistic Description and Computer Programme for Children's Speech. *208 pp.*

Reports of the Institute of Community Studies

Cartwright, Ann. Human Relations and Hospital Care. *272 pp.*
● Parents and Family Planning Services. *306 pp.*
Patients and their Doctors. *A Study of General Practice. 304 pp.*
● **Jackson, Brian.** Streaming: *an Education System in Miniature. 168 pp.*
Jackson, Brian, and **Marsden, Dennis.** Education and the Working Class: *Some General Themes raised by a Study of 88 Working-class Children in a Northern Industrial City. 268 pp. 2 folders.*
Marris, Peter. The Experience of Higher Education. *232 pp. 27 tables.*
Loss and Change. *192 pp.*

Marris, Peter, and **Rein, Martin.** Dilemmas of Social Reform. *Poverty and Community Action in the United States. 256 pp.*

Marris, Peter, and **Somerset, Anthony.** African Businessmen. *A Study of Entrepreneurship and Development in Kenya. 256 pp.*

Mills, Richard. Young Outsiders: *a Study in Alternative Communities. 216 pp.*

Runciman, W. G. Relative Deprivation and Social Justice. *A Study of Attitudes to Social Inequality in Twentieth-Century England. 352 pp.*

Willmott, Peter. Adolescent Boys in East London. *230 pp.*

Willmott, Peter, and **Young, Michael.** Family and Class in a London Suburb. *202 pp. 47 tables.*

Young, Michael. Innovation and Research in Education. *192 pp.*

● **Young, Michael,** and **McGeeney, Patrick.** Learning Begins at Home. *A Study of a Junior School and its Parents. 128 pp.*

Young, Michael, and **Willmott, Peter.** Family and Kinship in East London. *Foreword by Richard M. Titmuss. 252 pp. 39 tables.*

The Symmetrical Family. *410 pp.*

Reports of the Institute for Social Studies in Medical Care

Cartwright, Ann, Hockey, Lisbeth, and **Anderson, John L.** Life Before Death. *310 pp.*

Dunnell, Karen, and **Cartwright, Ann.** Medicine Takers, Prescribers and Hoarders. *190 pp.*

Medicine, Illness and Society

General Editor   W. M. Williams

Robinson, David. The Process of Becoming Ill. *142 pp.*

Stacey, Margaret, *et al.* Hospitals, Children and Their Families. *The Report of a Pilot Study. 202 pp.*

Monographs in Social Theory

General Editor   Arthur Brittan

● **Barnes, B.** Scientific Knowledge and Sociological Theory. *About 200 pp.*

Bauman, Zygmunt. Culture as Praxis. *204 pp.*

● **Dixon, Keith.** Sociological Theory. *Pretence and Possibility. 142 pp.*

● **Smith, Anthony D.** The Concept of Social Change. *A Critique of the Functionalist Theory of Social Change. 208 pp.*

Routledge Social Science Journals

The British Journal of Sociology. *Edited by Terence P. Morris. Vol. 1, No. 1, March 1950 and Quarterly. Roy. 8vo. Back numbers available. An international journal with articles on all aspects of sociology.*

Economy and Society. *Vol. 1, No. 1. February 1972 and Quarterly. Metric Roy. 8vo. A journal for all social scientists covering sociology, philosophy, anthropology, economics and history. Back numbers available.*

Year Book of Social Policy in Britain, The. *Edited by Kathleen Jones. 1971. Published annually.*

Printed in Great Britain by Unwin Brothers Limited
The Gresham Press Old Woking Surrey
A member of the Staples Printing Group